Youth Activism in Modern Politics in Ghana

CHARLES PREMPEH

WOELI PUBLISHING SERVICES
ACCRA
2024

Published by
Woeli Publishing Services
P. O. Box NT 601
Accra New Town
Ghana
Tel.: 0243434210
Email: woelipublishing@yahoo.co.uk

Designed and typeset by Woeli Publishing Services

To
JOSEPHINE
KWAME
ADWOA
YAA
and
WOELI

A Note from the Author

While editing this manuscript for external review, an Accra High Court in Ghana, on 15 March 2023, ruled against Anas Amereyaw Anas, upholding a charge against the investigative journalist that what he does with investigative journalism is 'investigative terrorism' (https://drive.google.com/file/d/1EUy6S5L7CjvwesulVe4VQfqfAm PHJYZ/view).

In 2018, Anas had filed a defamation suit against Kennedy Ohene Agyapong, a New Patriotic Party Member of Parliament for Assin Central. Anas, among other reliefs, was seeking monetary damages to the tune of Gh¢25 million.

(See: Ghanaweb of 16 March 2023. "Full Text: Court ruling on Anas' GH¢25 defamation suit against Ken Agyapong," https://www.ghanaweb.com/GhanaHomePage/NewsArchive/ Full-text-Court-ruling-on-Anas-GHC25m-defamation-suit- against-Ken-Agyapong-1731728)

Table of Contents

Acknowledgements

There are many people behind my writing of this book. First of all, my largest thanks go to my family for their support, patience and appreciation of my work as an academic and federal head of our family — according to our shared Christian faith. I am particularly grateful to my wife, Josephine Tweneboaa Afrifa (Jo), who continues to sacrifice her time and comfort, as I often travel to and from Ghana collecting data, and also for spending considerable time sequestered in my study, reading and writing. This book was made possible because Jo complemented by stepping in as mother, sister, and the economist in the home.

I also thank my children, Kwame Nhyira Amponsah, Adwoa Adom Mmoraa, and Yaa Nkunim Tweneboaa. They have endured my frequent absences from home. Apart from Yaa, the recent addition to the family, Kwame and Adwoa usually woke up to find that I was either in Ghana, giving seminar presentations or giving lectures on Zoom. In all, these children have been a blessing to me and I pray for God's continuous blessings for them.

I have incurred many debts in the course of writing this book. I would, therefore, like to thank Prof Jabal M. Buaben and his wife, Mrs Lydia Buaben. The Buabens have always provided for my family needs and encouraged us throughout our stay in Birmingham (UK).

I am equally grateful to my natal family, comprising my mother, Agartha Adjei and siblings: Patrick Adjei, Eric Amponsah, Frederick Prempeh, Sarah Adjei, Rebecca Ama Duah, and my twin sisters, Deborah Adwoa Boadua Prempeh and Dorcas Adwoa Boadua Prempeh. They have been there for me since I decided to go into academia. Their prayers have always encouraged me to push on. I thank my parents for instilling in me a sense of diligence, perseverance, and hard work. Most specifically, they introduced me to God at a tender age. I am grateful they did. I particularly appreciate my late father, Mr Anthony Prempeh, who always reminded me to internalize the wise saying, "A wise son brings joy to his father" (Proverbs 10:1a). I also thank my wife's family, especially her parents: Mr Sampson Afrifa and Madam Comfort Peprah, who have always urged me on. I register my appreciation to my wife's sister, Shirley

Afranewaa Afrifa and her husband, Mr Frimpong Boateng, and brother, Kofi Afrifa and his family.

I am particularly grateful to my publisher, Mr Woeli Dekutsey, who, after he had read the manuscript, readily accepted to publish it. I share with Mr Dekutsey the privilege of attending the same secondary school, to wit West Africa Secondary School. He completed in 1968; I completed in 2001 (as his 'grandson,' so to speak). Mr Dekutsey worked extraordinarily hard to ensure that this book is published. I want to extend my special appreciation to his family, especially his wife, Stella.

Next I wish to express my profound gratitude to Ernesto Yeboah, Mahmoud Jajah, and Oliver Mawuse Barker-Vormawor, whose friendship and interactions have enriched my understanding of the passion young people harbour towards building a flourishing human society. Similarly, I thank Prof Toyin Falola and Victor Angbah, who extended invitation to me to interview Ernesto Yeboah on "The Toyin Falola Interviews." My academic mentors also deserve to be appreciated for always encouraging and supporting my scholarship. For this, I want to thank Professors: Kwabena Akurang-Parry, Francis Nyamnjoh, Wilson Kwame Yayoh, De-Valera N. Y. M. Botchway, George M. Bob-Milliar, Joel Cabrita, Rev Canon Jeremy Morris (currently National Advisor, National Ecumenical Council of the Church of England), Mary Akosua Seiwaa Owusu, Timothy Quashigah, Stephen Owoahene-Acheampong, and Mr Mathew Quamey Alidza.

I thank all those who have read and commented on the manuscript at different stages, including Ernesto Yeboah, Stephen Kwame Ameko, Jane Cecil Dadzie, and Mariam Laruba Shaibu. Similarly, I thank my friends, Naidatu Hameed, Dr Theresa B. Dery, Kofi Semanu Atsu Adzei, Maxwell Amofa, Margaret Babirye, Dzifa Hukporti, and Susanna Adjei Arthur.

Finally, and most importantly, I thank the God Almighty, by whose grace and mercy alone my family and I have come this far. Indeed, the Lord has been good and kind to us. To Him alone belong the glory and honour, Amen!

List of Abbreviations

BNI	Bureau of National Investigations (Ghana)
CUGS	Cambridge University Ghanaian Society
CIA	Central Intelligence Agency (USA)
CDD	Centre for Democratic Development (Ghana)
CoP	Church of Pentecost
CPP	Convention People's Party
IAS	Institute of African Studies
KNUST	Kwame Nkrumah University of Science and Technology
MISR	Makerere Institute of Social Research
NDC	National Democratic Congress
NPP	New Patriotic Party
TVET	Technical and Vocational Education Training
UCC	University of Cape Coast
WHO	World Health Organization

CHAPTER 1

Introduction

"Fix the Country!" was the clarion call from some youth leaders to dramatize the oversized impact of the 2020 corona virus pandemic on the Ghanaian economy. Mobilizing first on social media, particularly Facebook, the young people of Ghana undertook offline street demonstrations to submit petitions about their discontentment with the various political elites about the slow pace at which Ghana was running to achieve appreciable human development. Several of these young men and women, who joined the street protests, felt the nation, Ghana, has failed them. In the major cities, the young people chanted the patriotic song, "Arise Ghana youth for your country!" Offering the youth much vaunted visibility, the print and electronic media, apart from those decidedly aligned with the ruling New Patriotic Party (NPP), amplified the anger of the street voices.

Predictably, therefore, the success of their mobilization reverberated across the Ghanaian communities in the Diaspora, namely USA, UK and Germany. The young and old joined protest marches to the Ghana High Commissions and Embassies in various countries of migration and shared memes on social media. Everywhere in the major cities of Ghana the situation was the same. It was hoped the agitations would kindle the vision of economic prosperity. Regrettably, but quite predictably, it appeared all the 'shout' of 'Fix the Country!' (#FixTheCountry) fell on deaf ears. Indeed, the protesters imagined Ghana to be a country of "One people with one destiny," that would identify with their demands to represent the 'collective vision' of the 1950s.

Nevertheless, the various chants all ended in a complex *cul de sac,* where the international convenor of the #FixTheCountry campaign, Oliver Mawuse Barker-Vormawor, is currently facing trial for treason.[1] After a few local and transnational rallies to call on the elites to fix Ghana, it appears Ghana remained stagnated; the politicians only offered a charade of assurance that they were responding to the demands of the young people. But after waiting in frustration on the usual political rhetoric, Oliver, became disenchanted, especially when the government imposed yet another tax, the unpopular Electronic Transfer Levy (E-Levy) on Ghanaians. Struggling to mobilize the young people who appeared to have lost their zest for yet another round of hitting the street, Oliver is reported to have scribbled words on his social media platform, which the political elites interpreted as desiring to organize a political coup.

Moments upon landing in Ghana on 11 February 2022, to ginger the young people to protest against the E-levy, Oliver was whisked away from the airport to an undisclosed security destination. The media promptly drew attention to Oliver's fate. The Ghana's Bureau of National Investigations (BNI), the internal intelligence agency of the country that had picked him up and arraigned Oliver before court and had him subsequently remanded. After several legal tussles, Oliver's lawyer secured a bail for him. The irony of Oliver's case is that when he was first arrested, nearly all the young people who supported the #FixTheCountry agenda converged at the court where they thought Oliver would be appearing, chanting the usual "Arise Ghana youth!" in solidarity. But after a few appearances, the supporters' numbers dwindled away, as happened in the case of Jesus Christ, whose disciples disserted him when he fell 'foul' of the Jewish law.

Such a desertion speaks volumes to me. I have had the occasion to work with Oliver as a co-executive member of the Cambridge University Ghanaian Society (CUGS) in 2019. I reflected over the oft-touted expression, "We the people of Ghana." How sincere are the individuals who often ride on public sympathy in the hope of securing the common good? The complexity of what constitutes Ghana has implications for the sufficiency of Pan-African alliance and constitutional chance of turning Ghana's fortunes for the better. Certainly, the expression, "We are Ghanaians," indicates simplicity in constructing the modern state and citizenship.

The goal of this study, therefore, is to interrogate the simplistic notions of the state and citizenship — investigating the extent to which the socio-cultural constitution of both the state and citizenship needs to inform the civic participation strategies of the youthful constituency of Ghana and, by extension, Africa. The study is anchored on the argument that an implicit understanding of the state and citizenry, as naturally given, would potentially frustrate young people's aspirations for economic democracy. Advancing a contextual analysis of the study's argument, the next section provides a historical and contemporary perspective of Africa's predicament. The section will aim at bringing to the fore, the complexity of Africa's challenges that defy simplistic binaries.

The African Predicament as Context

That the state and its concurrent citizenship is a social and cultural construct sheds insight on what has come to be called the 'Africa's predicament.' This provides the context for analysing young people's politics in Ghana and the diaspora. The condition of Africa before colonialism is well documented, largely by Arab travellers and explorers who visited different parts of the continent, especially the Medieval Western Sudanese Empires, including Ghana, Songhai, and Mali, beginning from the 9th century.[2] Another source of narratives about the continent comes from Europeans who visited the continent in the 15th century and anthropologists who visited several societies on the continent in the 19th century, to satisfy their curiosity about the so-called Dark Continent and noble savages.[3] This was after the Portuguese had touched base with the continent in the 15th century. Some of the accounts of the Arabs and Europeans before the beginning of the 20th century are quite contentious and often derogatory of Africans.

Complex expressions may have informed this bad reportage on Africa, including a need for both the Arabs and Europeans to justify the enslavement of Africans and the mercantilist exploitative economy. These reports also provided European armchair researchers, some of whom used stigmatizing terms such as paganism, fetishism and idolatry, to profile African traditions and belief systems. By the late 19th century, some of the reporters emerged as colonial anthropologists whose assumed cultural knowledge about African societies paved the way for the colonization of the continent.

At the turn of the 20th century, there was what is generally called the 'anthropological turn,' where African cultures came to be written in what appears to be 'in favourable light.' This major shift in Europeans writing about Africans was not necessarily because they felt any sense of remorse for what their forebears had done to the continent, rather it was to also celebrate the noble savage who had supposedly been spared the devastating impact of the Industrial Revolution in Europe since the middle of the 18th century. By the late 19th century, therefore, several African societies had been merged into colonial enclaves and given names chosen by the colonial powers.[4] What is now Ghana was named the Gold Coast, while other areas were named after celebrated colonialists, such as Cecil Rhodes – Southern Rhodesia (now Zimbabwe) and Northern Rhodesia (now Zambia).

Meanwhile, by the late 19th century, missionary work had reached a peak in several non-Muslim African European colonies.[5] The missionaries had established schools to support the proselytization agenda of the Christian faith.[6] The impact of the mission presence was mixed. First, the western-type of literacy that they provided several Africans became the basis for Africa's sense of nationalism — constructed around cultural recuperation.[7] Second, mission education allowed African scholars, especially since the 1960s, to write, using Christian or Greco-Roman imagery — indicating that Africans had what Europeans had, if not better.[8]

In the case of the Gold Coast, for example, the works of R. S. Rattray, who began writing extensively about the Asante, a major political force in the forest area of the colony, became a major source of reference to later writers.[9] It is through Rattray, in particular, that later Gold Coast writers, including J. B. Danquah and K. A. Busia began writing about Akan cultures from the Christian prism,[10] which Okot p'Bitek critiqued as "dressing African deities in Greco-Roman garbs."[11]

By the 1960s, several African historians had chronicled extensively, challenging western epistemic injustice to the continent. The Senegalese Cheikh Anta Diop became quite revolutionary, for example, in connecting Africans to ancient Egypt — claiming that Ancient Egyptian civilization was decidedly a black African civilization.[12] Martin Bernal also contributed to the Egyptology narrative with his *Black Athena* volumes.[13] In the 1970s, Africans and people of African descent, such as Leopold Senghor and Aimé

Fernand David Césaire championed a romanticism of African cultures in the cultural-philosophy of *Negritude*.[14] Beyond that, these writers indicated that Western civilization borrowed extensively from Africa. The works of these writers incurred the response of European scholars such Mary Lefkowitz, whose, *Not Out of Africa,* challenged the idea that Western civilization is decidedly African in origin.[15] Meanwhile, toward the turn of the millennium, other writers, including Peter Burke, had demonstrated that cultural hybridity is a historic fact across cultures; while Kwame Anthony Appiah discredited the idea of Western civilization as a convenient myth.[16]

Nevertheless, by the 1970s, debate raged among African scholars about the extent to which colonialism impacted Africans. Beginning with Ajayi's understanding that the colonial impact was episodic more than epochal, a set of scholarship churned out in response, given that colonialism did not last for even a century. Perhaps, the most revolutionary was Walter Rodney (in *How Europe Underdeveloped Africa*), who argued that colonialism did nothing but messed up Africa. He claimed that Africa entered into colonialism with a hoe and emerged out of it with a hoe.[17] Others, such as Adu Boahen and Ali Mazrui, have attempted giving a balanced sheet account of colonialism, highlighting areas of merits and demerits with the European incursion into Africa.[18]

In all this, and sometimes given the romanticism of the African past, it is becoming difficult to discern the state of Africa before colonialism and what would have been the continent's trajectory without colonialism. Nevertheless, the point is also true that Africans are also a socio-cultural construct of colonialism, borne out of African nationalist 'othering' European colonizers as the cause of Africa's plight. 'Africans' emerged out of a certain hope that the absence of Europeans — through political independence — would usher the continent into the dawn of prosperity.

Consequently, by the late 1950s, several African colonies, beginning with Ghana ceded ties of political disequilibrium associated with erstwhile European colonizing powers. But judging by the overwhelming psychological impact of colonialism on Africans, some writers, including Frantz Fanon doubted whether the postcolonial elites who took over from the Europeans could redeem their people from the legacies of colonialism.[19] Fanon concluded his analysis in several of his writings that new African elites could not engineer the aspirations of political decolonization as they themselves cherished to occupy the post that the Europeans had left without fundamentally changing it.

Nevertheless, in the early days of independence in the 1960s, the first generation of African leaders, considering capitalism to have formed the base of colonialism, espoused different ideas of socialism.[20] They also deployed symbolism and myths of historic heroic origins to foster imagined postcolonial states.[21] Further, they integrated entertainment, including popular music and sports, into the nation-building agenda.[22] Occasionally, they used legislation to marginalize dissenting voices through deportation and imprisonment.[23] With all this, the first-generation of African leaders recorded some successes — providing infrastructure: schools, roads, and hospitals. But by the end of the 1960s, nearly all of them began experiencing retrogression, including a surge in ethnic politics and polarization along religious lines, especially between Christians and Muslims. The decline of the various postcolonial states appeared to run faster than the elites could handle, as the elites were accused of corruption and abuse of power. Agitations from the citizens became louder than the elites could bear.

Admittedly, the first-generation leaders had the rhetoric of statecraft, including symbols, to their advantage, but they hardly had the brute military force of the colonizers. This means that while Max Weber may be right in his analysis that a major defining feature of the modern state is its use of coercive force, the attempts by the elites to deploy force rather suffered major pushback.[24] So, by the late 1960s, several postcolonial countries experienced military interventions, leading to a massive decline in progress towards nation-building and human flourishing.[25]

The woes of African countries hardly abated. It entered into the 1980s when the economies could not stand the force of draught and piled-up historic corruption. By the 1980s, several African countries, such as the so-called developing economies, had to seek the intervention of the International Monetary Fund and the World Bank. Called Bretton Woods institutions, these two international financial institutions imposed neoliberal policy on African countries.[26]

These included forcing the state to significantly withdraw from the 'market' through the removal of subsidies on education, health and agriculture.[27] Given that these are the key factors in nation building and indexes of human flourishing, the diminishing effect of state removal of subvention made life worse for several Africans.

Alongside came the 1990s when Africans leaders were forced to re-democratize, as agitations threatened to undermine the peace of the continent.[28] From one country to the other, several African countries under military regimes were forced to re-democratize. But the question is whether democracy has yielded the needed economic prosperity. Freedom of expression definitely broadened, but whether it broadened equally for everyone and ensured the relative economic prosperity of the masses remains a moot question altogether.

At the turn of the millennium, Africa, once again, became the epicentre and theatre of religious revivalism, mainly from the Arab and European worlds.[29] It also became the home of various levels of activism, including gender rights, children rights and, more recently, since 2007, minority sexual rights.[30] All this also comes against a surge in chieftaincy, which appeared to have lost much of its sting during the early days of postcolonial eras.[31] Consequently, as the millennium wore on, the idea of 'We' has become highly bastardized to represent competing interests of segments of African population. The onset of social media in the 2000s also amplified the voices of dissenters locally and globally.

To a significant extent, the idea of 'We' Africans has hardly been achieved. The imagined postcolonial Pan-Africanism appeared to have fallen into comatose. But some African countries appeared to be making progress until the sudden outbreak of the corona virus pandemic in March 2020. The pandemic had a global effect of upsetting nearly every aspect of human life, creating deep-seated anxieties. As part of the global efforts to curb the rapacious spread of the virus, the World Health Organization (WHO) promoted the imposition of lockdown rules and the wearing of facemasks by nearly every citizen of the world. Some individuals resisted the lockdown rules, including reading what may come across as conspiracies into the pandemic, but nothing much was achieved.[32] In the end, the pandemic reversed global economic gains, with several thousands of people losing their jobs, others becoming jobless soon after the pandemic, as they lacked new skills to survive economic regime change.

More specific to this study, the pandemic is believed to have presented an opportunity for higher education to foster both knowledge and human well-being.[33] Similarly, in the world where global capitalism is believed to be destroying peripheral states or set the states up for destruction through revolutions by billions of unemployed human workers, the outcome of the COVID-19 is compared with a possibility of a Fourth Industrial Revolution that would fast-track the process of destroying economies in peripheral states.[34] It is, therefore, assumed that COVID-19 could be understood as an obligatory passage point meant to force the world to transition in terms of global capital's rituals of renewal.[35] To the knowledge of some scholars,[36] the pandemic also overstretched many constitutional democracies.

But more specifically, governments everywhere invoked wide and intrusive emergency powers in responding to the public health crisis, leading to widespread and general concerns about the legal basis of emergency powers and their proper use for legitimate public health objectives (i.e. saving lives, preventing transmission, and protecting the health of the nation). Second, the constitutional balance that normally exists between the executive, the legislature, and the judiciary was disrupted, and the fundamental rights protected under international and national laws were restricted on a massive scale. To reset the disruption of constitutional governance, scholars suggest a need to understand how ordinary processes of constitutional government were disrupted during the pandemic.[37] In the Middle East and Africa, the impact of the pandemic was such that it impacted negatively on a region that was already struggling to recover from the effects of a decade of uprisings, failed or stalled political transitions, state fragility, economic decline, collapsing social safety nets, civil war, and international conflicts.[38] The global pandemic is wreaking havoc on welfare systems, institutions and societies throughout the region (Middle East and North Africa), with far-reaching social consequences.[39]

With the impact of the pandemic as context, the least

provocation in one country was likely to have a metastasizing impact in another country — the real experimentation with the domino effect theory. Sometimes some issues people reacted to raised concerns about people's genuineness. For example, in the early days of the pandemic, an American policemen, Derek Michael Chauvin and James Alexander Kueng brutally murdered an unarmed African, George Floyd, on 25 May 2020. The incident happened in the city of Minnesota, United States of America. Social media immediately whipped up pent up anger. The whole world experienced spontaneous outpouring of anger, resulting in pulling down of statues and busts of Euro-Americans believed to have contributed to contemporary racism and marginalization of minority groups.[40]

One wonders whether the sustained European interest in #BlackLivesMatter, as a result of Floyd's death, was sincere. This was because just recently, on 27 January 2023 another black man of 27 years, Tyre Nichols, was similarly murdered and given wide social media coverage, yet the response appeared to be a 'no one's business.'[41] Anyway, regardless of the complexities of racism, the pandemic provided yet another reason for Africa's challenges to be discussed, as layers of subdued local and global systemic discrimination in health, education and food cultures were made very visible. The conversation has been sustained by the Russia-Ukraine conflict, which has further deepened the economic woes of Africa.

Social Media and Digital Citizenship

From the foregoing, it could be argued that local and trans-local occurrences offered the #FixTheCountry Movement the kind of nation-wide support it received from Ghana's youthful constituency. The use of youthful constituency applies to persons of 18 years and above, both men and women, who are passionate about participating in public activism to cause a paradigm shift in governance in their respective African countries. The study also focuses on young men and women, knowledgeable in using various social media handles, such as Facebook, WhatsApp, and Twitter to form online communities to effect revolutionary change in the offline world.

We will now discuss how Ghana's young people are deploying

social media to overturn the overwhelming state control of offline political activities.

The study's argument is that social media has redefined the channels of communication, bringing the voices of otherwise marginalized individuals living at the extreme corners of the world to the epicentre of communication. Playing the role of amplifying voices, social media promotes complexities of both broadcasting and narrowcasting perspectives. In other words, through social media, individuals can get their views broadcast beyond their local reach; at the same time, social media can easily induce narrowcasting, forcing individuals to focus on aspects of information that resonate with their views. Either way, social media can entwine local conflicts with global networks; extreme voices can easily find support from dissenting voices worldwide. This trend could easily lead to individuals who live at different sides of the world, to fight for the same cause, supposedly, without even knowing or appreciating local contexts.

Social media's overwhelming benefits and challenges have similarly triggered complex forms of digital dictatorship. Considering that the political elites feel they are failing in their use of old offline structures, such as police and military brutalities to cow dissenting voices into submission, citizenship is being reconfigured as biometric registration to easily track people in the virtual world.[42] In other words, digitalization of citizenship has become more complex when the elite seek to operationalize dictatorship.[43] Technological advances have facilitated issues of individual 'privacy' to be easily subverted through digital surveillance and dictatorship. This also means that, rather than the old regime of the state recognizing the separation between private lives and public lives of its citizens, totalitarian regimes of the world have a totalizing control of the lives of citizens, as technology has served as an enabler in helping such regimes to bridge the gap between the 'private' and the 'public.' Through technology, the world appears to have come to a point where the idea of social contract, where citizens retain some rights in their private space, is collapsing under the prying and penetrating scrutiny of digital surveillance. The bureaucratic state of the 19th century, with the power of the army and legal documents, had a form of coercive power that pales in the face of the enablement that digitalization offers 21st century dictators. Through digital technology, freedom of communication appears to have come under constraint as technology has brought the elites into close proximity with the voices of the citizens, living far away. Social media, therefore, often serves as the channel, instead of the primary cause, of expressing discontentment against a regime.[44] This is precisely because just like any human invention, social media channels are ontologically neutral, since what they are used for are all informed by human agency.[45] In all this, young people around the world are constantly negotiating how to go around the multilayers of a digital dictatorship.

The study shall now focus on the centrality of social media in recalibrating politics in a way that brings both the periphery and epicentres of power into a conversation — even if on a disequilibrium scale.

Until the 21st century, communication across cultures, was largely mediated by material enablers. Either people travelled or wrote letters that had to be physically delivered across persons in communication. However, beginning with the Internet revolution of the 1970s, the channels of communication have broadened. Through the Internet, people across continents can now communicate easier and faster than previously anticipated. The onset of social media at the turn of the millennium has offered communication yet another boost. Merging digital communication, it is nearly impossible now to communicate without the mediation of social media. Similarly, social media has reconfigured political power dynamics, including redefining the grand ideas of globalization and citizenship. As part of the reposition of globalization on a different level, social media and other forms of digital communication has created a world of significant proximities, affecting politics and the networks of communication in what has been referred to as *pax technica*.[46]

Through digital communication, political power and its limits now orbit around the elites and young people negotiating over freedom. Moving beyond the usual elite's usage of bureaucratic structures to control offline political spaces, young people have largely succeeded in subverting such 'out-dated' state control structures as the gatekeeping role of regime-favoured media.[47] In 2005, Iranians, for example, elected Mahmoud Ahmadinejad as its sixth president.

But the election came across to several segments of the Iranian population, including the young people, as having been rigged and badly manipulated in favour of Ahmadinejad. Instead of just hitting the street to protest, the young people readily deployed social media or online space to stir protest against the elected president.[48] Thus, in Iran, a major power bloc in the Arab world had its power tested by the technology in the hands of the youth — a domino effect that metastasized into other countries including Indonesia, Kyrgyzstan, Kuwait, Egypt, Tunisia, Turkey, Malaysia and Kazakhstan. The relative successes of the young people form part of the usual understanding that digital technology has broadened the frontiers of democratic governance, offering alternatives to engage political power and diffuse the principles of democratic governance.[49] Specifically, social media has broadened the critical indexes of democracy, which include the unimpeded flow of information and education, discussion, deliberation, choices, and action.[50]

More importantly, social media allows policies to be scrutinized and analyzed and circulated beyond local reach by experts and those considered non-experts alike.[51] Elsewhere in North Africa, including Algeria, Tunisia and Egypt, the young people have employed social media to upset old authoritarian regimes that had used every offline bureaucratic mechanism to resist regime change.[52] The same could be said about Uganda, where urban young people usually use social media to challenge what they consider the dictatorial regime of Yoweri Museveni.[53] In Africa, the youth have also used social media to question the existing economic malaise, thus forcing a renegotiation of authority and control, addressing stability challenges in different ways.[54] On the other hand, students on university campuses,[55] for example, in South Africa have also leveraged social media to whip up disaffection against the statues of imperialist personalities such as Cecil John Rhodes.

But it is not all bliss with social media or digital communication as an enabler of democratic practices. It has been observed that digital communication could unleash the venom underpinning the process of decentralization, the weakening of mechanisms of power and control from dominant centres of power, facilitated by the dispersed, boundary-transgressing networks of new communication media.[56]

The perceived counterproductive impact of digital communication, inter alia, has armed the elites to overturn the governance technology against social media users. For this purpose, the elites have acquired advanced technologies that enable them to both routinize surveillance online and arrest and punish individuals behind dissenting voices.[57] Not only that, the Internet does not create the imagined liberal space that many have assumed. This is because the Internet, as a channel for social media use, relies on a hierarchical infrastructure that interlinks individual customers to the Internet, which then provides the state, as a key stakeholder in controlling such infrastructure, with control opportunities.[58] This makes various states in Africa to mainstream Internet shutdowns during elections.[59] Several times the state compels Internet operators to shut down, thus demonstrating its militarized authoritarian control.[60]

The state or individuals, through social media, enhance the practice of propaganda where disinformation and misinformation are complexly brought together to inform action and inaction, from a particularly partisan unidirectional perspective. This gives rise to what we earlier stated as the broadcasting and narrowcasting effects of social media, also known as computational propaganda.[61] Other scholars have also expressed concerns about the extent to which the ubiquitous visibility of social media, as an integral part of the web evolution, could cause civil disturbances, strategic insecurity, and military operation to develop a model to structure information warfare. The potential of social media generating security threats is precisely because of the issues of malicious coding and social engineering.[62] State control of the infrastructure of the Internet and social media alter the relationship citizens have with the state. In several African countries, the state imposes heavy taxes and fosters slow Internet access to social media handles such as Facebook, Twitter, and WhatsApp as a way of disciplining citizens and controlling them.[63] The state also exerts its responsibility of controlling cross-border traffic and safeguarding of freedom of expression and access to information and pursues a controlling agenda of interfering with and blocking the free flow of information.[64] On the whole, the vision that social media affords multiple channels of communication to foster democratic governance is far from conclusive. The surge of digital dictatorship with the political elites controlling the infrastructure of online communication through censorship and shutdowns of the Internet could set democracy in a relapse mood. As a solution, some authors have recommended a need to re-assess and redesign the operations of Internet providers and regulators to ensure that they are adept at managing complex, ambiguous, and evolving realities that sit at the intersection of technology, politics and governance.[65]

In Ghana, the various political parties have, since the turn of the millennium, deployed social media to advance their interest, that is to say, to capture political power. But given that the channel is also riddled with challenges such as invasion of privacy, peddling of unsubstantiated claims, and publishing false news without due diligence, some academics have suggested that politicians should rather depend more on traditional media and use social media as an additional communication channel to advance their political interest.[66] Given all the negative challenges associated with the politicization of social media, it is reported that in the face of competitive democratic elections, Ghana's democratic reputation will, in no small measure, depend on how successfully the country navigates the challenges of the digital age.[67] This is against the background that other academics assume that broadening the channels of communication that social media provides, enhances youth participation in governance — hence promoting democratic discourses and participation.[68] From the perspective of political marketing, social media has been identified as positive and significant in ensuring the dissemination of political messages across social media that enables political participation, political knowledge and political efficacy of young voters.[69] But all said, it is still suggested that much as social media holds the potential for broadening the frontiers of Ghana and Africa's democratic credentials, the state needs to invest in cyber security to regulate and combat fake news and propaganda. Failure could spell the nemesis of the digital age.[70]

A Renewed Research Intervention

The discussion above has highlighted the complexities of the challenges that have burdened postcolonial Africa shortly after independence. The reasons for Africa's challenges are varied, ranging from leadership ineptitude, corruption and neo-colonialism. In all, it appears that liberal democracy and neoliberal economic answers that the Western world recommended to the continent, have not yielded the desired results. The situation has rather impacted the young people socio-psychologically. Several of them are increasingly disillusioned about their respective country's prospects. Some of them are daring the consequences of crossing the Sahara and traversing dangerous water bodies to greener pastures, in the hope that their futures will be better. Several African youths are deceived by images of the 'good' life out there, to see the 'grass being greener' at the other side. Many of them, particularly several of the youths in Ghana have jettisoned the lyrics of an old religious song that stipulates that, "Life in this world is a great struggle for both the young and old; rich and poor." They challenge religion itself.

Since the turn of the millennium, Ghana has seen a surge in new religious movements, particularly the historic religions such as Islam and Christianity, some of which are a complex mixture of the New Age movements, along with aspects of indigenous cosmogony. Others also see indigenous political structures, such as chieftaincy, as part of the tools in the hands of the elites to further marginalize the youth. Also, there is, what young people (especially university graduates), think is the failure of the schooling system to offer them value for the money on account of their investment in education. Not only that, the fact that attaining postgraduate education before one is promoted at work, regardless of whether postgraduate education is needed in that sense, has also had two main implications. First, several young men and women, some of whom 'think' they are underemployed and have invested more in postgraduate education in anticipation of securing work, have become disillusioned eventually. Second, several tertiary institutions such as the Kwame Nkrumah University of Science and Technology, tend to run courses to meet the demand for postgraduate certificate without sometimes getting the course duly approved.[71] Thus education has become monetized and captured within the bracket of economic neoliberalism.

Additionally, the country is currently promoting technical education with less emphasis on the humanities, thereby assuming that they are responding to claims that graduates do not meet technical the requirements of industry. Many think that technical education is the way to go. In consequence, Ghana has turned nearly all its polytechnic institutions into technical universities. But the question that has hardly been satisfactorily addressed in the Ghanaian context is whether the solution to the country's teeming challenges lies only in technical education. Whatever it is, the case of India that has heavily invested in technological education and yet remains one of the most unequal societies carries useful instruction for Ghana's philosophy of education.[72] Certainly, the lingering and residual effect of India's caste system might continue to mainstream inequalities,[73] but the point is that the 'why'-answers to the questions of life weigh more heavily than the 'how'-questions.

Nevertheless, to re-assert what we stated in the introductory section, the COVID-19 pandemic's devastating impact worsened the plight of the marginalized in Ghana. Much as the pandemic enriched the pockets of a few individuals, who already had pre-existing skills and structures to renew their employable skills, majority of the Ghanaian populace in the informal sector, especially those in urban slums, were nearly kicked out of jobs without the possibility of economic recuperation. The whole issue is compounded by the fact that given the elaborate and significant impact the pandemic had on work culture, individuals needed renewed social and eclectic technical skills to survive the next world of work. There are questions about whether or not technologies would take over jobs and intensify inequalities. Nevertheless, the fear of technologies, particularly Artificial Intelligence (AI) replacing human beings appeared to be overstretched, since historically, technology is supposed to generate more jobs than destroy.[74] Going forward, however, and contrary to Ghana's fixation with technical education, it is highly recommended that social, digital, and technological trends will drive the future. Most importantly, we need to be more human and cultivate social skills that would foster conviviality.[75]

Considering that the future is hardly known and usually offers no clear crystal ball for discernment, young people tend to be frustrated with the daily sense of hopelessness that seem to take hostage their ambition. Ordinarily, the youth tend to be hopeful, on account of age, yet in the case of Ghana, the future for the youth seems to be perpetually bleak. One of my interlocutors, a 40-year-old man, who was heading a private media house in the city, disclosed:

> Ten years ago, I made a decision to stay and help build Ghana. I was almost ostracized by my close family. I, on the other hand, was appalled by their seeming lack of patriotism. Ten years on, I wonder if I have not been stupid. Nothing seemed to be working. Reading posts everyday on social media about Ghana I become depressed. I don't share in the sentiments expressed in those posts. I am sorry to say that Ghana's future is bleak. You will sink trying to save it.

One of them also said, "Give anything to the African and they'll treat it like Esau did his birth right. We've long sold our 'living right.'" Out of frustration about the huge sums of money that politicians have sunk in the February 2023 Nigerian elections vis a vis the poor sanitary conditions around, the same person wrote:

> When some of us talk about the animal nature of the African, we know what we are talking about. We 'kill' each other for money as monkeys do for banana. And oh, the African Union should stop issuing vacuous statements. Once they stop their monkey posturing, the rest of the world will stop taking us for monkeys!

From the foregoing, we could argue that African leaders need to factor into governance the future of the youth as regards citizenship, their birth rights of belonging to a nation and stakeholder improvements in their living conditions. In his inaugural speech as the elected president of Ghana on 7 January 2017, Nana Dankwa Akufo-Addo charged Ghanaians to be "citizens rather than spectators."[76] This call assumed that the idea of citizenship is not handed across, as several people think. What is rather not often take into consideration is how the state enforces the idea of citizenship, especially after persuasion has failed. We shall take this up in the next chapter, but suffice it to say now that the state is a socio-cultural construct that is predicated on convenient myths and 'sacralized' state emblems. Citizenship is also not given,[77] as people have multiple kinship ties based on social covenant rather than the legal relations informed by the social contract they have with the state.

For the above reason, the idea of democracy is an index of the right use of language on social media and young people's compliance with what they consider as gerontocratic dictatorship. At any rate, it is not uncommon that bad language and fake news saturate social media, for which reason people think the youth are abusing digital technology.[78] Historically, some cultures in Ghana, including the Akan and Ga, allowed various insults, to ensure checks and balances in societal formation.[79] Perhaps, one may raise the issue of timing: that such insults were cultural and period specific. Much as that is true, young people also see insult as a 'necessary evil,' to navigate bureaucratic regimes that overreach themself beyond the offline space to control the virtual world.

The goal of this study is to move away from what we consider as simplicities of social media and politics to also discuss the issues of state and citizenship. More specifically, we are interested in how the young people of Ghana construct their philosophies about life and governance to reconfigure their engagement with the entity called Ghana. We are also interested in how the digital world or cyborg is also replenishing the primordial idea of citizenship as both social and fluid. At the moment, the digital world has enabled Ghanaian youth to 'travel without travelling'; their voices are criss-crossing geo-spatial locations to participate in governance without easily becoming victims of a particular legal constraint of Ghana or the other world.

We will discuss two main groups, the Economic Fighters League and #FixTheCountry Movement that have deployed different philosophies and merged them with social media to overreach themselves as citizens of the particulars and universals. We also focus on yet another youth group known as ZongoVation, which deploys digitalization to fashion their vision of community development through training young men and women in tech-related skills. Our argument is that the digital age is helping young people to reinvent their historic notions of citizenship in Ghana and Africa as more socially constructed than legally determined. Historically, African citizens could move into different spaces and assimilate and be assimilated into them. However, colonialism ushered in legal citizens who, through documentation, must be limited to a particular space[80] such as a husband in Togo and a wife in Ghana. Even though both might be Ewe, they cannot consider themselves citizens of the same ethnic group. What digital media has done, in my view, is that it has created 'visual beings,' who are nibble-footed globally without being constrained within any particular space.

With the foregoing as context, the book is structured as follows: Chapter 2 discusses Ghana's formation. It poses the question about why it is simplistic for Ghanaians to assume that young people would easily see Ghana as a natural entity. The chapter leverages both the traditions of state formation among the Akan and Western philosophies to posit that Ghana is a social construct that will demand more than just the state use of coercive force to cow people into submitting to a particular 'national' vision.

To ground the study's argument in historical context, a historical tapestry of the country is provided, highlighting instances where Ghana is simply a social construct that never existed as a natural entity. The Chapter 3 discusses Ernesto Yeboah, one of Ghana's revolutionary leaders whose leaning towards Nkrumaism informs his quest to reformulate Ghana away from capitalist ideology. Assuming that Nkrumah embodied the collective vision of the founding fathers and mothers of Ghana, Ernesto Yeboah seeks to refurbish Nkrumah's ideas, taking into consideration contemporary philosophies as a complement. Currently, a doctoral candidate in intellectual history at the Institute of African Studies, University of Ghana, where he formally began his political activism as a student in the 2000s, Yeboah comes across to several Ghanaians as one of the highly sophisticated young philosophers and activists who 'alone' challenged the Parliament of Ghana with his #DropThatChamber campaign and won against the state. He has succeeded as an eclectic public intellectual, whose activism traverses national and transnational boundaries, aligning with another socialist movement globally to birth the utopian ideals of Karl Marx.

Having felt the frustration of reforming Ghana through what he later described as a discredited revitalized Nkrumah's Convention People's Party, after having served as the party's youth leader, he founded the Economic Fighters League as an apolitical Movement to achieve economic democracy. Chapters 4 and 5 discuss the Economic Fighters League, which embodies Ernesto's socialist idea of establishing a free and economically democratic country with national and continental impact. Much as Yeboah's leaning repudiates institutional religion as potentially oppressive, his Movement is as religious as an institutionalized religion. This, as we shall argue, is because it takes politics to manage differences, but religious promises of an eschatological bliss tends to harmonize people for governance. We conclude the chapter by arguing that Ernesto, contrary to his vision, is also investing in the old idea of state construction based on the myth of 'we, the people' thus making the attainment of his ideals in the material sense quite complex, if not problematic.

Chapter 6 discusses a cognate group, #FixTheCountry Movement, which based on a brief stint with Ernesto, similarly seeks to reform Ghana through constitutional change. Dominating Ghana's social media during the episodic movement of the pandemic, the convener of the Movement, Oliver Mawuse Barker-Vormawor, a doctoral researcher in International Law at the University of Cambridge, challenged the nation to overturn the 1992 Constitution that has governed the nation for a little over three decades. We discuss the #FixTheCountry for many reasons, including the fact that it marked the Movement in Ghana's recent history that deployed social media and offline street demonstrations to merge multiple social segments as supporters: politicians, traditional authorities, religious figures, the Ghanaian and African diaspora. However, the Movement did not go beyond simplistically chanting Ghana's patriotic song of "Arise Ghana youth for your country!" Only a few individuals leveraged it to meet their self-centred ends. After several betrayals and frustrations, Oliver found himself on the wrong side of the law; he was charged with treason due to his purported comments on social media. Following his arrest, his network of #FixTheCountry started declining.

Analyzing the #FixTheCountry Movement, together with the Economic Fighters League, we argue that, instead of the usual suggestion for the state to further control online spaces, which is nearly impossible, and instead of the state assuming citizenship and nationalism are fossilized and given, we explore the importance of Nkrumah's Consciencism and adaptive leadership as critical in recuperating Ghana's imagined community.

Chapter 7 discusses the tapestry of stagnation of urban slums in Ghana, focusing particularly on Muslim inner-cities in Accra (known historically as 'Zongos' i.e. 'strangers' quarters'). The Chapter 7 discusses the different use to which yet another millennial Mahmoud Jajah has pioneered the deployment of the digital age to foster community development. The main argument is that since the Zongos have had their citizenship often intertwined with partisan politics, the communities have lagged behind in the state's provision of social services. The deprivation of the Zongos, indexed by poor sanitation and squalid living conditions, high levels of illiteracy, and low-intensity violence, has induced some of its youthful constituency to indulge in violence and Internet-related fraud. Against this background, Mahmoud Jajah recuperated the Zongo citizenship away from over-reliance on the state, to rather focus attention on self-initiated projects as part of reconstructing the Zongo self-identity as a people capable of using tech-skills to support human flourishing.

The last chapter (Chapter 9) provides reflections on the entire discussion, indicating a need for the various youth groups to invest in the philosophy of 'why' as opposed to the usual resort technology 'how' in defining their place in the world.

Methodological Approaches and Theoretical Consideration

This study stems out of a long-standing academic and practical interest in young people's leadership in Ghana and Africa. Thus, to gather data for this research, ethnographic data collected since 2006 was compiled. The data collection included this researcher's travelling across some of the major cities in Ghana, including Accra, Cape Coast, Kumasi, and Tamale from 2011 to 2013. Several young men and women, including leaders of youth associations were engaged. Not left out were his students over a period of about a decade. The researcher teased out his students' ideas about what constitutes 'Ghana' and citizenship and realized that their youthful ideas were far more idealistic than the two concepts being socio-culturally constructed. Their expectations that the elected political elites would deliver on the promises made at voting time, are rather a romanticism of human altruism. In theory, the youths have a social contract with the state, but in reality, this contract does not necessarily translate into anything that significantly affects their lives. The excessive monetization of the country's politics, the competitive partisanship nexus and the legacies of pre-colonial and postcolonial regimes predispose politicians towards themselves, their party, their constituencies and 'their' country. This deviation recently has pricked the conscience of one student of the Kwame Nkrumah University of Science and Technology (KNUST) who said his uncle asked him to defect from the New Patriotic Party (NPP) to the National Democracy Congress (NDC). According to this student, his uncle, a member of the NPP, opined that he was concerned with 'him' (the student first) and 'family' before anything else. Since it was promising for our student to take up a leadership position in his constituency in NPP-dominated Asante Region, at the time of the interview in September 2022, he had followed through with his uncle's advice; he had defected from the NPP and won as a youth leader in the NDC.

To ensure the researcher really properly grasped the philosophy about the youth's vision and aspirations, this researcher decided to do a biographical analysis of Ernesto Yeboah — following and talking to people around Ernesto Yeboah, especially during his student days at the University of Ghana, Legon (2003-2007). But Ernesto caught this researcher's attention when the latter was campaigning to become a student leader on the Legon campus. Yeboah became 'involved' with fighting against examination malpractices, leading to University of Ghana's Vice-Chancellor's being relieved of his work. This researcher finally met Yeboah formally on 14 April 2022 during a panel discussion. This researcher was selected to host a panel discussion comprising other radio personalities such as Afia Pokua (a major voice in Ghana's media space), Nana Ansah Kwao (Chief of Akwamu Adumasa) and the host of 'That's My Opinion' on Joy FM. The interview was part of Falola's "The Toyin Falola Interviews" — a series created and aired over Zoom and streamed live into the homes of millions of viewers and listeners. The series interviewed opinion leaders, scholars, and policy-makers whose work, opinions and research are particularly relevant to the African continent and its people, including those in the diaspora. When it was this researcher's turn to interview Ernesto, the researcher examined Yeboah's activism and academic background, to understand Yeboah's philosophy as a youth leader.

At the end of the session, which drew much interaction from the audience, this researcher decided to write formally about Ernesto. A week after the interview, the researcher met Yeboah on the campus of the University of Cape Coast (UCC) where Yeboah was then doing his doctoral studies before transferring to the University of Ghana. The researcher followed most of Yeboah's public activities and patronized the website of the Economic Fighters League. On 5 March 2023, the researcher had three hours of in-depth Zoom interview with Ernesto. Before then, the researcher sent him an interview guide, allowing him a week to reflect on the questions before the interview. With his permission, the researcher recorded the proceedings and listened to it many times, to ensure Yeboah's views were not misrepresented. After the interview, the researcher ran a series of follow-up phone-calls to clarify any gaps. After writing the chapters (in this book) on Yeboah and his Economic Fighters League, the researcher sent the write-up to him for vetting, to make assurance double sure.

For Oliver Mawuse Barker-Vormawor, the international convenor of the #FixTheCountry Movement, the researcher relied on his experience of working with him (Barker-Vormawor) as an executive member of CUGS. Beyond that, when Barker-Vormawor initiated the idea of calling on Ghanaians to fix Ghana, this researcher personally had a few WhatsApp exchanges, inquiring from him about whether Ghana could be fixed the way he and his friends anticipated. Later on in June 2021, when Barker-Vormawor extended his ideas about fixing Ghana on CUGS's WhatsApp platform, where this researcher shares common membership, it generated several conversations which, as expected, took a partisan turn. After a few days of discussion that engendered contrary opinions about the whole initiative to fix Ghana, the conversation died a 'natural death' until news broke that Barker-Vormawor had been arrested in Ghana. But even though the conversation ended on the CUGS' WhatsApp platform, this researcher decided to write an academic paper on the #FixTheCountry Movement. Later, this researcher had about two hours of phone conversation with Barker-Vormawor over his (the researcher's) analysis of the #FixTheCountry Movement.

Next is Jajah. This researcher has known him since the early 1990s at Maamobi, Accra and later at the West Africa Secondary School where they were students (Jajah being a junior school mate). The researcher had a series of interviews and WhatsApp messages with Jajah when the researcher was collecting data for this book.

Regarding the methodological approach on Barker-Vormawor's #FixTheCountry Movement, this researcher relied on secondary material, online news sources, and the Movement's website. Since the researcher does not have the permission of Barker-Vormawor and the various persons who contributed to the discussions on the #FixTheCountry Movement on CUGS's platform, we will not use the group's WhatsApp messages. Concerning the theoretical foundation for the book, the researcher used a mixture of theories, which he discusses extensively at the start of the chapters. But suffice it to state that this researcher builds on his Akan philosophical background to draw theories about human nature, the constitution of the state and the Akan non-binary worldview to discuss young people's civic participation in politics. The researcher then reflected on theories, mainly Anthony Giddens' structuration thesis to demonstrate that structures of society are not non-negotiable, and contrary to the Foucauldian school of thought, they are not necessarily oppressive.[80] Instead, within the structures of society, individuals exercise their agentic capacity to negotiate their interests amid competitive societal interests. Within this theoretical framework, the researcher argues that the state is a socially and culturally constituted, leveraging the works of Benedict Anderson and Ernest Gellner, which also create space for cultural innovativeness.[81] State structures, which recently include social media as a means of administration, is highly negotiable — bringing young people and the political elites into a dialogue. Even if the dialogue is tilted in favour of the ruling elites who tend to control Internet connectivity, young people exercise their agency in assuming 'virtual' citizenship, enabled by the Internet to subvert offline legislations and punitive measures.

On the whole, this book contributes to an on-going discussion about digital technology, humanity and the future of governance in both the private and public spheres.

NOTES/REFERENCES

[1] Ghanaweb (29 October 2022), "Oliver-Barker Vormawor faces two court rulings on felony charges November 11," https://www.ghanaweb.com/GhanaHomePage/NewsArchive/Oliver-Barker-Vormawor-faces-two-court-rulings-on-felony-charges-November-11-1652387.

[2] Ousmane Oumar Kane (ed), *Islamic scholarship in Africa: New directions and global contexts* (New York: James Currey, 2021); Ousmane O. Kane, *Non-Europhone intellectuals* (Dakar/Senegal: Council for the Development of Social Science Research in Africa, 2012).

[3] Toyin Falola and Christian Jennings (eds), *Sources and methods in African history: Spoken, written, unearthed* (Rochester, NY.: University of Rochester Press, 2003).

[4] Albert Adu Boahen, *General History of Africa: Africa under colonial domination, 1880-1935*, Vol. 7 (London: Heinemann, 1985).

[5] Bengt Sundkler and Christopher Steed, *A history of the church in Africa* (Cambridge: Cambridge University Press, 2000).

[6] C. K. Graham, *The history of education in Ghana: From the earliest times to the declaration of independence* (London: Frank Cass, 1971); Elizabeth A. Isichei, *A history of Christianity in Africa: From antiquity to the present* (London: Society for Promoting Christian Knowledge, 1995).

[7] Edward H. Berman, "African responses to Christian mission education," *African Studies Review,* 17, 3 (1974): 527-540.

[8] Okot p'Bitek, *African religions in Western scholarship* (Nairobi: East African Literature Bureau, 1970.

[9] R. S. Rattray, *Ashanti* (Oxford: Clarendon Press, 1932); *Ashanti law and constitution* (Kumasi: Basel Mission Book Depot; London: Oxford University Press, 1923).

[10] Charles Prempeh, "Decolonising African divine episteme: A critical analysis of the Akan divine name of God (Twereduampon Kwame)," *Journal of Religion in Africa,* 52 (2022): 269-291.

[11] p'Bitek, *African religions,* p. 41.

[12] Cheikh Anta Diop, *The African origin of civilization: Myth or reality* (trans. Mercer Cook) (Westport: Lawrence Hill, 1974).

[13] Martin Bernal, *Black Athena: The Afroasiatic roots of classical civilization: The fabrication of ancient Greece, 1785-1985*, Vol. 1 (New Brunswick: Rutgers University Press, 1987); *Black Athena: The Afroasiatic roots of classical civilization: The archaeological and documentary evidence,* Vol. II (New Brunswick: Rutgers University Press, 1991); *Black Athena: The Afroasiatic roots of classical civilization: The linguistic evidence,*

Vol. III (New Brunswick: Rutgers University Press, 2006).

[14] Irele Abiola, *The negritude moment: Explorations in francophone Africa and Caribbean literature and thought* (Trenton, N.J.: Africa World Press, 2011); Aimé Fernand David Césaire, *Discourse on colonialism* (trans. Joan Pinkham) (New York: Monthly Review Press, 1955).

[15] Mary R. Lefkowitz, *Not out of Africa: How Afrocentrism became an excuse to teach myth as history* (New York: BasicBooks, 1996).

[16] Kwame Anthony Appiah (19 November 2016), "There is no such thing as western civiilization," https://www.theguardian.com/world/2016/nov/09/

[17] Walter Rodney, *How Europe underdeveloped Africa* (Nairobi: East African Educational Publishers, 1972).

[18] Albert A. Boahen, *African perspective on colonialism* (Baltimore: Johns Hopkins University Press, 1987); Ali A. Mazrui, *The Africans: A triple heritage* (London: BBC Publications, 1986).

[19] Frantz Fanon, *The wretched of the earth* (trans. Constance Farrington) (Harmondsworth: Penguin Books, 1963).

[20] Idris Cox, *Socialist ideas in Africa* (London: Lawrence & Wishart, 1966); Abdul Rahman Mohamed Babu, *African socialism or socialist Africa?* (Dar es Salaam/Tanzania: Tanzania Publishing House; London: Zed Press, 1981).

[21] Harcourt Fuller, *Building the Ghanaian nat ion-state: Kwame Nkrumah's symbolic nationalism* (New York: Palgrave Macmillan, 2014).

[22] Paul Darby, "'Let us rally behind the flag': Football, nation-building, and Pan-Africanism in Kwame Nkrumah's Ghana," *Journal of African History*, 54, 2 (2013): 221-246.

[23] Roger Gocking, *The history of Ghana* (Westport, Conn.: Greenwood Press, 2005).

[24] Max Weber, *Economy and society* (A new translation by Keith Tribe). Cambridge, Mass.: Harvard University Press, 2019, 75.

[25] William Guttridge, *Military regimes in Africa* (London: Methuen, 1975).

[26] Kwame Akonor, *Africa and IMF conditionality: The uniqueness of compliance, 1983-2000* (New York: London: Routledge, 2006).

[27] Ibid.

[28] Stephen N. Ndegwa (ed), *A decade of democracy in Africa* (Leiden: Brill, 2001); Kwame Boafo-Arthur (ed), *Ghana: One decade of liberal democracy* (London: Zed Books, 2007).

[29] Bernard Sallah and Charles Prempeh, "Charismatic Christianity in Ghana: A relook at some pertinent issues," In Matthew A. Ojo (ed), *The dynamics of charismatic Christianity in Ghana and Nigeria: Essays in honour of Rev Professor Emmanuel Kingsley Larbi*, 30-56 (Accra: Pentecost

Press Ltd., 2022).

30 Charles Prempeh, "African agency, human rights and issues of homosexuality: Biden and Africa" In Bob Wekesa (ed.) *Africa's Policy Towards the US: The Biden Era,* Johannesburg: African Centre for the Study of the United States, 137-157 (University of the Witwatersrand, 2021).

31 Charles Prempeh, "Religious innovations of chieftaincy in Ghana: Pentecostal Christianity and the complex persistence and transformation of Akan chieftaincy" *Religion Compass*, (2021): 1-13, DOI: 10.1111/rec3.12426.

32 Charles Prempeh, "Religion and the state in an episodic moment of COVID-19 in Ghana", *Social Sciences & Humanities Open*, Vol. 4, Issue 1 (2021), pp. 1-8.

33 Charles Prempeh, "Covid-19 and the philosophy of education: Recuperating Africa's triple heritage," *Millah: Journal of Religious Studies*, 22, 1 (2023): 95-126.

34 Rewai Makamani, Artwell Nhemachena and Oliver Mtapuri (eds), "Introduction," in Rewai Makamani, Artwell Nhemachena & Oliver Mtapuri, *Global capitalist's 21st century repositioning: Between Covid-19 and the fourth industrial revolution on Africa,* 1-18 (Bamenda/Cameroon: Langaaa Research & Publishing CIG, 2021), p. 1.

35 Ibid., 4

36 Derek M. Powell and Ebenezer Durojaye, "Constitutional resilience and the Covid-19 pandemic," In Ebenezer Durojaye and Derek M. Powell, *Constitutional resilience and the COVID-19 pandemic: Perspective from Sub-Saharan Africa,* 1-78 (Cham: Palgrave Macmillan, 2022), p. 1.

37 Ibid., 2.

38 Anis Ben Brik, "Introduction: Facing the wave: A journey in the shadow of the pandemic," in Anis Ben Brik (ed), *The COVID-19 pandemic in the Middle East and North Africa,* 1-20 (New York: Routledge, 2023), p. 2.

39 Ibid. 2.

40 Alisha Ebrahimji (7 June 2020), "These controversial statues have been removed following protests over George Floyd's death," https://edition.cnn.com/2020/06/03/us/statues-removed-george-floyd-trnd/index.html.

41 CBS News (8 March 2023), "What we know about Tyre Nichols' death and the Memphis officers charged with murder," https://www.cbsnews.com/news/tyre-nichols-death-investigation-memphis-police-officers-charges-what-we-know/

42 Séverine Awenengo Dalberto, Richard Banégas (eds), *Identification and citizenship in Africa: Biometrics, the documentary state and bureaucratic writings of self* (London: Routledge, 2021).

[43] Yuval Noah Harari (October 2018), "Why technology favors tyranny," https://edisciplinas.usp.br/pluginfile.php/4906801/mod_resource/content/1/Yuval%20Noah%20Harari%20on%20Why%20Technology%20Favors%20Tyranny%20-%20The%20Atlantic.pdf.

[44] Miriyam Aouragh, and Anne Alexander (2011). "The Arab Spring: The Egyptian Experience: Sense and Nonsense of the Internet Revolution." *International Journal of Communication* 5: 1344-58.

[45] Philip N. Howard (2011). *Information technology and political Islam.* Oxford: Oxford University Press, p. 17.

[46] Philip N. Howard (2015). *Pax technica: How the internet of things may set us free or lock us up.* New Haven and London: Yale University, p. xix.

[47] Bruce Mutsvairo (2016), "Dovetailing desires for democracy with new ICTs' potentially as platform for activism," in Bruce Mutsvairo (ed.), *Digital activism in the social media era: Critical reflections on emerging trends in sub-Saharan Africa.* Cham: Palgrave Macmillan, p. 3.

[48] Philip N. Howard (2011). *Information technology and political Islam.* Oxford: Oxford University Press, p. 3.

[49] Ibid, p. 11; Sonia Pedro Sebastiaõ (2014), "Preface," in Bogdan Pã trut & Monica Pã trut, *Social media in politics: Case studies on the political power of social media.* New York and Dordrecht London: N Springer Cham Heidelberg, p. vii; William Gumede, "How technologies boost democracy and development in Africa," *Journal of African Media Studies,* 10, 1 (2018): 135-144.

[50] Morrisett, L. (2003). "Technologies of freed?" in H. Jenkins and D. Thorburn (eds.), *Democracy and new media.* Cambridge, MA and London: The MIT Press.

[51] Samuel C. Woolley & Philip N. Howard (2019). "Introduction," in Samuel C. Woolley & Philip N. Howard (Eds.), *Computational propaganda: Political parties, politicians, and political manipulation on social media.* Oxford: Oxford University Press, p. 4.

[52] James L. Gelvin, (2012). *The Arab Uprisings: What everybody needs to know.* Oxford: Oxford University Press, p. 50-52.

[53] Mathias Kamp (2016). "Introduction," in Mathias Kamp (ed), *Reality check: Assessing the impact of social media on political communication and civic engagement in Uganda.* Kampala: Konrad-Adenaur-Stifung, Uganda Programme, p. 1.

[54] Akin Iwilade (2013). "Crisis as opportunity: youth, social media and the renegotiation of power in Africa." *Journal of Youth Studies,* 16(8), 1054-1068.

[55] Tanja Bosch, "Twitter activism and youth in South Africa: The case of #RhodesMustFall," *Information, Communication & Society,* Vol. 20,

no. 2 (2017), pp. 221-232.

[56] Mudhai F. Okoth, Wisdom J. Tettey & Fackson Banda (2009). *African media and digital public sphere.* New York: Palgrave Macmillan, p. 3.

[57] Ibid, pp. 3-4.

[58] Tina Freyburg and Lisa Garbe, "Blocking the bottleneck: Internet shutdowns and ownership at election times in Sub-Saharan Africa," *International Journal of Communication,* 12 (2018): 3896-3916.

[59] Ibid.

[60] Admire Mare, "State-ordered internet shutdowns and digital authoritarianism in Zimbabwe," *International Journal of Communication,* 14 (2020): 4244-4263.

[61] Mudhai F. Okoth, Wisdom J. Tettey & Fackson Banda (2009). *African media and digital public sphere.* New York: Palgrave Macmillan, p. 4.

[62] Brett Van Niekerk, "Social media and information conflict," *International Journal of Communication,* 7 (2013): 1162-1184.

[63] Clovis Bergère, "'Don't tax my megabytes:' Digital infrastructure and the regulation on citizenship in Africa," *International Journal of Communication,* 13 (2019): 4309-4326.

[64] Rolf H. Weber, "Politics through social networks and politics by government blocking: Do we need rules?" *International Journal of Communication,* 5 (2011): 1186-1194.

[65] Ronak Gopaldas, "Digital dictatorship versus digital democracy in Africa," *South African Institute of International Affairs* (2019): 1-18.

[66] Ransford Edward Van Gyampo, "Social media, traditional media and party politics in Ghana," *African Review,* (2017): 1-15: (2019): 1-18; DOI: 10.1080/09744053.2017.1329806

[67] Elena Gadjanova, Gabrielle Lynch, Jason Reifler and Ghadafi Saibu, *Social media, cyber battalions, and political mobilisation in Ghana* (Exeter: University of Exeter, 2019).

[68] Wilberforce S. Dzisah, "Social media and elections in Ghana: Enhancing democratic participation," *African Journalism Studies,* 39, 1 (2018): 27-47.

[69] Justice Boateng Dankwah and Kobby Mensah, "Political marketing and social media influence on young voters," *SN Social Sciences,* 152 (2021): 1-19.

[70] Harrison Kofi Belley, "Advances in social media and political campaigns in elections: An assessment of the 2016 general elections in Ghana," *Asian Journal of Education and Social Studies,* 12, 1 (2020): 20-28.

[71] Ghanaweb (1 September 2022), "Why KNUST and UG were cited for running unaccredited courses in A-G's report," https://www.ghana web.com/GhanaHomePage/NewsArchive/Why-KNUST-and-UG-were-

cited-for-running-unaccredited-courses-in-A-G-s-report-1614827.

72 Martha C. Nussbaum, *Women and human development: The capabilities approach* (Cambridge: Cambridge University Press, 2000).

73 Ashwini Deshpande, *The grammar of caste: Economic discrimination in contemporary India* (Oxford: Oxford University Press, 2011).

74 James Cook (14 February 2023), "Future-proofing careers and business in the changing world of work," https://www.businessleader.co.uk/ future-proofing-careers-and-business-in-the-changing-world-of-work/.

75 Ibid.

76 TV3 Ghana (2017), "Prez Nana Addo's inaugural speech [Full] – 7/1/2017," https://www.youtube.com/watch?v=jUX_Z03LX3M.

77 Matthew Akon-Mensah, Citizenship in Ghana: Understanding its cultural and political construction (PhD Diss., Universidade do Minho (Portugal), 2019); Akosua Perbi, "'Who is a Ghana?' – A historical perspective," in *Ghana Academy of Arts and Sciences, National integration: Proceedings, 2003*, 29-38 (Accra: The Ghana Academy of Arts and Sciences, 2006).

78 Agana-Nsiire Agana and Charles Prempeh, "Of farms, legends, and fools: Re-engaging Ghana's development narrative through social media," *Media, Culture & Society* (2022): 1-17.

79 Moses Nii-Dortey and Edward Nanbigne, "Tabooing insults: Why the ambivalence?" *Journal of Philosophy and Culture*, 8, 1 (2020): 1-11; Kofi Ermeleh Agovi, "Words, music, dance and parody in confusion: The performance of Nzema Avudwene songs," *Research Review*, 6, 2 (1990): 1-7.

80 Anthony Giddens and Philip W. Sutton, *Essential concepts in sociology.* Cambridge: Polity Press, 2014, p. 56; Anthony Giddens, *The Constitution of Society: Outline of the Theory of Structuration.* Cambridge: Polity Press, 1984, pp. 16-40.ß

CHAPTER 2

The Ghana Establishment: An Understanding of a Nation's Politics

Introduction

The youth in Ghana have expressed total discontent with the nation's progress. They have complained about how the political elites have deliberately sunk the nation into a morass of corruption. Using collective indexes such as "We the youth of Ghana" and "We Ghanaians," the youth have attempted to push to the fore their concerns and assert their right to be given attention. Perhaps, this explains the difficulties that have encumbered youth activism in their bid to transform the country. Even though political scientists, governance experts and sociologists might be familiar with the issues discussed in this chapter, we nevertheless consider it important that the young people understand the complex interface of what constitutes Ghana, by way of ethnicity, religion, and politics. We must also state that it is crucial to understand the Ghanaian Establishment as an imagined community, bounded together by the 'sacralization' of state emblems, institutions and coercion. This might help the young people reconstruct their online presence. Finally, understanding Ghana as a socio-cultural construct devoid of conflicted personal interests would put in a different perspective the demand for constitutional change as a remedy.

The rest of this chapter is structured as follows: First, there will be a brief account of pre-modern state formation, where we will argue that religion or the appeal to the metaphysical imagination has played a major role in state formation. This will be followed by the colonialist establishment of Ghana in the late 19th century and how all these morphed into the formation of postcolonial Ghana. The chapter will conclude with the basic argument that the postcolonial state combines the ethos of premodern state formation (an aspect of the colonial regime) to govern. The lessons adduced will then provide an important context for Ghana's political dispensation at the turn of the millennium — which is heavily marked by digitization or online politics.

The Precolonial State Formation

The hallowed place of culture in human society is a fact that cannot be denied. The point, however, is the interface between culture and human beings. Are human beings just the product of culture or producers of culture? This question is important in answering how the pre-modern state was established. In answering this question, Peter Berger argued convincingly that there is a dialectic nexus between human beings and culture. Human beings create culture, and culture, in turn, creates or determines human actions and inactions.[1] More importantly, instead of seeing culture as an arbitrary creation, as sometimes advanced by post-modernist analysts such as Jean Paul-Sartre and Michel Foucault,[2] Berger argues that cultural creations are intentionally formulated to perform a pre-determined function. This point has been firmed by Anthony Gidden's structuration theory, which states that societies thrive on practices that are "ordered across space and time" through which structures are produced.[3]

Reducing the above theoretical foundation to the formation of states, pre-modern society deployed the metaphysical imagination to structure people into communities. Through an appeal to both real and imagined ancestors, a concatenation of people who ordinarily were warring factions were put together as one people. Among the Asante, for example, the idea of a Golden Stool that descended from the skies provided an important transcendental justification for the political elites.[4] The religious domain, which is also believed to be equally accessible to all, was also a domain of elite control. For example, the Asantehene Osei Tutu — the pioneering founder of Asante — monopolized the idea of 'Nyame' to exercise a firm grip of the Asante spiritual world.[5] Groups in other parts of Ghana and Africa also share the Asante state formation. In all this, the political elites had their bodies sacralized and their legitimacy to rule entwined with the cult of primordial ancestors.[6] This allowed the ruling class to also control commerce through taxation and demand from royalty other forms of social control, including regulating marriages of youngsters.[7]

The issue was not only about the sacralization of the political regime but also about how power was used and controlled. Western thinkers such as Thomas Hobbes, John Locke, and Jean-Jacques Rousseau have disagreed over the state of nature — whether human beings who constitute the state of nature are ontologically good or not.[8] Irrespective of their disagreement, they appeared to have agreed on the need for power to be regulated, which Lord Acton aptly firmed that "absolute power corrupts absolutely."[9] The various indigenous cultures had a good understanding of the riddles of power. They may not have written about it, but they left no doubt about their philosophy of power and governance. Whether through complex forms of theocracy, where an appeal to common ancestors such as the earth priest of the Tendana of the Tallensi group or the symbolism of the linguist staff of the Akan chief, it was considered important to build restrictions around power. While the Tallensi did not have an institutionalized established army, the Tendana appealed to the ancestral cult to upset the feud.[10] By appealing to the fact that the people worshipped the same ancestors and the derivative ancestral taboo against bloodshed, the Tendana was generated ensured governance without bloodshed.[11] The appeal to the ancestral cult for peace and appeasement was important because the notion of forgiveness was alien to nearly all cultures until the Judeo-Christian incursion into world civilization.[12]

Among the Akan, the need to regulate the elite's use of power was routinized in the symbolism of the linguist staff — which, inter alia, includes a palm holding an egg. If the palm held the egg very hard, it breaks; and if it held it loosely it breaks, all the same. Either way, the linguist's staff indexes the delicate nature of chiefly authority, emphasizing the need for power to be regulated.[13] Nevertheless, pre-modern societies were hardly free from conflicts and altercations.

The conceptualisation of power in the pre-modern state was balanced on the social formation of the state. Instead of totalizing economic enrichment and partisan politics at the public sphere, the pre-modern state emphasized social conviviality. Among the Asante, for example, development was more about social cohesion, which undergirded rules that tabooed uncovering a person's ancestry.[14] Cultural alienation was also limited through a social system that ensured that even war captives and slaves could be assimilated to occupy important offices, to enable them rise through the ranks.[15] Unlike the Arab and European introduction of chattel slavery in the 14th and 15th centuries, pre-modern slavery did not result in the enslaved suffering from social alienation or de-personalization, which Orlando Patterson referred to as social death.[16] Definitely, the point is not that slavery in any form is any good nor was the institution very easy to define or conceptualize.[17] Instead, we surmise that, historically, reducing some people to servitude status — however regrettable that is — the point is about whether those in servitude are still treated as human beings. Here, we argue that pre-modern societies perhaps did better in incorporating differences than the contemporary world, ridden with racist-inspired multidimensional social exclusion.[18]

Complexly called communitarian or societies with a predilection towards Ubuntuism, the Akan believe that "all human beings are children of God."[19] This assertion provides an entry into the pre-modern state issues and rights ideas. Rights, in several pre-modern states, were more about community flourishing than the libertarian idea of individual liberties.[20] Among the Akan, for example, all public delitescence such as murder and sexual infractions were punished by death or excommunication.[21] That is also not to say that pre-modern societies were ethically unblemished. For example, as opposed to popular notions, pre-marital sex was allowed among adolescent Akan men — except that it was regulated.[22]

Every segment of society was also part of governance. Women played important roles — though the extent to which they influence public decision is highly contested among academics.[23] Young people also played an important role, especially in the so-named acephalous societies. Societies, such as the Asante and the Mole-Dagbani, depended on the energy of young people to form the warrior group (known in Fante/Akan as Asafo).[24] Formed into an important group, the youth wing leader was called Nkwankwaahene.[25] Among the Akan, he was very influential and together with his group, they determined the stability of the ruling regime.[26] In Akan societies, where chiefs sat in a palanquin to symbolically demonstrate their authority over the people, young people carried the palanquins.[27] Often this militia of young people are really opinion leaders.[28] In the extreme, they could throw off a chief they have a disgruntle against. Since it is a taboo for a chief to walk barefooted, a chief thrown out of his palanquin this way, is deemed to have been destooled (or de-throned). In age-set societies such as the Nuer, the young people similarly form the warrior group. Considering the young people's critical role in state formation and consolidation, they were hardly ignored in governance.

Much as the young people could not be easily dismissed in governance, a complex form of gerontocracy limited their extent of their influence. Through the older generation's control of the materials of marriage and possessing cultic knowledge about the spirit world, the elderly exercised control over the younger generation. Also, ethical practices that deferred ultimate decision-making to the older generation limited the sphere of young people's control. Concurrently, there were cases of inter-generational conflicts in pre-colonial societies against oppressive rulers.[29] As we shall discuss extensively in Chapter Three, insults and invectives, a practice which is occasionally allowed, formed part of the channels of communication available to young people.

The socio-political structures of the pre-modern governance underwent seismic change during the colonial era. In the next section, we shall discuss Ghana's colonial experience. We shall argue that while the colonial regime marked a major turn in societal formation, the arsenals of governance — religion and force (though at different degrees of expression) remained nevertheless.

The Colonial Interlude and Formation of State

It has been argued that the pre-modern state was formed on an imagined unity of a people —routinized through myths and practices. The situation was also far from occasional disruptions and disputations. However, the ethos of social conviviality that was held in the pre-modern world diminished significantly during the colonial rule. Since the 1960s, marking the independence decade and the rise of nationalist scholars, African academics have disagreed over the extent to which colonialism exerted influence over African people. The issue is rather complex and cannot be answered in simple chronological terms. We mean that while colonialism, as Ajayi argued, did not last for more than a century — making it an episode, it would be glib to limit the colonial regime to just the beginning of the late 19th century.[30] Certainly, until the 19th century, the British, in the case of Ghana and much of West Africa (apart from Sierra Leone and Liberia), were hardly involved in the direct political governance of the colonies, neither did they make any attempt to establish any political presence into the interior, apart from the coastal area. But that is far from arguing that the British did not exercise any form of influence over the local population. In fact, by the 1840s, the British had established the Bond of 1844, which involved about 14 coastal chiefs ceding part of their cultural sovereignty to them.[31] This initial British imperialism was part of the colonial ethos of 'civilizing' the local population — making the colonial encounter more of a cultural engagement than military.[32] Colonial cultural imperialism has been profiled differently in terms of its impact on Africans. But generally, the fact remains that it has had a lingering impact on Africans, including what some Africans have described as the enslavement of the African mind.[33] The cultural epistemicide that the colonies experienced was aided and abetted by the so-called 'anthropologists' because they claimed to have studied a supposedly 'primitive' and non-literate culture.[34]

The above context implies that by the time the British took over from the Dutch in the 1870s and later reinforced their political grip over the colonies, the stage had been prepared to cower the colonized into the grid of Eurocentrism. Concomitantly, when Europeans resolved their internal conflicts to present a common front in the pillaging of Africa through the Berlin Conference of 1884/85, the British had yet another reason to colonize their West African protectorates. Following one of the rules of the Berlin Conference, the issue of colonial powers demonstrating effective control of a colony in spite of Asante incursions and disruption of the coastal state, the British went all out to conquer the colony. They deployed tactics such as 'divide and rule,' which in settler colonies was expressed largely in their introduction of legal pluralities — creating natives and settlers who subsisted under different legal regimes.[35] They also recognized pre-existing governance structures. In the case of the Gold Coast (now Ghana), the British expressed their use of the pre-colonial governance structures as: "The chiefs and people of the Gold Coast."[36]

The British recognition of the chiefs was pragmatically informed. First, it was to cut down the cost of governance, and second, to disrupt internal unity that could have upended the colonial enterprise. For this reason, under the banner of Indirect Rule, the British ended up creating chiefs whom Mamdani designated as 'decentralized despots.'[37] Mamdani's conclusion is generalized and has no universal application in all colonies. At least, not in non-settler colonies like the Gold Coast, where some chiefs resisted colonial rule.[38] It was because of the strong resistance from some chiefs that informed the next layer of subduing colonial subjects — the use of violence. The British deployed violence, including exiling an Asante chief such as Prempeh I, whose people did not yield to British imperialist demands.[39] Besides exiling local political elites, a common practice of colonialism was for the British to resort to a security regime using foreigners. The British flirtation with using foreigners whose loyalty they could count on was such that they even used enslaved Hausa people to form the Hausa Gold Coast Constabulary in 1874.[40] They also used legislative strategies such as the Land Bill of 1897, which was designed to concentrate the so-called 'empty land' in the British imperialist rule.[41] Elsewhere, the colonialists, particularly the Belgians deployed brute force in violent areas such as the Congo.[42]

Aside from the carving out the Gold Coast by leveraging and altering pre-existing political regimes, the British hardly involved themselves in the religious itinerary of the people. This non-interference with the religious map of the colonized Gold Coast could have been informed by two main reasons: First, in the late colonial era of the 19th century, the British was advanced in the secularization of its politics.[43] Second, the British recognized the important role of religion in legitimizing the authority of the chiefs through whom they routed the Indirect Rule system. Possibly, it may be for this reason that the British did not readily allow the Christian missionaries into the Northern Territories, where Islam had been established about a century before the European incursion in the 15th century.[44] It may also explain why the British allowed some flexibility of indigenous religious practices but only interfered in those that they considered infractions of human rights.[45]

So, like the pre-colonial state, the British allowed religion to feature in governance. The missionaries were diplomatic in mediating the colonial government and the local population. Nevertheless, the missionaries were also careful to curate an image away from confusing the colonized that they were part of the colonial regime. This development led some of the missionaries into trouble, for example, the Basel missionary Andreas Riis, whom the Danish Governor of Accra stopped from going to the Akuapim Area because Riis refused to hoist the Danish flag on his mission compound.[46] However, when we look at the role of religion, the point remains that the colonialists allowed indigenous cosmogony, Islam and Christianity to operate as a unifying factor in colonial governance.

Nonetheless, the devices of the colonial regime made it an alien institution to the colonized. It was seen as *aban*, a power wall, which aliens erected against indigenes.[47] Coupled with the colonialists' siting development projects only in areas they could exploit, the colonial state was set for collapse in the postcolonial era. Apart from deliberately delinking the people from governance, the postcolonial leaders hardly contemplated that their days were numbered.

At the turn of the 20th century, the colonial regime had shown signs of decline. The outbreak of two World Wars towards the middle of the century reignited the resolve of the colonized to demand political independence — a return to the status quo, as they were free before the colonial intrusion. But at this time, the idea of Asante, Mole-Dagbani and Ga were progressively capitulating to a sense of "we the people of the Gold Coast." Through Islam and Christianity, which both went beyond ethnic boundaries, religious identification became an important channel for constructing Gold Coast nationalism. It is, therefore, comprehensible that at the height of nationalist contestation in the late 1940s, Kwame Nkrumah deployed religious sentiments to whip up national sentiment. He inverted the Christian exhortation by Jesus: "Seek ye first the kingdom of God," into "Seek ye first the political kingdom." By this Nkrumah garbed his political ambition in appealing to religious colouration against colonialism.[48] He also sought ritual cleansing from such religious functionaries as Jehu Appiah of the Mosama Disco Christo Church after his 1951 imprisonment; from Oparebea of Aburi for spiritual protection; and from the Senegalese Sufi leader, Ibrahim Niass for the construction of the Akosombo Dam in 1963.[49]

At the same time, a section of the Gold Coast also used religion against Nkrumah. For example, the elite youth and older elites invoked the sovereignty of the Golden Stool as the soul of Asante state to mobilize support against Nkrumah.[50] They did this through the formation of the National Liberation Movement (NLM) in 1954 by conjuring the Asante religiosity and nationalism symbolized by the Golden Stool in their clamour for federalism. For this reason, while economic reasons may have triggered Asante nationalism, religion formed the base of Asante agitations. This flies in the face of Nkrumah's quest for a postcolonial unitary state for the Gold Coast. Nkrumah stuck to his call of "We are Ghanaians," so let us forge on as one country and led the people of Ghana into independence.

Meanwhile, Nkrumah inherited from a colonial state power that was fragile and susceptible to collapse. Nkrumah did not change the colonial governance system in any revolutionary way. Instead, he deployed it to reconstruct the nascent and precarious state into an amalgam of ethnic groups in the mantra of "We are Ghanaians." In the pursuance of this agenda, Nkrumah sought to eliminate all persons who stood in his way of achieving his goal of building a unitary state. Even chiefs were not spared. He threatened that he would cause any chief who would oppose him to runaway 'leaving their sandals behind.' To this end, Nkrumah passed laws to ban the formation of political parties around ethnic and religious lines.[51] Second, he passed a law to politicize citizenship which resulted in the expelling some Hausa leaders, namely Ahmadu Baba and Alfa Lardan who dissented with him.[52] He also passed the Preventive Detention Act in 1958 to detain without trial political dissenters, thereby alienating some 'friends' such as Ako Adjei and J. B. Danquah (who is considered as the doyen of Ghanaian politics).[53]

Beyond using the colonial strategies of laws and intimidation, Nkrumah invested in symbolism to reorient Ghana's postcolonial state away from 'colonial mentality', 'tribalism', or destabilize the possibility re-tribalization.[54] It is at this point that Nkrumah instrumentalized religion in a way that marked his socialism as very distinct from Marxist socialism. Whereas Karl Marx profiled religion as an opium that enhanced false consciousness and further oppression of the marginalized, Nkrumah saw religion differently. To him, a religious person is a non-denominational Christian and a Marxist socialist.[55] This might appear contradictory, but one could read this as Nkrumah's eclectic creativity in deploying religion instrumentally and pragmatically for nation-building. Measured against his philosophy of Consciencism, which Ali Mazrui relabelled as Africa's Triple Heritage, Nkrumah's intension was to assemble indigenous religions (Islam and Christianity), as existential postcolonial reality to build a nation.[56] From the perspective of religion, Nkrumah imbued symbolism with the aura of the sacred. That is why the 'red' in Ghana's flag was interpreted to imply the blood of those who sacrificed their lives for the country.

While it is true that the death of three ex-servicemen in 1948 became a major catalyst towards Ghana's independence, there is hardly any evidence to show that the march of ex-servicemen on that fateful 28 February 1948 was intended to fight for Ghana's independence. Unlike settler colonies such as South Africa and Kenya, Ghana was a non-settler colony. So, instead of the militant strategy of the Mau Mau of Kenya,[57] Ghana's journey towards independence was hardly about armed struggle. Even Nkrumah's declaration of Positive Action in 1950, a year after he formed his political party, the Convention People's Party (CPP) in 1949, it was tempered with Gandhi's non-violence approach to protest. Against all odds, Nkrumah achieved for Ghana political independence from British colonialism. There are people in Ghana today who raise an outcry that it is inappropriate to call Nkrumah as a 'founder' of independent Ghana; that it would rather be more appropriate to speak of 'founders' of Ghana, thus belittling the immense contribution of Nkrumah. It has been a tradition to celebrate Nkrumah's birthday of 21 September as the founder's day in Ghana. Some elements in Ghanaian politics vehemently oppose this. They say it is more appropriate to commemorate the day as founders'[58] day. The argument, therefore, is reduced to one of pettiness — the position of an inverted comma! Away from the commemoration of who founded Ghana, the family of the three ex-servicemen have demanded that the nation should formally recognize the fallen soldiers by having a statue or bust made in their honour in addition to the cenotaph already erected at Osu Kinkawe where they fell.

On the nation's television news (GTV) on 28 February 2023, a family member of one of the deceased charged the nation of playing ethnic politics against the Ga, the indigenes of Accra. He argued that while the nation had decorated the city of Accra with the statue of non-Ga J. B. Danquah, K. A. Busia and more recently Major Maxwell Adam Mahama, who was grotesquely murdered by a mob in Twi Praso in 2017, not a single Ga indigene, including the ex-servicemen has had that honour. He argued that if these ex-servicemen did intentionally pay with their blood for Ghana's independence, why have they not been honoured all this while?

Recently, on 13 March 2023, addressing Allan Kyerematen, the presidential aspirant of the New Patriotic Party (NPP), the Ga Mantse, Nii Teiko Tsuru II (the Paramount Chief of the Ga people) agitated over what he described as people's disregard and mistreatment of the Ga people on Ga land. He authoritatively stated that, "Accra is Ghana and Ghana is Accra."[59] Second, as part of the commemoration of the ex-servicemen, the current leader of the Veteran Association of Ghana said he would not consider dying for Ghana, as the country does not honour its heroes and heroines. Instead, when choosing between his family and the state, he would choose his family.

Returning to Nkrumah and the formation of postcolonial Ghana, while Nkrumah used law to silence his critics and religion to promote an imagined unity of "We are Ghanaians," he embarked on several developmental projects. He started an aggressive industrialization agenda and provided social services.[60] The nascent nation enjoyed the euphoria of a united people until the beginning of the 1960s when the 'political kingdom' or economic prosperity that independence promised appeared to have limited beneficiaries. Government overspending and sometimes ill-planned industrialization projects began crippling the economy. There were also allegations of corruption against Nkrumah's government. All this sparked agitations and threats on Nkrumah's life, including his escape of two assassination attempts. When all failed in Nkrumah's attempt to build a nation of one Ghana, he reinvested in ideologically reorienting Ghanaians towards socialist philosophy through his establishment of the Ideological Institute at Winneba in 1961. He also reinvested in his Pan-African agenda by appealing to all Africans to unite. In 1963, he wrote *Africa Must Unite* to keep aflame his vision of Pan-Africanism.[61]

Under the guise of protecting himself and the nation from those he considered as neo-colonial stooges, Nkrumah declared a de facto one-party Ghana as a de jure one-party state in 1964.[62] To mobilize the youth to his cause of one Ghana, Nkrumah established the Ghana Young Pioneers' Movement in 1964.[63] During this time, a book surfaced that bore Nkrumah's name as the author, while, in fact, it was believed to have been authored by one William Emmanuel Abraham, a Ghanaian philosopher. The book, *Consciencism* was published in 1964 and is highly philosophical. It critically reflects on the human constitution as a factor of nation-building.[64] Considered as philosophically complex, the book did not gain traction even among the intellectuals at the time, not to talk of the masses — the so-called 'Veranda Boys.'

With agitations from every corner of the country, Nkrumah's declared *de jure* Ghana came under fire from opponents. Given that the declaration may have gone through a Parliamentary process and approval, it hardly solved the political contention that was tearing the new state apart. Against all expectations, Nkrumah's socialist philosophy incurred the ire of the established religious institutions, which garnered mass support against Nkrumah. They charged him for afflicting the nation with what appears to be 'godlessness' by means of his Young Pioneers' movement. In short, Nkrumah became an anathema and enemy of religious freedom. To one Ghanaian academic, Peter Omari, Nkrumah was the epitome of dictatorship.[65] Ali Mazrui profiled Nkrumah as ultimately "good for Africa, but not for Ghana."[66]

Internal politics, metastasizing to include the bi-polar world of the time, saw an ideological battle between America's capitalist leaning and Russia's socialist predilection. Nkrumah wrote his book, *Neo-colonialism* in 1965.[67] The book critiqued America and the erstwhile European colonial powers for interfering in and undermining Africa's quest for human flourishing. As a result, America became more aggressive towards Nkrumah. Emerging as an economic power bloc after the Second World War, America's economic prosperity proved stronger than Russia could withstand. The collapse of erstwhile colonial powers, particularly of France, Germany and Britain, America rose to superpower status. Backed by intense propaganda and the lure of capitalist gifts, several leaders in Africa were divided over how to relate with Nkrumah. America's policy towards African countries veering towards socialism varied.[68] Julius Nyerere of Tanzania practised socialism and yet was favourably treated by Americans. Meanwhile, Nkrumah was considered the bad socialist in the annals of American surveillance.[69]

Failing to win support at home and abroad Nkrumah ran the risk of being toppled. America was ready. Nkrumah's government was considered a threat to America's capitalist interests in Africa. It is well documented that United States of America's Centre for Intelligence Agency (CIA) colluded with the military and police in Ghana to overthrow Nkrumah. On 24 February 1966, Nkrumah was booted out through a military coup d'etat while he was on a mission to broker peace in Hanoi. Reflecting on his post-coup life while serving as Sekou Toure's co-president in Guinea, Nkrumah wrote a few more books, namely *Dark Days in Ghana* in 1968 where he responded to several of the allegations that the joint military cum police junta leveraged against him to justify their takeover.[70] In the final analysis, Nkrumah did return to Ghana, but not alive. He was brought home dead. A mausoleum now marks where he was finally laid to rest in Accra.

Concluding Thoughts

We have dwelt extensively on Kwame Nkrumah for several reasons. First, he was Ghana's first president whose political activism reverberated across Africa and the rest of the world. Declared the African personality of the 20th century, Nkrumah's ideology and activism inspired decolonization struggles across Sub-Saharan Africa, such that by the 1960s, virtually the entire African continent was free from the jaws of colonialism. Second, among the leaders who have ruled Ghana, Nkrumah, perhaps was the most revolutionary in seeking to change the narrative of Africa — curating the continent from its position as a periphery continent to the centre stage, where Africans could manage their own affairs. He was perhaps the most daring and a force to reckon with in the Western mind. Third, he was a pioneer West African leader to have experimented with the idea of constructing citizenship away from the divisive colonial politics of 'divide and rule.' Finally, Nkrumah remains the icon and a major point of reference for many Ghanaians. Nearly all the political elites of Ghana since the country's major re-democratization in the 1990s have identified with Nkrumah. With reference to youth political activism, Nkrumah remains an iconic figure to almost all the revolutionary youth groups in Ghana, including the two that we shall discuss as case studies in this volume.

Therefore, Nkrumah set the stage for all the leaders who came after him. Whether the post-Nkrumah leaders professed liberalism or different versions of socialism, they all inherited a 'failed' nascent state that had relapsed into different levels of polarities — ethnicity, religion and partisan politics. They also claimed to have inherited an economy in near comatose. The economic and political morass of post-Nkrumah Ghana should also be measured against some of the marked achievements of the Nkrumah's regime. Nkrumah's rule lasted for nine years —what these days would be equivalent to two terms. Yet he established many corporations (for example, Ghana Publishing Corporation, State Hotels Corporation, Ghana Film Industry Corporation, etc.); he set up Ghana Education Trust (GET) schools, Ghana Airways, Black Star (Shipping) Line, Builders' Brigade (to harness employable skills), Workers' College (to encourage the youth to acquire higher degrees while working), Kwame Nkrumah University of Science and Technology at Kumasi, University of Cape Coast, to train teachers; he built a hydro-electric dam at Akosombo to power a dizzy conglomerate of factories all over Ghana, constructed the Tema township with an enviable motorway, and embarked on an ambitious industrialization agenda unequalled by his successors. It appears all the youth groups in Ghana draw inspiration from Nkrumah's achievements, which many think are revolutionary and unprecedented.

Without going into details about how the post-Nkrumah leaders fared, suffice it to state that nearly all of them tried to rebuild the country and nearly all have failed. Many of them were overthrown through coups d'état. Even during the democratic era, many of the leaders appeared to be running in circles, in spite of good intentions. The youth largely felt betrayed, and a good number perish in the wilds of Sahara desert in their bid to seek greener pastures in Europe. Against this context, the next chapter discusses Ghana's politics since the turn of the 1990s, focusing largely on how different segments have pointed the country in different directions — almost stultifying the idea of "We are Ghanaians."

The following chapters will focus on how segments of the youth express their discontent against the country's post-COVID morass, to start new movements to jettison the clueless and old flotsam.

NOTES/REFERENCES

[1] Peter L. Berger, *The sacred canopy: Elements of a sociological theory of religion* (New York: Anchor Books, 1967), Chapter 1.

[2] Jean-Paul Sartre, Existentialism is humanism (trans. Carol Macomber) (New Haven: Yale University Press, 2007); Michel Foucault, *Discipline & punish: The birth of the prison* (trans. Alan Sheridan) (New York: Vintage Books, 1977).

[3] Anthony Giddens and Philip W. Sutton, *Essential concepts in sociology.* Cambridge: Polity Press, 2014, p. 56; Anthony Giddens, The Constitution of Society: Outline of the Theory of Structuration. Cambridge: Polity Press, 1984, pp. 16-40.

[4] K. A. Busia, *The position of the chief in the modern political system of Ashanti: A study of the influence of contemporary social changes on Ashanti political institutions* (Oxford: Institute of Social and Cultural Anthropology, 1951).

[5] Emmanuel Akyeampong & Pashington Obeng, "Spirituality, gender, and power in Asante history," *The International Journal of African Historical Studies*, 28, 3 (1995): 481-508.

[6] Busia, *The position.*

[7] Kwame Arhin, *West African traders in Ghana in the nineteenth and twentieth century* (London: Longman, 1979); T. C. McCaskie, *Asante identities: History and modernity in an African village,* 1850-1950 (Edinburgh: Edinburgh UniversityPress, 2000); Jean Allman, "Rounding up spinsters: Gender chaos and unmarried women

in colonial Asante," *The Journal of African History,* 37, 2 (1996): 195-214.

[8] Thomas Hobbes, *Leviathan* (edited with an intro. &. Notes by J. C. A. Gaskin) (Oxford: Oxford University Press, 1996/165), p. 84; John Locke, *The second treaties of government in two treaties of government* (edited by Peter Laslett) (Cambridge: University of Cambridge, 1988/1689); Jean-Jacques Rousseau, *The basic political writings* (Indianapolis: IN: Hackett, 1987); Jean-Jacques Rousseau, *The basic political writings* (Indianapolis: IN: Hackett, 1987).

[9] Roland Hill, Lord Acton (New Haven: Yale University Press, 2000), p.xxiv.

[10] Meyer Fortes, "The political system of the Tallensi of the Northern territories of the Gold Coast," in Meyer Fortes and E. E. Evans-Pritchard (eds), *African political systems*, 239-271 (London: Oxford University Press for International African Institute, 1970).

[11] Ibid.

[12] David Konstan, *Before forgiveness: The origins of a moral idea* (Cambridge: Cambridge University Press, 2010).

[13] Kwesi Yankah, *Speaking for the chief: Okyeame and the politics of Akan royal oratory* (Bloomington: Indiana University Press, 1995).

[14] Wilks, One nation; Charles Prempeh and Lydia Amoah, "Secular governmentality and the court of the Asante Ahemaa in 21st century: An ethnographic account of Ejisu and Juaben traditional areas". In Edmund Abaka & Kwame Osei Kwarteng (Eds.), *The Asante World*, 281-300 (London/New York: Routledge, 2021).

[15] Akosua A. Perbi, *A history of indigenous slavery in Ghana: From the 15th to the 19th century* (Accra: Sub-Saharan Publishers, 2004).

[16] Orlando Patterson, *The sociology of slavery; an analysis of the origins, development, and structure of Negro slavery society in Jamaica* (Rutherford, N.J.: Fairleigh Dickinson University Press, 1967).

[17] Suzanne Miers, "Slavery: A question of definition," *Slavery & Abolition,* 24, 2 (2003: 1-16.

[18] Perbi, *A history.*

[19] Kwame Gyekye, *African cultural values: An introduction* (Accra: Sankofa Publishing Co., 1996).

[20] Ibid.

[21] K. A. Busia, *The challenge of Africa* (New York: F. A. Praeger, 1962).

[22] Emmanuel Akyeampong, "Sexuality and prostitution among the Akan

of the Gold Coast, c. 1650-1950," *Past & Present*, 156 (1997): 144-173.

[23] Charles Prempeh and Lydia Amoah, "Secular governmentality and the court of the Asante Ahemaa in 21st century: An ethnographic account of Ejisu and Juaben traditional areas". In Edmund Abaka & Kwame Osei Kwarteng (Eds.), *The Asante World*, 281-300 (London/New York: Routledge, 2021).

[24] Ransford Edward Van Gyampo and Franklyn Obeng-Odoom, "Youth participation in local and national development in Ghana: 1620-2013," *The Journal of Pan African Studies*, 5, 9 (2013): 129-150.

[25] Ivor Wilks, "'Unity and progress': Asante politics revisited," Ghana Studies, 1 (1998): 151-179; Anshan Li, "Asafo and destoolment in colonial southern Ghana, 1900-1953," *The International Journal of African Historical Studies*, 28, 2 (1995): 327-357; Busia, *Position of the chief.*

[26] Busia, *The position.*

[27] Charles Prempeh, Christianity, Culture, and Pentecostalism in Ghana: An Ethnographic Study of Pentecostal Traditional Authorities in Contemporary Akan Society (1990s–Present) (Unpublished PhD Dissertation submitted to the University of Cambridge, 2021).

[28] Busia, *Position of the chief.*

[29] Jean Marie Allman, *The quills of the porcupine: Asante nationalism in an emergent Ghana* (Wisconsin: The University of Wisconsin Press, 1993); Agnes A. Aidoo, "Order and conflict in the Asante empire: A study in interest group relations," *African Studies Review*, 20, 1 (1977): 1-36; Manuel J. Manu-Osafo, "'The days of their heedless power were over and done': Dynamics of power in the military structures of the precolonial Asante state, 1874-1900," *The Journal of African History*, 62,2 (2021): 254-270.

[30] J. F. Ade Ajayi, "The place of African history and culture in the process of nation-building in Africa south of the Sahara," *Journal of Negro Education*, 30, 3 (1961): 206-207; Rodney, How Europe; Ali A. Mazrui, *The Africans: A triple heritage* (London: BBC Publications, 1986).

[31] J. B. Danquah, "The historical significance of the Bond of 1844." *Transactions of the Historical Society of Ghana*, 3, 1 (1957): 3-29.

[32] Aimé Césaire, *Discourse on colonialism* (trans. Joan Pinkham) (New York: Monthly Review Press, 1972).

[33] Kofi Asare Opoku, "Independence of the mind," *Journal of Black*

    Studies, 1, 2 (1970): 179-186.

34 Mwenda Ntarangwi, David Mills and Mustafa H.M. Babiker (eds), *African anthropologies: History, critique, and practice* (London: Zed Books, 2006).

35 **Mahmood** Mamdani, Citizen and subject: Contemporary Africa and the legacy of late colonialism (Princeton, N.J.: Princeton University Press, 1996).

36 E. A. Boateng, *Government and the People: Outlook for Democracy in Ghana* (Accra: Institute of Economic Affairs, 1996), p.144.

37 Mamdani, *Citizen and subject.*

38 Adu A. Boahen, *Topics in West African history* (Harlow: Longman, 1986).

39 Joseph K. Adjaye, "Asantehene Agyeman Prempe I and British colonization of Asante: A reassessment," *The International Journal of African Historical Studies,* 22, 2 (1989): 223-249; Emmanuel Akyeampong, "Christianity, modernity and the weight of tradition in the life of 'Asantehene' Agyeman Prempeh I, c. 1888-1931," *Journal of International African Institute,* 69, 2 (1999): 279-311; Robert Aldrich, *Banished potentates: Dethroning and exiling indigenous monarchs under British and French colonial rule, 1815-1955* (Manchester: Manchester University Press, 2018).

40 Sarah Balakrishnan, "Of debt and bondage: From slavery to prison in the Gold Coast, c. 1807-1957," *Journal of African History,* 61, 1 (2020): 3-21.

41 S. K. B. Asante, "The neglected aspects of the activities of the Gold Coast Aborigines Rights Protection Society," *Phylon,* 36, 1 (1975): 32-45.

42 Adam Hochschild, King Leopold's ghost: A story of greed, terror, and heroism in colonial Africa (Boston, Mass.: Houghton Mifflin, 1998).

43 John Dunn and A. F. Robertson, *Dependence and opportunity: Political change in Ahafo* (Cambridge: Cambridge University Press, 1973).

44 Nana James Kwku Brukum, Northern territories of the Gold Coast under British colonial rule, 1897-1956: A study in political change (PhD thesis submitted to the University of Toronto, 1997).

45 E. K. Quashigah, "Legislating religious liberty: The Ghanaian experience," *BYU Law Review,* 2, 6 (1999): 589-609.

46 Effah K. Ababio, Conflict, identity and co-operation – The relations of

the Christian church with the traditional, colonial and national state in Ghana with special reference to period 1916-1966 (PhD thesis submitted to the University of Edinburg, 1991).

[47] Baffour Agyeman-Duah, "Ghana, 1982-6: The politics of the PNDC" *The Journal of Modernn African Studies*, 25, 4 (1987): 613-642.

[48] Charles Adom Boateng, *The political legacy of Kwame Nkrumah of Ghana* (Ontario: The Edwin Mellen Press, 2003).

[49] Okomfo Ama Boakyewa, Nana Oparebea and the Akonnedi shrine: Cultural, religious and global agents (PhD thesis submitted to the Indiana University, 2014); John S. Pobee, *Kwame Nkrumah and the church in Ghana, 1949-1966* (A study in the relationship between the socialist government of Nkrumah, the first Prime Minister and first President of Ghana and the Protestant Christian Churches in Ghana (Accra: Asempa Publishers, 1988); Charles Prempeh, Nima-Maamobi in *Ghana's Postcolonial Development: Migration, Islam and Social Transformation* (Bamenda/Cameroon: Langaa RPCIG, 2022).

[50] Kwame Arhin, "The Asante praise poems: Theideology of patrimonialism," *Paideuma*(32(1986):163-197; JeanMarieAllman,"'Hewers ofwood, carriers of water': Islam, class, and politics on the eve of Ghana's independence," *African Studies Review*, 34, 2 (1991): 1-26.

[51] Allman, "'Hewers," p.10;

[52] Ibid.

[53] Harcourt Fuller, *Building the Ghanaian nation-state: Kwame Nkrumah's symbolic nationalism* (Basingstoke, Hampshire: Palgrave Macmillan, 2014), p. 33.

[54] Ibid.

[55] Ebenezer Obiri Addo, "Religion and politics in Africa: An assessment of Kwame Nkrumah's legacy for Ghana," in Nimi Wariboko and Toyin Falola (eds), *The Palgrave handbook of African social ethics*, 185-201 (Cham: Palgrave Macmillan, 2020).

[56] Kwame Nkrumah, *Consciencism: Philosophy and ideology for decolonization and development* (London: Heinemann, 1964); Ali A. Mazrui, *The Africans: A triple heritage* (London: BBC Publications, 1986).

[57] Robert I. Rotberg and Ali A. Mazrui (eds), *Protest and power in black Africa* (New York: Oxford University Press, 1970).

[58] Edem Adotey, "A matter of apostrophe? Founder's day, founders' day, and holiday politics in contemporary Ghana," *Journal of West African*

Studies, 5, 2 (2019): 113-139; Mary Akosua Seiwaa Owusu, Nationalism in question: A study of key categories in Ghanaian history, 1863-1965 (PhD thesis submitted to Dalhousie University, 2020); Charles Prempeh (5 August 2019), "Founders or founder? The lies and the lies we have believed for long! Enough of the lies," https://www.modernghana.com/news/948858/founders-or-founder-the-lies-and-the-lies-we-have-believed.html.

59 Emma Ankrah (13 March 2023), "We have been mistreated on our own land for far too long – Ga Mantse fumes," https://www.myjoyonline.com/we-have-been-mistreated-and-sidelined-on-our-own-land-ga-mantse-fumes/

60 Fuller, *Building the Ghanaian nation-state.*

61 Kwame Nkrumah, *Africa must unite* (London: Heinemann, 1963).

62 Ibid.

63 Ibid., p. 122.

64 Kwame Nkrumah, *Consciencism: Philosophy and ideology for decolonization and development* (London: Heinemann, 1964).

65 Peter T. Omari, Kwame Nkrumah: *The anatomy of an African dictatorship* (London: C. Hurst, 1970).

66 Ali A. Mazrui, "Nkrumah: The Leninist Czar," Transition, 26 (1966): 8-17.

67 Kwame Nkrumah, *Neo-colonialism: The last stage of imperialism* (London: Thomas Nelson & Sons, Ltd., 1965).

68 Emmanuel Akyeampong, "African socialism; or, the search for an indigenous model of economic development?" *Economic History of Developing Regions*, 33, 1 (2018): 67-87.

69 Ibid.

70 Kwame Nkrumah, *Dark days in Ghana* (London: Panaf Books, 1968).

CHAPTER 3

Young People and Ghana's Politics Since the Millennial Turn

Introduction

From the foregoing, provision has been made for a detailed account of the extent to which the Ghana establishment is a social contract reflecting historical and global state formation realities. It has been argued that, much as the idea of Ghana as a social contract is a given, it appears not to have reflected in the political mobilization and activism of the country's youth. This chapter asserts that this trend in youthful political activism has seen the state often deploying every means, including digital surveillance, to dismiss and clamp down on youth quest for reforms. To put all this in context, this chapter provides an account of Ghana's politics since the turn of the millennium and how the country has resorted to social media as a strategy.

An Overview of Ghana's Politics Since 2000

After Nkrumah's government was overthrown in 1966 by a military-cum-police coup, Ghana has had many coups that derailed and ruined all prospects of a desired economic prosperity. However, with the coming of Rawlings, who staged a coup in 1981 against Dr Hilla Limann, a democratic leader, Ghana was in the grip of Rawlings' military regime until 1992. To his credit, as a military leader, Rawlings succeeded in securing Ghana's political stability since the 1980s. This stabilization enabled democratic governance to take root and has fostered a culture of regime change. For this reason, the country's re-democratization came with a renewed understanding of Ghana as an imagined united country of "We are Ghanaians."

Unlike the military era, which mainstreamed Rawlings's deployment of decrees and random use of force to cow Ghanaians into submitting to his ideas, the 1992 Constitution ushered in a new socio-political regime. The new dawn expanded communication channels to citizens. The new political era also ensured a significant shift by Rawlings from sympathizing with a segment of the citizenry such as the Vincent Damuah's Afrikania Movement, while he discredited chiefs and Christianity.[1] This means that until the country's re-democratization, Rawlings succeeded in overcoming the two main forces, namely ethnicity and religion that made an imagined "We are Ghanaians" nearly impossible.

Nevertheless, the liberalization of Ghana's political space and the ushering in of relative media freedom did not necessarily resonate with economic prosperity. Ghana continued to reel under the overwhelming economic morass that undermined both the aspirations of independence and the expectation of the country's youthful populace. At the time Rawlings ended his service to the nation as a democratic leader on January 2001, Ghana had made modest progress in its quest for human flourishing. Nevertheless, for the majority of the country's citizenry, particularly the youth, the realities of unemployment, rising cost of living, nepotism, ethnocentrism, partisan politics and what several of them labelled as gerontocratic politics, the chances of the youth ever getting out of their woes, have continued to blur.

Consequently, with all hindrances in the way of religion and ethnicity significantly removed, the country experienced a rise in re-tribalization and religiously informed partisanship. As we have mentioned, during the colonial times and under the regime of Kwame Nkrumah, a combination of force and legislation was used to block the polarizing impact of ethnocentrism and conservative religious aspiration. But as the millennial turn hardly impacted the fortunes of several Ghanaians, citizens have constantly re-established touch with their ethnic groups and religions. Since the 2000s, Ghana has seen a sharp rise in people rallying in support of their chiefs to demand their share of the 'national cake.' This means that much as the country has sought to curb ethnocentrism by barring chiefs from active politics in its 1992 Constitution, several chiefs across the country have hardly remained aloof in matters of politics. At every major presidential election, several chiefs have flouted the state's imposition of non-involvement partisan politics on them. On a few occasions, some figures have successfully leveraged the influence of their chiefs to bar a particular political party from campaigning in their traditional area.

The issue of ethnicity is also nuanced by the fact that citizens of Ghana who have kins across national borders have had their citizenship politicized. Historically, late colonial rule, armed by the Berlin Conference of 1884/85, legitimized the European scrambling for and partition of Africa.[2] The result was the splitting of erstwhile cohesive ethnic groups across national borders. Contrary to the much-vaunted argument about the arbitrariness of colonial boundaries, such demarcations are social contracts.[3] Nevertheless, splitting largely homogeneous groups across national boundaries has challenged the unity of post-colonial states in several African countries, thus instigating border conflicts.[4] Citizens of Ghana who have kin-members in neighbouring countries such as Togo (to the East), Côte d'Ivoire (to the West) and Burkina Faso (to the North), have freely crisscrossed borders to participate in sociogenic and economic activities with their trans-national kin-members. For example, the Akan in Côte d'Ivoire and Mossi in Burkina Faso have often moved across national boundaries to trade and organize joint festivals and funerals of prominent members. The cultural ties among trans-national ethnic groups have deepened since the United Nations declared the 1990s a decade for indigenous cultures' recuperation.[5] The concurrent surge in chieftaincy in Ghana as the constitutional body serving as a bastion of culture has also fostered trans-national cultural ties.

But all these are also encumbered with ethnocentrism.[6] While ethnic groups such as the Akan and Mossi have not significantly struggled to re-unite their kinship ties across national borders, the Ewes have rather struggled to achieve the same. Largely for partisan reasons, which date back to the 1950s when a section of the Ewe group had to decide in a plebiscite whether to join Ghana or Togo, the political elites have complexly politicized Ewe citizenship.[7] The Ewe people have spread across Ghana, Togo and Benin. Of the two countries, it is Togo, which for the reason of geographical proximity, have sustained a continuing tie with kinsmen and women in Ghana. On several of our visits to the Volta Region, where the Ewe people are located as a major ethnic group, we find Ewes who, for example, farm in Ghana but sleep in Togo and vice versa. Whereas these Ewe people often cross 'artificial' borders to transact social and economic activities across borders, the political participation of Ghanaian Ewes is often complicated. Since the turn of the millennium, almost every registration towards election has fostered controversies over who is truly a Ghanaian Ewe.[8] The general perception that the Ewes support the National Democratic Congress, a party founded and led by Jerry John Rawlings, burdens the Ewe inclusion in national politics. As a section of the Ewe feel they are marginalized for partisan reasons (a reality that, as we said, was not properly addressed in the 1950s), speculations have arisen in public discourses that a few discontented Ewes have sought to organize coups, while others have subscribed to a secessionist agenda.[9]

Revising the historical strategy of politicizing citizenship, since the turn of the millennium, Ghana has embarked on a progressive digitalization agenda, which has crystallized under the New Patriotic Party (NPP), perceived also as an Akan-dominated party.[10] The digitalization agenda of state institutions to fight corruption and enhance efficiency of state institutions has involved the digitalization of citizenship. Reflecting a global trend of nations taking advantage of the Internet Revolution of the 1970s, biometric data has become a major strategy for politicizing citizenship.[11] Whether shifting from paper document or combining it with biometric data, it is now more common and easy for states to regulate and police citizens and trans-national migrations.[12] Against the background of what was said previously that trans-national social ties remain strong among border ethnic groups, the digitalization of citizenry may be read as a complex way of either breaking trans-national ethnic ties or policing citizens and their migration choices.

Needless to say, since Ghana introduced biometric citizenship (known as a National Identity Card) at the turn of the millennium, ethnic-related politics has surged. Marginalized ethnic groups, including a section of the Ewe people, have re-membered and reinterpreted their history to secede from Ghana or promote 'ethnic nationalism.' It is against this background that one could understand the rise of a group known as the Homeland Study Group Foundation (HSGF), founded and led by Charles Kormi Kudjordji, Martin Asiama Agbenu and Divine Odonkor in 2017. The HSGF has often stood against the Ghanaian state. According to Weberian theory of the state using coercing force, the police have been deployed to arrest and detain the leadership of the HSGF. Since the Ewe group, like any ethnic group in Ghana, is internally polarized, the HSGF has struggled to draw support from a significant number of other Ewe groups in Ghana.[13]

On the religious front, the idea of "We are Ghanaians" has also been very challenging. The surge in the activities of Pentecostal-charismatic Christianity at the turn of the millennium, with leaders who hardly concede to aspects of indigenous practice in urban areas, has divided the nation. For example, the tension between the Ga indigenous people of Accra and a section of Pentecostal Christians over an annual ban on 'noisemaking' that precedes the Ga *Homowo* traditional festival has often led to conflicts between the two groups.[14]   Similarly, elsewhere in the country's Western Region, Pentecostal Christianity has had a violent confrontation with traditional authorities on the eve of the millennium.[15] Nevertheless, religious tensions have been pronounced in Accra for several reasons. First, the colonial administrators in 1877, for health and sanitation reasons, made Accra its administrative capital.[16] This ensured a continuous flow of other ethnic groups into the city, who eventually have certainly shaped Ga culture.[17] The city has retained its political and social status as the heartland of both economic activities and seat of government since independence in 1957.

Additionally, the state failed to decentralize development, implying that migration into Accra continues to increase. Since the 1980s, Rawlings' regime, as part of the country's quest for nationwide development, mainstreamed the idea of decentralization; but such a project had hardly succeeded at the turn of the millennium.[18] Its failure includes the inability of political elites to fund state institutions and traditional authorities to advance regional developments. Accra remains the epicentre of all major state institutions. People have continued to move to Accra to access quality health and education. The plurality of the city has also sustained religious tensions. The politicization of its chieftaincy has also fractured its ability to secure a commom interest. Against this background, Pentecostals have had difficulty living cordially with the Ga traditional constituency since the turn of the millennium.

Beyond Pentecostals and indigenous Ga authorities, internal disputes have also rocked the Muslim community.[19] Historically, by the 1830s, the city of Accra has had a small segment of Muslims made up of freed Muslim slaves from Brazil. The colonial government had fostered divide and rule tactics by reserving the Muslim North as a source of labour supply.[20] Muslim role in nationalist politics has not been recognized to an appreciable level in the country's history.[21] Meanwhile, during the struggle for independence, the Muslims (sometimes homogenized as Hausa) played an important role Ghana's politics. During the heydays of the nationalist struggle for independence, the Muslims, fearing emerging marginalization, formed the Ghana Muslim Association as a cultural and educational organization in 1938. But given the ethnic polarization that dogged the nationalist struggle, the Muslims redefined their association into a political party — the Muslim Association Party (MAP) in 1954.

The MAP largely identified with the Asante National Liberation Movement (NLM) against Nkrumah's Convention People's Party (CPP). The alliance was mainly due to a long history between the Asantes and Muslims. The Asante Empire, which was very powerful since the 18th century, had established both military and administrative ties with the Mole-Dagbani Kingdoms.[22] For this reason, the Asante attracted several Muslim clerics and scholars who provided both ritual and administrative services to the Asante political elites.[23] This meant that in the late colonial era, Asantes had an overwhelming presence of Muslim population and migrants from the Northern Territories and other West African countries. To unite the migrant group for effective administration and also foster the divide and rule strategy, the British established the first recognized migrant community (known as 'Zongos') in 1896.[24] The ethnically diverse community was united on the use of the Hausa language, first, and second, the appointment of influential persons, mostly the Hausa as headsmen. As the latter subsisted under the Asante, they ultimately were loyal to the British colonial administrator. The issue was also complex because at the time of the establishment of the Zongos, the British had exiled Asantehene Prempeh I in 1900 and nearly succeeded in breaking the Asante into small units. Given this history, some of the leaders of the MAP readily aligned with the Asante when Nkrumah agitated against the Asante NLM over the constitution of postcolonial Ghana.

Considering Nkrumah's discontent with the leadership of NLM and how he thought they had delayed the country's independence struggle, he intensified his efforts at polarizing the Muslim front by establishing a rivalry group, the Muslim Youth Congress, led by Z. B. Shadow and Mallam Mutawakilu.[25] Later, at independence, Nkrumah passed laws to exile vocal Hausa figures. Since independence, therefore, the Muslim community has hardly united on anything.

All this has historically been compounded by inter-sect conflict in Islam. The Ahmadiyya Muslims have been in Ghana since 1920. They established schools and translated the Qur'an as part of their modernization agenda. But since the so-named orthodox Muslim hereticized the Ahmadiyya, the Muslim community has hardly appeared united.[26]

All the inter-Islamic tension crystallized towards the end of the 1990s when a reformist religious group, the Ahlu Sunna, led by Hajj Umar Ibrahim, discounted the Tijaniyya as altering the validity and sanctity of Islamic doctrines, morphing into the Sunni charge of the Tijaniyya as dabbling in *bida* (innovation).[27] Much as scholars seem divided over whether the Muslims are united or not,[28] national politics and its tendency towards divisiveness has burdened the Muslims and their integration. Since the turn of the millennium, the Muslims have struggled to get the state to recognize Muslim women's use of the veil (headscarf) in public institutions, particularly schools.[29] There have also been allegations of historic Christian mission schools disallowing Muslim students from fasting. Such mission schools have also been accused of compelling Muslim children to participate in Christian rituals. It is also reported that such imposition of Christian rituals forced a final year Muslim student, Mustapha Abdul Gafaru, to jump from a classroom block to his death when he saw a Senior House Master approaching.[30]

President John Mahama's admission into Ghana of controversial Arab detainees in America brought Muslims and Christians into a collision in 2016.[31] Also, simmering internal tension has affected the possibility of a Muslim president. Ghana's population is overwhelming Christian, who command 71.26 percent of the country's segment, while Muslims command 17 percent.[32] Much as the Muslims have nearly disputed all national censuses since the 1990s, they have had a good representation in politics. The political elites, especially of the NPP, a major force in the country's politics since the millennium, have ensured that the Vice Presidential slot is secured as an office for a Muslim. This NPP strategy is more pragmatically informed than a clearly stated mandate. But the Muslims have disputed the identity of such a Vice President. For example, the first Muslim Vice President, Alhaji Aliu Mahama, had his Islamic identity questioned by a section of Muslims. In Maamobi (where this researcher had resided since 1984 when he was two years old), Alhaji Aliu Mahama was ridiculed. At a Moslem gathering, the Imam had said, *"Atakbir."* Instead of responding *"Allahu akbar,"* the Vice President rather said, *"Sallelehu alehi wasalem."* This was taken to mean a breach of protocol and that Alhaji Aliu Mahama did not represent the Muslim front.

More recently, Muslims have disputed over their support for yet another Muslim Vice President — Dr Mahamudu Bawumia. He is known for often patronizing Christian programmes and receiving prayers from Christian leaders. Several of these incidents have been streamlined on social media. A conservative section of Muslims sees that as a betrayal of his Islamic identity — polarizing the Muslim community against his ambition to become the president of Ghana on the ticket of the NPP. All this is because the NPP is considered as an Akan as well as largely a Christian party. Not only that, under Kofi Abrefa Busia, a Christian and Akan civilian leader of Ghana after Nkrumah, a section of 'aliens' was expelled under what came to be known as the 'Alien Compliance Order.' When it was promulgated on 18 November 1969, all aliens without resident permits were given two weeks to rectify their stay or leave the country.[33] This resulted in the expulsion of several Muslims. While the incident took place in the late 1960s, it has often been politicized against the NPP as anti-Muslim and anti-Northerners. No amount of NPP offering Muslim important national appointments appeared to have assuaged some Muslims who continue to hold the notion that the NPP is anti-Islam.

To say the least, all the tensions discussed so far, have undermined the country's quest for development. But they have also cascaded into national politics — especially as it involves the young people of marginalized Muslim enclaves in Accra. It has been mentioned that Accra has had a Muslim presence since the 1830s; besides, the British relocation of the administrative capital of the colony from Cape Coast to Accra further brought in more migrants. It could, therefore, be argued that since the Hausa (usually used as a loose term to designate all Northern migrants) had demonstrated loyalty to the British, they were the favourites of the British. In Accra, the British offered leadership positions to Hausa leaders in newly emerging urban areas, which became the extension of Zongos in Accra in the late 19th century. These communities included Sabon Zongo, Cow Lane, and Tudu. At the turn of the 20th century, the communities expanded to include areas such as Nima, Maamobi,

Accra New Town and Madina in the 1950s.[34]

The British used all strategies, including introducing cemeteries in the city; the Ga traditional philosophy of admitting migrants ensured the growth of the Zongos.[35] But the leadership of the Zongos also secured more freedom. It ensured that Islam was practised devoid of all 'pagan' influences and mainstreamed the location of Zongos away from the city centre. So, until later in the 1950s, the Zongos were hardly part of the administration of Accra. The consequence of this included the fact that the Zongos were starved of development. Second, for political reasons, which included Nkrumah's complicated relationship with the Hausa and the historic Hausa people's role in the colonial establishment, Hausa is not considered a national language. Presently, much as the Hausa language is spoken everywhere in Ghana among the Muslims, the language has not achieved the status of a lingua franca in several West African countries. This is because Hausa is not taught and studied in secular schools.[36] Besides, Muslims reject, as missionary propaganda, Christian education; and the Zongos still remain impoverished in the supply of social services. In 2017, the New Patriotic Party (NPP) government established the Ministry for Zongo and Inner-City Development. Religion occupies an important place in Zongo life. Several residents are prepared to invest in undertaking pilgrimages to Mecca several times at the expense of educating their children. This trend, which has been politicized at the national level, flies against the fact that in Islam one should not go on pilgrimage if one cannot provide for his or her family. Regrettably, in Nima, Maamobi, and Accra New Town, several Muslims pride themselves on how many times they have gone on the *hajj*.

Merged with a subdued and continuing intra- and inter-religious tension, which should have subsided significantly after the COVID-19 pandemic, the Zongos have all been characterized by poor sanitation and squalid living conditions, a relatively high level of illiteracy and ignorance and reported cases of criminal activities and youth consumption of illicit herbs and substances. The issues become grimmer when politicians continue to support ventures such as promoting Arab language education and building of Astro-turf football pitches that do not immediately solve the historical marginalization of the Zongos. As the city's continuing economic challenges set in and weighed heavily on the Zongo young people, several of them took the path of the internet fraught known locally as *Sakawa*, which was very popular at the turn of the millennium, especially in 2007. Beyond Accra's land disputes, which involve multiple sale of land by some Ga traditional personages, conflicts in the city have abounded over land claims. For this reason, some traditional and political elites formed Zongo youth into groups known as 'land guards' to protect their lands. The result had been a rash of several conflicts among these land guards, some of whom have been drawn from the Zongos. This has divided the Zongo front on matters that do not directly inure to the communal good of the Zongos.

Over time, both land guardism and *Sakawa* lost their appeal when the police began to clamp down on the youth. Making a significant dent on *Sakawa*, specifically was the advanced digital surveillance technology which has been developed in the West and offered to Ghanaian and African leaders to fight internet fraud. To survive the never-ending economic difficulties, several of the youth mobilized themselves to participate in politics from the periphery. Consequently, in Nima and Maamobi, these young people, majority of whom had little or no Western education, formed groups to pragmatically support the NPP and the NDC — the two political parties, which have dominated politics in Ghana since the 1990s. Initially, as was the case with Accra, Kumasi and other cities, the youth mobilized under the guise of weekend 'Keep fit' exercises to rally support for their respective political parties. Sometimes, they creatively composed songs to render their parties popular. But because of their limited education and the general marginalization of the Zongos, the young people got 'forgotten' when the parties they supported came into office. They were given a pittance as a wage; some were given gifts of food for their efforts.

Denied the juicy pickings, the dispirited youth expressed their discontent through resorting to violence. In the Zongo communities, the youth embarked on violent acts such as burning, gunshots, stoning and seizing state institutions such as toll booths on highways and taking over public toilets.[37] As a result, the youth groups were labelled severally as 'vigilante groups' and 'foot soldiers.'

The troubles of these youth groups have been a major concern to the political elites for two main reasons. First, the West African sub-region is increasingly becoming the epicentre of religiously inspired mass groups such as Boko Haram and ISIS.[38] With reported cases of a few Ghanaian Muslim youth joining such groups, the elites found a reason to disband the so-called foot soldiers as breeding grounds for religious extremism. Since the 11 September 2001 terrorist attack on the US, the latter has been actively involved in supporting Ghana to curb terrorist activities.[39] The second reason is that the economy of Ghana is still not growing to ensure relative decentralized development for a large section of the Ghanaian populace, of which the Zongos are an integral part. This means that more agitations would emanate from marginalized communities.

In consequence, public discourse arose on how to end the activities of the foot soldiers. Politicians who also need the youth when their parties lose an election often betray the aspirations of the youth. A case in point was the disastrous consequence of a parliamentary by-election at the Ayawaso West Wuogon in Accra in 2019. The election was marked by low-intensity violence, which, it was said, was fuelled and sustained by foot soldiers.[40] A committee of experts was formed whose findings led to the passage of the Anti-Vigilante Law in Ghana in 2020.

With the activities of foot soldiers clamped down, the youth were left with nearly nothing to cling to, even as elitist politics surged. All this was happening within the context of civil society organizations such as the Ghana Centre for Democratic Development, whose activities several youths think fostered the interest of the elite and western neo-colonial aspirations. Cumulatively, the social construction of the postcolonial state of "We are Ghanaians" hardly united Ghanaians. Whether through legislation or the state use of force, the multidimensionality of social exclusion has polarized the country into silos defined around partisan politics, ethnicity and religion.

The result has been the youth, who are highly disillusioned about their future, are compelled to seek greener pastures in Europe and in the Arab world, where they are subjected to complex forms of modern-day enslavement. They would work on tomato plantations in Italy, break their backs working in care homes or be reduced to domestic slaves in some Arab countries.[41] Social media is awash with stories and pre-recorded videos and audios about young Ghanaian women who lament about how their Arab taskmasters sexually and physically abuse them. Between 2022 and 2023, several Ghanaian nurses complained about their frustrations while working in England. Since the outbreak of the coronavirus pandemic, several recruitment organizations have emerged (and old ones revitalized) to recruit Ghanaian nurses for work abroad. For example, in their hurry to escape the economic hardships at home, women pay huge sums of money — not less than £6000 — to secure a highly contentious English work permit. Several of them arrive in England only to languish in hostels after a month of their arrival.

In February 2023, a young nurse, who was pregnant, came through that route, and got stuck. Coming ahead of her husband (who joined her a few months later), the young lady and her husband found themselves stranded in a hostel, not knowing where to turn to deliver their baby. Meanwhile, she was ejected from her hostel because in England women are not allowed to deliver in hostels — they need a permanent residential address for postnatal care. The irony is that Ghanaians are quick to criticize Arab countries for bad treatment meted to their compatriots, but are mute when it comes to the maltreatment in the colonial metropolis.

Regrettably, highly educated Ghanaians acquiesce to do menial jobs such as sweeping streets in Europe and taking up roles that are far below their qualification; they live on 'hand-to-mouth' basis. What is painful is the way Artificial Intelligence (AI) technology is rendering some jobs, such as business administration, quite redundant.

In addition, the Western world has relocated several of its industries to the Asiatic world and many African migrants are struggling to survive working there. In the case of England, the commonest job available for even highly educated Africans, who hold a Masters degree, is the care industry. It is no wonder that Ghanaian youth has resorted to social media to re-negotiate their stake in the country's politics.

Social Media and Politics in Ghana

An increasing number of Ghanaian young men and women who find themselves in the cusp of life's limbo have embraced social media to their advantage. Ghana connected to the internet in the late 1990s. In 2001, several secondary school graduates ponder the possibility of re-membering or re-gathering after graduating from school. Several fear that, upon finishing school, they might not meet again; some break down in tears. This was the case in August 2001 when students at the West Africa Secondary school finished their final exams. They formed on WhatsApp an old students association handle. There they re-membered, asserted their collective identity as early millennials and used the internet to organize online meetings, mobilizing resources to help members in need.

Elsewhere, the youth wing of ethnic groups has re-invested in historic ethnic movements to advance ethnic interests.[42] As Ghana becomes more and more segmented along partisan, religious and ethnic lines, several ethnic groups have had their traditional leaders mobilize online for offline sociogenic activities. Continuing with old ethnic associations in Accra in the early days of independence and home-town associations abroad, online ethnic associations have broadened. A study of the Asante Kotoko Society WhatsApp group noted that since the middle of the 2000s, Asante young men and women, intelligent in their cultural histories and savvy in the use of the internet, have aligned with the older generation to rejuvenate the historic early 20th century Asante Kotoko Society — an ethnic nationalist group.[43] The revitalized Society, inter alia, discusses matters that primarily affect Asanteman's development, including canvassing politically for Asante political national aspirants.

In Accra's multi-cultural setting, young people have leveraged social media to transcend ethnic barriers to form political pressure groups that break them into either lending their support to one of Ghana's two major political parties, namely the NPP and NDC. Several researchers have explored the various ways young people use social media for political purposes. Our concern is how social media now serves as a dual space where online activities tend to metastasize into offline street demonstrations and protests. Online spaces are saturated with partisan politics, using language that the older generation considers highly offensive. Nevertheless, since Ghana clamped down on foot soldiers' type of political mobilization, backed by ever-increasing cost of political party organization obscuring the prospects of any alternative political party other than the duopoly ever wining an election,[44] young people have found social media a safe home. Through social media, they overreach their local spaces to involve themselves in transnational politics.

As we shall see, the proliferation and global use of social media has also helped young people to reconfigure their citizenship. Through social media, citizenship among the youth is now virtual, possessing a semblance of pre-modern citizenship, which, as previously stated, was more about social conviviality than legislation, belonging and identity. Citizenship, like the nation-state is a socio-cultural construct. And yet, through biometrics and digitization, an illusion of naturally constructed nature of citizenship arms the elite to police bodies and migrations. Since the turn of the millennium, Ghanaian migrants abroad with interest in participating in local politics, have had their dreams ended because of legislation against dual citizenship and active politics in the Ghanaian context. Similarly, the Ghanaian diasporan community have struggled in vain to get the chance to vote during elections in Ghana. More complex is the prosecution of the diasporan person who, for various reasons, including maybe ignorance of citizenship laws in Ghana or pragmatism, skip the rule of renouncing their citizenship to the countries abroad in which they domicile. This is even after they have won competitive parliamentary elections to represent their people, including bringing their acquired skills and resources to support human flourishing.

The overreaching arms of social media have challenged dual or multiple citizenships that law and partisan politics have hampered. Furthermore, social media is transnational in coverage, while creating human beings as virtual beings who also subsist in the fluid cyborg or virtual world. The virtual world is a fluid, malleable, transitional, hardly conforming to any particular law. It is hardly sociogenic in the sense of undertaking social events. But it also helps to reinvent the creation of an imagined community of people of diverse backgrounds, who may hardly know themselves or hardly meet and yet mobilize around an ideology that is mainstreamed online. It is part of this virtuality and inter-penetrable disposition of social media world that trans-national citizenship has been rendered more possible than ever imagined.

Theoretically, the social media world affirms the Akan people's understanding of the human family as a forest with clusters of trees that looked very much closer and homogenous but autonomous as one gets closer. At the same time, the virtual world ensures the relevance of two main theories, for example, Anthony Giddens structuration and James Clifford 'travel without travelling.'[45] Giddens deconstructs the simplicity of the Foucauldian idea that structures simply oppress, leaving individuals in 'social imprisonment.'[46] From the perspective of Foucault, this imprisonment is structured through language and social webs of socialization and state institutions, including the schools and prisons. Jean-Paul Sartre, on his part, advanced existentialism as a theory to arm human beings against the dictates of natural boundaries. For both Foucault and Sartre, structures are human inventions to perpetuate multidimensionality of marginalization.

Nevertheless, from Anthony Giddens structuration theory and Peter Berger's idea of cultural dietetics, one could argue that structures are not just overwhelmingly invincible with a totalizing oppressive verve. Instead, much as structures are intentionally cultivated, there are rooms for human beings to exercise their agency. Certainly, it is not to argue that the idea of agency is given, as it is to posit that it is possible for human beings to negotiate around structures to advance their interest. Unlike deconstructing structures, as Sartre and Foucault or even Marxist revolutionary ideas would have supported, human beings can use structures to challenge structured-induced oppression. This context allows for an analysis of various creative ideas that young people have incorporated into their use of social media.

To provide some examples of the capacity of social media to negotiate complex structures, transnational virtual citizenship helps Ghanaians across the world to overstep the boundaries of legal restriction. In Ghana, the elites are accused of deploying the judiciary to gag freedom of expression — sometimes as part of the complex framing of defamation. Much as Ghana's re-democratizing has markedly broadened freedom of expression and its channels over print and electronic media, a residue of criminalizing speech has continued from colonialism as the criminal libel.[47] Invectives, which predated colonialism as a communication device in checking regime excesses, is often criminalized and punished in Ghana. The democratic principle of speaking the truth is frowned on and obstructed by political regimes through the elites' instrumentalization of law.

But in the diaspora, especially in America that has a relative advanced form of liberal democracy that affords broader spectrum of freedom of expression, invectives are highly proscribed. Ghanaian youth in the US have leveraged the legal regime away from home through the use of invectives that might qualify readily as defamatory in Ghana. Kevin Taylor, a Ghanaian in the US, who operates an online company, Loud Silence, titled "With all due respect," uses words that may readily count as insult in Ghana to profile high-ranking politicians and traditional authorities. In July 2021, for example, he said that, "Akufu (*sic*) Addo's government is an indication that not all grey hair is a sign of wisdom."[48] Taking on everyone, Taylor profiled a Member of Ghana's Parliament, representing the people of Assin Central (Central Region of Ghana) as a "murderer, drug addict, thief, and green card fraudster." Considering Taylor's words as defamatory,[49] Kennedy Agyapong filed a suit against Taylor at the District Court of the Eastern District of Virginia. Contrary to Agyapong's expectation, the US court dismissed his case as lacking merit, as the plaintiff failed to prove that the comments were defamatory. The case between Taylor and Kennedy Agyapong indexed the contradictions in two worlds under two legal regimes without citizenship necessarily losing the rights to function beyond national boundaries.

Apart from the elites, traditional authorities have also struggled, almost without success, to recuperate indigenous spiritual world map to clamp down on how the young people circumvent customary norms. In Ghana, several societies allow for the use of invectives to critique chiefs occasionally. But generally, it is tabooed and treated as sacrilegious to insult the person of the chief. As an intermediary between the ancestors and the mundane world, chiefs are inviolable, until they violate ancestral customs. Meanwhile, trans-national Ghanaian citizens, including Kevin Taylor and Twene Jonas (also domiciled in the US), have never shied away from insulting and attacking the person of chiefs.[50] Given that the laws in their jurisdiction cover transnational Ghanaian citizens, some chiefly figures have resorted to imprecation and invocation of ancestral spirits to cow such young men into submission.[51]

Put together, social media has blurred physical boundaries and allowed young people to challenge what they consider as outdated customs and conventions. It is also argued that social media has allowed for greater civic participation in governance by overcoming both the pre-modern mystification and modern reconfiguring of power to police freedom of expression.

Nevertheless, because power reproduces itself, social media has not been absolutely out of the reach of state and elite control. Through complex surveillance system and intelligence gathering (which are also enhanced by biometric citizenship), it is possible for the state to both track and undermine youth political activism online. Given that young people use social media to influence electoral outcomes in several countries. A case in point is Uganda, which shut down social media during elections.[52]

In conclusion it could be argued that the advent of the millennium did not yield the idea of "We are Ghanaians" to foster a relatively equitable distribution of resources. The two main political parties — NPP and NDC have also succeeded firmly in controlling the political space, alternating power between them, and also using state institutions to overcome political dissidents. In frustration, the young people both locally and trans-locally have invested in social media to reconfigure their citizenship — creating opportunities to overreach their spatial boundaries. Through social media, the frontiers of civic participation in governance have increased, but not without the threats of digital dictatorship, engendered through shutdowns and censorship of social media. All this has also demonstrated the fluidity of citizenship, enhanced by social media that allows transnational participation in governance usually from the immediate reach of state control. The result is that structures of society are far from being oppressive and invincible, as young people have negotiated around structures to advance their civic participation in politics. The next chapter discusses Ernesto Yeboah and analyzes his role as one of Ghana's revolutionary young men in redefining and broadening the frontiers of civic participation in governance. The chapter will also examine his socialization, education and how in 2016 Nkrumah's ideologies influenced his formation of the Economic Fighters League.

NOTES/REFERENCES

[1] Marleen de Witte, "Afrikania's dilemma: Reframing African authenticity in a Christian public sphere," *Etnofoor*, 17, ½ (2004): 133-155.

[2] J. D. Hargreaves, "Towards a history of the partition of Africa," *The Journal of African History*, 1, 1 (1960): 97-109.

[3] A. I. Asiwaju, Artificial boundaries (An inaugural lecture delivered at the University of Lagos on Wednesday 12 December 1984).

[4] J. Barron Boyd, Jr., "African boundary conflict: An empirical study," *African Studies Review*, 22, 3 (1979).

[5] Charles Prempeh, "Religious innovations of chieftaincy in Ghana: Pentecostal Christianity and the complex persistence and Transformation of Akan chieftaincy" *Religion Compass*, (2021): 1-13, DOI: 10.1111/rec3.12426.

[6] Naomi Chazan, "Ethnicity and politics in Ghana," *Political Science Quarterly*, 97, 3 (1982): 461-485.

[7] Ibid.

[8] Edem Adotey, "'Operation eagle eye': Border citizenship and cross-border voting in Ghana's fourth republic," *Journal of Borderlands Studies*, 38, 1(2023): 21-38.

[9] Edem Adotey, "'9th may 2017 is our day': The homeland study group foundation and contested national imaginaries in post-independence Ghana," *Nations and Nationalism*, 28, 2 (2022): 662-679.

[10] Pamphilious Faanu and Emmanuel Graham, "The politics of ethnocentrism: A viability test of Ghana's democracy?" *Insight on Africa*, 9, 2 (2017): 1-18.

[11] Engin Isin and Evelyn Ruppert, *Being digital citizens* (London: Rowman & Littlefield International Ltd., 2015).

[12] Btihaj Ajana, *Governing through biometrics: The biopolitics of identity* (Basingstoke, Hampshire: Palgrave Macmillan, 2013).

[13] Adotey, "9th May 2017 is our day."

[14] Abamfo Ofori Atiemo, "International human rights, religious pluralism and the future of chieftaincy in Ghana," *Exchange*, 35, 4 (2006): 360-382.

15 Stephen Sintim-Koree, *The God who answers by thunder: An account of Christian persecution in Nzemaland during the ban on drumming 1993-1996* (Accra: SonLife Press, 2013).

16 Ato Quayson, *Oxford street, Accra: City life and itineraries of transnationalism* (Durham: Duke University Press, 2014).

17 Irene Odotei, "External influences on Ga society and culture," *Research Review*, 7, 1&2 (1991): 61-71.

18 Charles Prempeh, *Nima-Maamobi in Ghana's Postcolonial Development: Migration, Islam and Social Transformation* (Bamenda/Cameroon: Langaa RPCIG, 2022).

19 Yunus Dumbe, "Islamic polarisation and the politics of exclusion in Ghana," *Islamic Africa*, 10, 1-2 (2019): 153-180.

20 Nana James Kwku Brukum, Northern territories of the Gold Coast under British colonial rule, 1897-1956: A study in political change (PhD thesis submitted to the University of Toronto, 1997).

21 Misbahudeen Ahmed-Rufai, "The Muslim Association Party: A test of religious politics in Ghana," *Transactions of the Historical Society of Ghana*, NS, 6 (2002): 99-114.

22 Ivor Wilks, *Asante in the nineteenth century: The structure and evolution of a political order* (Cambridge: Cambridge University Press, 1975).

23 David Owusu-Ansah, "Islamic influence in a forest kingdom: The role of protective amulets in early 19th century Asante," *Transafrican Journal of History*, 12 (1983): 100-133.

24 Enid Schildkrout, *People of the Zongo: The transformation of ethnic identities in Ghana* (Cambridge: Cambridge University Press, 1978), p. 67.

25 Yunus Dumbe, *Islamic revivalism in contemporary Ghana* (Södertörns högskola, 2013), p. 38.

26 John H. Hanson, *The Ahmadiyya in the Gold Coast: Muslim cosmopolitans in the British empire* (Bloomington: Indiana University Press, 2017).

27 Yunus Dumbe, "Islamic polarisation and the politics of exclusion in Ghana: Tijaniyya and Salafist struggles over Muslim orthodoxy," *Islamic Africa* 10 (2019): 153-180.

28 Ousman M. Kobo, "Shifting trajectories of Salafi/Ahl-Sunna reformism in Ghana," *Islamic Africa*, 6, 1-2 (2015): 60-81; Yunus Dumbe, "Islamic polarisation and the politics of exclusion in Ghana,"

Islamic Africa, 10, 1-2 (2019): 153-180.

[29] Charles Prempeh, "'Hijab is my identity': Beyond the politics of the veil: The appropriations of the veil in an inner-Muslim area of Accra (Ghana) since 1980s", *Journal of Africana Religions*, 10, 1 (2022): 20-46.

[30] Godwin Yaw Agboka, "Ghana: Letter to the Speaker – Curbing religious imperialism in our nation," https://allafrica.com/stories/ 200803311320.html.

[31] Cameron Duodu (8 February 2015), "Mahama's Guantanamo deal angers Ghanaians," https://newafricanmagazine.com/11610/.

[32] https://statsghana.gov.gh/docs/countrypdf_gh.pdf

[33] Margaret Peil, "The expulsion of West African aliens," *The Journal of Modern African Studies*, 9, 2 (1971): 205-229.

[34] Charles Prempeh, *Nima-Maamobi in Ghana's Postcolonial Development: Migration, Islam and Social Transformation* (Bamenda/Cameroon: Langaa RPCIG, 2022).

[35] Sarah Balakrishnan, "Building the ancestral republic: Cemeteries and the necropolitics of properties in colonial Ghana," *Journal of Social History* (2022): 1-25; Samuel Ntewusu, "Co-existence in turbulent times: Migrants and the making of Ghana's Madina," *Anno*, LXXXVI, 2 (2020): 365-382.

[36] Prempeh, *Nima-Maamobi*.

[37] Millicent Adzimah-Alade, Charity S. Akotia, and Francis Annor, "Vigilantism in Ghana: Trends, Victim Characteristics, and Reported Reasons," *The Howard Journal of Crime and Justice*, 59, 2 (2020): 194-213.

[38] Muhammad Dan Suleiman, Hakeem Onapajo and Ahmed Badawi Mustapha, "Eternal influence, failed states, ungoverned spaces and small arms proliferation in Africa," in Usman A. Tar and Charles P. Onwurah (eds.), *The Palgrave handbook of small arms and conflicts in Africa*, 161-185 (Cham/Switzerland: Palgrave Macmillan, 2021).

[39] Interview with Wallee Ibrahim on 7 September 2021.

[40] Ghanaweb (2 February 2019), "Ayawaso West Wuogon by-election: Violent acts frightening, worrisome – CSOs," https://www.ghanaweb. com/GhanaHomePage/NewsArchive/Ayawaso-West-Wuogon-by-election-Violent-acts-frightening-worrisome-CSOs-720226.

[41] Emilia Mellosi, "'Ghetto tomatoes' and 'taxi drivers': The exploitation and control of Sub-Saharan African migrant tomato pickers in Puglia, Southern Italy," *Journal of Rural Studies*, 88 (2021): 491-499; Leandar

Kandilige, Joseph Kofi Teye, Mary Setrana and Delali Margaret Badasu, "'They beat us with whatever is available to them': Exploitation and abuse of Ghanaian domestic workers in the Middle East," *International Migration* (2022): https://doi.org/10.1111/imig.13096

[42] Charles Prempeh, "From offline to online imagined community: Recuperating Asante culture and history for development in Ghana" *Question*, Issue 06 (2021), pp. 36-44.

[43] Ibid.

[44] Ransford Edward Gyampo, "Public funding of political parties in Ghana: An outmoded concept?" *Ufahamu*, 38, 2 (2015): 3-28.

[45] James Clifford, "Travelling cultures," in Lawrence Grossberg, Carl Nelson and Paula A. Treichler, *Cultural Studies*, 96-116 (London: Routledge, 1992).

[46] Michel Foucault, *Discipline and punish: The birth of the prison* (trans. Alan Sheridan) (Harmondsworth: Penguin, 1977).

[47] Samuel Appiah Darko, "Ghana's law on publication of false news is vague and easily abused," https://eprints.lse.ac.uk/113932/1/africaatlse_2022_02_25_ghana_law_publication_of_fake_news_vague.pdf.

[48] News Reporter (13 July 2021), "Akufo Addo's government is an indication that not all grey hair is a sign of wisdom–Kevin Taylor," https://loudsilencenews.com/akufo-addos-government-is-an-indication-that-not-all-grey-hair-is-a-sign-of-wisdom-kevin-taylor/.

[49] Edna Agnes Boakye (25 March 2022), "US Court throws out Kennedy Agyapong's $9.5M defamation suit against Kevin Taylor," https://citinewsroom.com/2022/03/us-court-throws-out-kennedy-agyapongs-9-5m-defamation-suit-against-kevin-taylor/

[50] Ibid.

[51] Agana-Nsiire Agana and Charles Prempeh, "Of farms, legends, and fools: Re-engaging Ghana's development narrative through social media," *Media, Culture & Society* (2022): 1-17.

[52] Rita Abrahamsen and Gerald Bareebe, "Uganda's 2016 elections: Not even faking it anymore," *African Affairs*, 115, 461 (2016): 1-15. The researcher personally experienced this when he was a postgraduate student at the Makerere Institute of Social Research, Makerere University.

CHAPTER 4

Ernesto Yeboah: The Man and His Socio-Political Philosophy

Introduction: A Theoretical Foundation

Chapter Three fleshed out the trajectories of Ghana's politics since the beginning of the millennium and how it meshes with Ernesto's life, philosophy and experiences. This chapter provides a biographical account of Mr Yeboah and how the various episodes in his life shaped and informed his activism, culminating in the formation of his Nkrumahist movement — the Economic Fighters League (EFL). Analytically, the chapter weaves in the various general philosophical and historical tapestries that have formed and consolidated Ernesto's social and political philosophy of life. This chapter establishes the philosophical foundation of the Akan ethnic group of Ghana and their cognate expression in western philosophies — about the social embeddedness of human beings.

The Akans hold the philosophy that every human being is a social being whose identification relates to other persons. This is obvious from the way they name their babies. Through the primacy of naming new entrants into the world, one can glean entitlements to rights of care and the responsibility to care for others. Through the practice of naming, individuals become both social and legal beings who can sue and be sued; who can elect and be elected to occupy an important position and whose rights cannot be violated and who cannot also violate the rights of others without consequences.[1]

Through socialization, which the Ghanaian sociologist, Max Assimeng, understands as the transformation of a biological being into a social being, an individual becomes culturally and socially competent to live with others.[2] Socialization, therefore, grounds individuals in the worldview of their societies and yet offers a chance to negotiate. However, their negotiation is not expected to violate some clear ethical and ontological boundaries, defined around both private and public delitescent. Murder and wanton destruction of the natural vegetation are not within the rights of individuals — violation of which are severally punished through death or ex-communication.[3] Composition of African societies has raised issues about individual agency and rights. This contention emerges out of the idea of communitarianism, which African philosophers, including Kwame Gyeke, have championed.[4] But others, like Emmanuel Eze, for example, have contested the idea of communitarianism and argued that individuals are constitutive members of society.[5]

All these come into interaction with the western idea of individuals. Indeed, until the Christian Reformation of the 16th century, the idea of communitarianism was universally shared among Europeans. The Reformation broke ecclesiastical power and initiated the Western pathways into its modernity, characterized by the rise of the modern state and the idea of human rights.[6] Since then, Western philosophers such as Jeremy Bentham and John Stuart Mill of the 18th century have argued for individual libertarians, making them pioneers of libertarianism. These individuals considered doing anything by reason of custom and tradition as a form of enslavement.[7] Since the 18th century, the Western world's idea of individual liberties has increased to include total freedom that profile social structures as oppressive. As discussed already, Jean-Paul Sartre and Michel Foucault advanced this position of structures as oppressive. The 1960s marked yet another watershed in the Western sense of libertarianism, which Robert Bellah, arguing from the perspective of America, referred to as 'expressive individualism' and which Charles Taylor called the 'age of authenticity.'[8]

Nevertheless, social scientists, including Anthony Giddens, Robert Putnam, and Pierre Bourdieu have reconstituted the idea of humans as social beings. To Giddens, individuals act within a social construct. Putnam discussed the idea of social capital where individuals leverage other's social skills to advance themselves.[9] Bourdieu, on the other hand, posits that individuals are socially constructed through different layers of interactions with a habitus that determines their existence and worldview.[10]

Needless to say, by the 14th century, an Arab philosopher and historian, Ibn Khaldun had developed the concept of Asabiya,[11] which had preceded all these Western philosophers. He used the concept of Asabiya to explain the rise and fall of civilization. He said Asabiya is about social cohesion, based on what Nyamnjoh called incompleteness, where conviviality is established for human flourishing.[12] Asabiya begins to collapse when society gravitates from the subsistence level of agriculture to industrialization. With industrialization, Asabiya is overstretched to the point of splitting individuals into silos — which then marks their collapse. Leveraging all these theories, it is argued that Ernesto Yeboah is a social being whose philosophy is a concatenation of his interactions with his family, friends and national politics. His social and political philosophies are, therefore, hardly stable and fossilized. As he said, he and his EFL are open to superior ideas —much as they lean towards Nkrumaism.

The Man Ernest Yeboah: His Biography and Philosophy

Mr Ernesto Yeboah was born in Accra in 1982. He grew up at Nima under a single parent — his mother. (Nima is one of the oldest Muslim inner-cities in Accra). As the last child of his mother's three children, Ernesto bore his father's English name, 'Ernest.' However, when he started school, his teachers (mis)spelled his name, 'Ernesto.' So, he grew up with that name, only to realize later in life, after his secondary education in 2001, that his aspiration towards revolutionary transformation in favour of the poor, reflected that of the revolutionary Ernesto Che Guevara. In his own words,

> Much as I do not read history with a predisposition towards predestination, soon after secondary school, I realized that my life and what I stood for had been prefigured by the Cuban revolutionary, Ernesto Che Guevara.

Nima, as already mentioned in Chapter Two, is a Muslim enclave that has evolved since the 1940s.[13] The multi-layered deprivation in urban slums in Africa is very much evident in Nima. The community's deprivation and marginalization are marked by poor sanitation and extreme poverty.[14] Beyond that, a segment of the youthful population is prone to gangsterism.[15] As a result, Nima dwellers have developed a strong sense of self-defence. Therefore the young Ernesto was forced to strategize to stoutly defend himself under challenging circumstances even though he confessed he loathed violence. His mother ensured that her son stood up to anybody who sought to bully him. His mother insisted that he fought back his 'oppressors,' learned to protect himself and assert his independent-mindedness.

Later, as a trained History student from the University of Cape Coast (Ghana's third oldest public university since October 1962), Ernesto does not subscribe to providential largese. His philosophy is a complex mixture of Marxist materialism and Nkrumah's Consciencism. From the Marxist perspective, Ernesto believes that history is largely marked by natural laws as well as class struggle between the 'haves' and the 'have-nots.'[16] He believes that human agency is a crucial stimulus for things to happen. He argues that nothing happens in life unless one takes action. He eschews fatalism and apathy. He gave an illustration of the ant, which he had picked up. Philosophically, he said, granted the ant was destined to die; but it is yet to be proven whether the ant in his hand should die or live. But if he should ask the opinion of two people about the ant's fate, one of them would answer that the ant would die, and in defiance, he would let the ant live. But if the other should answer that the ant was destined to live, he would crush the ant.[17] The human factor is an influencing agency in determining human events.

But far from simply submitting to the total bracketing of the world away from any transcendental control, Ernesto tempers his Marxist historiography with Nkrumah's *Consciencism*. Nkrumah, who was a Marxist, combined his materialist reading of history with the African non-binary world. Educated by the Catholic missionaries, Nkrumah is reported to have developed a passion for the priesthood.[18] While studying at the Lincoln University in the United States of America in the 1940s, he preached on a few occasions.[19] But later in life, possibly influenced by the extent of oppression and his reading of Lenin, Nkrumah developed an eclectic religious position. He merged Africa's three religious postcolonial legacy — indigenous cosmogony, Islam and Christian — to form his idea of Consciencism. So, Nkrumah became president of Ghana and when his life came under several threats, he wrote a book on Consciencism. The book, believed to have been co-authored with one of Ghana's postcolonial philosophers, William Emmanuel Abraham, is deeply philosophical and complex to decipher its philosophical bristles. As a philosophical treaty, the book takes up complex subjects such as the nature of human beings and a philosophy about history.

In *Consciencism*, therefore, Nkrumah moves away from Marxist construction of matter as sole reality to constructing matter as primary to the ultimate reality. It is against this background that Nkrumah's *Consciencism*, which Ali Mazrui reframed as Africa's Triple Heritage in the 1980s, informed Nkrumah's pragmatic and personal deployment of religion. He is said to have been deeply spiritual, visiting various African independent churches, including Jehu Appiah's Mosama Disco Christo Church at Mosano in the Central Region.[20] He also visited the Akonnedi shrine at Akropong, under the spiritual authority of the priestess, Nana Oparebea for personal protection when his life often came under threat in the 1960s.[21] Similarly, he appealed to the Sufi spiritual leader from Kaola in Senegal, Sheikh Ibrahim Niass to complete the Akosombo Dam in 1963 — when spiritual forces were believed to be working against completing the project.[22]

Taking inspiration from Nkrumah and leveraging his own pneumatic (spiritual) experiences, Ernesto repudiates every attempt by materialists to bracket the world out of the control of the spirit world. As a child under the care of a single mother, Ernesto said his mother often invested in prayers whenever his family had nothing to feed on. Born in the 1980s when Ghana's economy had taken a nosedive after several accumulated cases of mismanagement and corruption and coping with the western imposition of neoliberal policies, life in urban Accra was very challenging. As Ernesto said, there were several times his family had nothing to feed on. During those times, his mother would urge all of them to kneel down and pray. Often, those prayers paid dividends — a benefactor from nowhere would pop up to give them either food or money. In personal life, especially when he was at the Ghana Secondary School (established by Fred Addae and Francis Adjei as boys' school in the 1940s), Ernesto had encounters with the divine through dreams in ways that affirmed his belief in the existence of a personal God. According to him, when he and his classmates were preparing for their final exams, he had a dream about an examination subject, Government — one of the General Arts (or Humanities) courses read at the senior high school level of education in Ghana. According to him, the Lord appeared to him in the dream and revealed to him the questions that would be set for the exams. But he did not take the question seriously. However, in the exam hall, when he attempted to solicit help from a friend, the invigilator announced that time was up.

When he woke up, he brushed off the dream, thinking it was just a happenstance. However, during the real examination, the questions which were revealed to him in the dream were the very questions that were set for the Government paper; and when he attempted to ask a friend seated next to him for help, the invigilator rang the bell to signal that time was over for the exams — exactly as happened in the dream!

Unfortunately, he got grade 'D' (credit). Upon re-siting the paper the following year, he got grade 'A'. Thus, the following year, while he and a few friends were feverishly preparing for the paper, he told them his dream experience the previous year and informed them that he had asked God to reveal the questions to him again. What he was not sure about this time was whether God would comply, considering that he, Ernesto, had dismissed the first one. He was not sure whether God would use him as a channel this time, so he charged his friends to open-minded about the possibility of receiving a dream about the pending exams. He added that whoever had the dream should share it with the rest. According to Ernesto, true to his prayers, God revealed the exam questions to a friend, whom they all considered as less deserving as a channel. The friend was not known to be a strong academic performer in the subject. This time, he, Ernesto, obeyed and followed the dream, and he passed his exams successfully.

Indeed, in the Ghanaian context, and true to several cultures around the world, dreams are interface for the metaphysical as well as the material world. Unlike Freudian psychoanalytical assumption that sought to demystify dreams as illusion or disguised fulfilment of a repressed wish, operating in the sub-conscious mind,[23] for several

Ghanaians, dreams index the non-binary universe. Dreams operate as the boundary between the material world and the spiritual world, such that spiritual beings deploy dreams to communicate their will to their loved ones. In the Ghanaian religious landscape or spiritual map, dreams remain very important to all the various religious groups, including Christians, Muslims and persons who subscribe to an ancestral cult and would go lengths to seek interpretations for their dreams. On radio and television, there are religious functionaries from all the three major religious heritage of Ghana, who claim to have the capacity to interpret dreams.

Dreams also align with complex philosophy of 'destiny' among the Akan. Could one's destiny be altered through one's deployment of agency? The Akans answer this question in the affirmative, positing that much as God created a world and designed its governance, human beings wield the capacity to deploy their agency to determine the contours of life in a manner that advances human progress. Resigning to fawning fatalism is, therefore, uncharacteristic of the Akan —particularly when the Akan has not eschatological vision of life in a blissful 'heaven.' For the Akan, human beings are created as earthly beings and their ontological abode of existence is here under the sun — literally rendered as 'Ɛwiase.' The duty of the Akan is, therefore, to aspire to bring God to earth, instead of going to God in the skies. This explains why the Akans conceive dreams as channels for formulating both vertical and horizontal relationships to bring 'God to earth' — in other words, to make life here and now better for all human beings.

During the missionary era in the 19th century, some missionaries, especially from the Bremen Mission who worked among the Ewe in what became known as the Volta Region in post-colonial Ghana, discounted dreams and other indigenous spiritualities as 'pagan.' Much as the missionaries proscribed these practices, they did not adopt a completely rationalistic posture as part of the legacies of the European enlightenment of the 19th century.[24] As Birgit Meyer, who has written extensively about Ewe spirituality has argued, the missionaries were rather worried that the Ewe Christian converts would conflate the work of the pneumatic work of the Holy Spirit and ancestral spirits.[25]

The missionary suppression of indigenous pneumatic practices did not imply the end of such beliefs. Instead, like their other Ghanaian Christians, several Ewes continued to hold their enchanted worldview that reinforces their belief in dreams, visions, and divination. The rise of so-named African independent churches in the Gold Coast, such as Jehu Appiah's Musama Disco Christo Church and Grace Tani's Twelve Apostles' Church, restored dreams and their interpretation into the religious regimen of Ghanaians. Later in the 20th century, the Pentecostal movement began at the end of the 19th century through the Gold Coaster reading of Alexander Dowie's the weekly newspaper, Leaves of Healing.[26] But it crystallized in the 1920s under Peter Anim. Through Peter Anim, who later received the assistance of the Irish missionary, James McKeown, Pentecostalism restored the pneumatic experiences of 'Pentecostalism' — characterized by dreams, visions, and speaking in tongues.[27]

Since the 20th century, Ghana's religious constituency in dreams have been retained through the rise of 'one-man' church founders or the so-named neo-Pentecostals who have deployed dreams as a means through which they receive prophecies for the nation. Since the turn of the millennium, such religious figures, including Rev Isaac Owusu Bempah and Nigel Gaisie, have participated in public governance through their annual end of year prophecies, some of which have proven problematic. Much as these prophets' activities are sometimes considered 'fake' by some analysts,[28] they maintain a strong influence in the Ghanaian religious landscape. Some of these so-called prophets are consulted by key political figures. Small public bookshops are filled with books and pamphlets written by such self-styled religious figures, who claim they have authority over dream interpretations. Dreams have their own political economy because when a religious figure claims the ability to interpret dreams, they also recommend answers to those dreams that are potentially fatal. At this point, such religious figures prescribe all forms of spiritual antidotes through their guidance, known in Twi (Akan) as *akwankyire* — literally 'to show the way.' It is against the importance of *akwankyire*, as a form of divination to access the will of the divine, that Nkrumah is reported to have sought interpretation to his dreams and headaches from the priestess Oparebea in the 1960s, which entailed subjecting himself to herbal and spiritual purification.[29]

With dreams serving as the web for the material and the spiritual to bond, Ernesto does not regard dreams as a comedy of illusions to jettison any belief in God. This informs the spirituality he invests in some of his activities. As he explained, whenever he had to undertake any major public protest, he first prays and consults his inner being — which signals personal conviction of the rightness of what he plans to do. One such incident that happened was when he was to undertake the #DropThatChamber campaign in 2019. According to Ernesto, when he decided to undertake the #DropThatChamber protest against that state's decision to invest $200m in expanding the country's parliament, he knew the risk involved would be overbearing.[30] First, it would involve a counter-intuitive mobilization of mass protest to 'invade' Parliament. Second, he knew he could return home to his family, either dead or alive. These reasons were also because of the Parliament of Ghana's democratic dispensation. The president of Ghana, Nana Addo Dankwa Akufo-Addo, in his March 2023 State of the Nation address, affirmed that the nation's parliament is the symbol of the country's democracy. This is also because it is filled with persons who ideally represent the various constituencies in the country. Concurrently, nearly all the military regimes in Ghana since the 1966 coup that toppled Nkrumah's government, had suspended the function of the country's parliament and instead ruled by decree.[31]

Having weighed the risk involved in marching against the country's Parliament, Ernesto said he invested in prayers and consulted his inner being — and once he felt convinced, he embarked on his mission. True to his calculation, he was arrested and handcuffed in full public view. His 'comrades,' as they call themselves — according to Nkrumahist ethos — publicized his arrest widely on social media, particularly on Facebook, to draw public attention and sympathy. Against the possibility of the state charging him with treason for 'invading' the country's Parliament while plenary was in session, Ernesto was freed.

Ernesto believed in the Bible. In 2 Timothy 1:7, Paul wrote to Christians that, "For God hath not given us the spirit of fear; but power, and of love, and of a sound mind."[32] Nkrumah (in Chapter 2) also used the Bible to create an imagined community of "We are

Ghanaians." Ernesto seemed to be doing the same thing. Fear is a major challenge to revolution; it undermines the willingness of people to upset oppressive structures. Similar to Marxist idea of the superstructure of false consciousness, which is often mainstreamed through religion, fear, according to Ernesto, cripples and cows people to accept and kowtow to injustice.[33]

Nevertheless, Ernesto did not discount the reality of fear, as he himself has had several reasons to rethink some of his actions for fear of the consequences. Instead of submitting to fear and allowing an oppressive regime to subsist, he invests in the Bible text, reminding himself that "God has not given him fear, but power and sound mind." For him, the fact that God does not give fear, but allows oppressive regimes to exist, he needed not to give in to threats. Second, 'sound' mind also means that he has to be convinced about whatever he intends to do. For this reason, he said that, "I do things not to win popular support or be celebrated. But rather, I always weigh whatever I do against what is right. I often ask myself: "Will what I am going to do fulfil a just cause?" Once he feels in his 'sound' mind that what he intends to do is just, he throws caution to the wind and goes ahead.

Much as Ernesto does not dismiss the transcendental element in his life, he thinks that the individual bears the responsibility, not the external elements. So, he does not believe in providence or any idea that a predetermined timetable governs his life. While his discounting of predestination is strong, his philosophy in this direction is not well formulated. He diverged from his work as a 'revolutionary' to pursue a business venture through a friend who tried to dissuade him from politics. He disclosed that, for about a year, he was not involved in any public activism and did not also comment on any public issue, including very contentious ones.

But he said after a year of venturing into a successful business, he came back to politics. When asked to interconnect the various episodes in his life, including the dreams, his name, among other influences, and whether he was convinced there were no divine interventions lurking behind what he does, he at first admitted that there might be providential interventions. But he added that, as part of his philosophy and that of the Economic Fighters League (EFL) soon to be discussed they accede to 'superior' philosophies, so he would not rule out the element of providence in his life.

Much as Ernesto admits to a personal God whom he relates with through prayer and meditation, he does not think that God is judgemental and limited to any particular religious construction. He said that God is love and kind, contrary to the God of established religions, who throws people into a burning hell fire for wrongdoing. He also said that God does not wear religious garb of any particular faith. The fact that hell does not literally exist is shared by other religious groups, including millennial ones like the Jehovah's Witnesses (JWs), a 19th American-originated church founded by Charles Taze Russell, that has been operating in Ghana (then the Gold Coast) since the 1930s.[34] Unlike the JWs' predisposition towards pacifism, Ernesto shares the vision of a revolution (including militant ones) to overturn oppressive regimes. Concurrently, it could be inferred that he identifies with the Communist vision of the "formation of the proletariat into a class, to overthrow the bourgeois supremacy, conquest of political power by the proletariat."[35]

Considering himself a 'fighter' in support of the economic freedom of the oppressed, Ernesto assumes that the proletariat had a better understanding of the idioms of economic oppression than the bourgeois who may have never tasted poverty. Indeed, Nkrumah believed that the elitist approach of the country's first political party, the United Gold Coast Convention, formed in 1948, was not revolutionary enough. He profiled them as espousing a gradualist approach towards independence with their motto, "Independence within the shortest possible time." Instead, Nkrumah identified with the masses, calling them the 'Veranda Boys' — who bore the brunt of oppression from the ruling class.[36] This led Nkrumah to espouse socialism, which unlike Karl Marxism, assimilated religion.[37] But when Nkrumah became the leader, it became clear that his philosophy of socialism was not readily digestible by some of his own party members. It became almost obvious to him that the human composition, including the so-called proletariat, was not as benign and selfless as he had assumed. It is also reported that Nkrumah was supposed to have borrowed £1,800 from the chairman of the Finance Committee of the CPP to pay for the importation of a Cadillac. When the issue was investigated under his watch, he was said to have conceded that it was "a new ruling class of self-seeking careerists."[38] It is also reported that some of the members of his government were very corrupt, to which he admitted. Krobo Edusei's wife was said to have gone to the extreme of importing a gold-plated bed from Great Britain.[39] Nevertheless, as Killick admitted, corruption was a minor reason for the poor performance of state enterprises under Nkrumah.[40]

Also, soon after independence, Nkrumah suffered what he considered betrayals from the Ghanaian public, indexed by the assassination attempts on his life. In the end, it could be said that Nkrumah's socialist idea curtailed the freedom and liberty of people, through the passing of restrictive laws, especially the Preventive Detention Act in the 1950s. Alongside his passage of the legislative instrument that declared Ghana a de jure one-party state in 1964, Nkrumah denied himself the service of sometimes well-meaning persons, including his old political friend, Komla Agbeli Gbedemah, who could have helped solidify the "We are Ghanaians" project. And while in exile serving as co-president with Sekou Ahmed Sékou Touré's Guinea, Nkrumah wrote his *Class Struggle in Africa* in 1970.[41] Until this time Nkrumah had hardly admitted the advanced capitalist form of classism even among the masses in Ghana. Meanwhile, historically, classism or the quest to accumulate wealth has been part of the Ghanaian persona except that it differed markedly from capitalist classism. Largely, Ghana's (or for that matter) Africa's capitalism tends to foster the creation of clients that cascaded into the economy of affection. Western capitalism, on the contrary, is largely about money and its fetishization in mediating social relations — as Marx discussed in his magnum opus, *Capital.*[42]

Certainly, Ernesto is not ignorant of Nkrumah's mistakes and failures. He had encountered Nkrumah through an accidental discovery of Nkrumah's biography in a pile of debris in 2001. This was just when he had completed his secondary school education and was on his way home. As he said, he had read about Kwame Nkrumah in his Government class. Still, when he started reading Nkrumah's biography, he realized that several of the things he had read about Nkrumah were not factual. They were rather convenient myths and selective chronicling of history to justify the anti-Nkrumah regime of the bourgeois class. As Ernesto said, he became aware that he could not trust the nation to tell him anything factual about Nkrumah — a realization that has informed his decision to write his doctoral thesis on the decolonization of Ghana's education, which he is currently engaged in at the Institute of African Studies, University of Ghana. Since encountering Nkrumah's biography, he has systematically mastered Nkrumah's philosophies —by reading nearly all of them.

Nevertheless, Ernesto's anthropological perspective is that human beings are intrinsically good and that if, for any reason, one does anything bad, it is because of one's moral weakness. Ernesto's anthropology resembles that of Nkrumah and other Marxist groups. By claiming that human beings are intrinsically good, it provides a justification for blame culture to be directed at the ruling class. In other words, the so-called working class has a justification for working to overthrow the elites who are considered as oppressors. It also helps the working class or the marginalized class to ask, "Who is causing our suffering?" instead of "What have we done to bring this suffering unto ourselves?"

By shifting responsibility or penitentiary culture into blame culture, Ernesto, just like Nkrumah, has suffered multiple betrayals. When he completed secondary school education and enrolled at the University of Ghana (UG) to read courses in Bachelor of Arts in Philosophy, Classics, History and Political Science in 2003, he tested his revolutionary ideas. Having read Nkrumah's biography in light of his own experiences in urban Accra, and inspired by ideals of socialism, Ernesto's initial registering of activism was when he attempted mobilizing against a new residential policy the University of Ghana sought to achieve.

The University of Ghana was established in 1948 to provide higher education to the emerging set of national leaders of the Gold Coast and, by extension West Africa.[43] Established just at the end of the Second World War and also at the beginning of political party nationalism, the university campus became an extension of nationalist politics. Nascent student politics on campus crystallized with the opening of the Commonwealth Hall, which later became popular and was called Vandal Hall, for only-male residents in 1958.

During Nkrumah's regime, university students, who appeared to have been relatively passive and almost spectators in national politics, witnessed the metastasizing impact of socialist politics on campus. The rift between the liberal political tradition of J. B. Danquah and the socialist leaning of Nkrumah manifested on the campus, where some of the university dons, including Akilakpa Sawyerr (later Vice Chancellor of the UG), Prof. Martin Owusu, Kwamina Ahwoi, Modibo Ocran (later Supreme Court judge), Fui Tsikata, Kojo Tsikata, Obed Asamoah, Kwesi Botchwey, and later John Evans Atta Mills (who later served as Ghana's president — 2008-2012 but died in office in July 2012) were avowed socialist and leftist academics.

Around 1958, Ghanaian students at the University of Ghana also protested against the unequal sharing of eggs at the various dining halls.[44] Prior to that at the Legon hall, students protested against attending church before eating.[45] This protest was framed around the mantra, 'No chop chop, no halleluiah.'[46] As the postcolonial politics reached a high pitch in Ghana, threatening to divide the student front, students on the various campuses formed the National Union of Ghana Students (NUGS) in 1962. Their aim was to protect the interest of Ghanaian students both home and abroad. In line with their established objective, in the 1960s, some students protested against Ghana's first president, Kwame Nkrumah's attempt to destroy university autonomy, as his party sought to subject the entire society under the control of the Convention People's Party ideological framework, using food as a metaphor. One student was reported to have said, "We are fed 'Nkrumah' for breakfast, lunch and dinner; 'Nkrumah á la mode' is not tasty and lacks essential vitamins, but it is the only food we can get, even though it gives us indigestion."[47] Under the regime of K. A. Busia, university students protested against the monotony of free rice and chicken meal in 1971. The tension was not just about food, but it was part of students' expression of disaffection with some of the policies of the Busia's government, such as the dismissal of 568 workers.[48]

From 1971, the governance of Ghana fell under a military leader, General Ignatius Kutu Acheampong who overthrew the civilian government of K. A. Busia. As part of recuperating the industriousness of Nkrumah to revitalize the agricultural base of the country's economy, Acheampong began the "Operation Feed Yourself" project,[49] which attracted several university students who went into the interior to hauled cocoa to the port for export. Others also joined their compatriots to plant trees. Nevertheless, students joined as corruption hit the regime and agitations started among the public in the late 1970s. As Acheampong's regime became quite unpopular, and calls for re-democratization were intensifying, Acheampong decided to introduce a mixture of civilian and military government known as Unigov — or the Akan version of "Nkabom aban."[50] Unfortunately, that initiative did not save the regime. On 5 July 1978, Acheampong was deposed in a palace coup and was succeeded by his Chief of Defence Staff, Lt General Fred Akuffo.

On 15 May 1979, Jerry John Rawlings, a young military officer, with the help of six other soldiers, overthrew General Akuffo's government. As a young man, Rawlings deployed populist rhetoric, which further endeared him to the youth. He was arrested by the military, which tried him at a military tribunal. During the trial, he made a famous statement, which readily resonated with Ghanaian youth, including students: "Leave my men alone!"[51] This statement showed him as a selfless leader who was willing to take responsibility, exonerating the young officers whom he led into insurrection. The youth thought this was a brave man who sought the interest of the ordinary man. Again, at the same tribunal, Rawlings was reported to have made an important statement that received thunderous applause from the youth:

> I am not an expert in Economics, and I am not an expert in the law, but I am an expert in working on an empty stomach while wondering when and where the next meal will come from, I know what it feels like going to bed with a headache, for want of food in the stomach.[52]

Students held Rawlings as a hero. The masses in general heaped on him a messianic accolade such as 'Junior Jesus.'[53] But by the late 1970s, ethnocentrism had begun eating deep into student politics. As previously stated, by the 1950s, ethnocentrism had characterized Ghanaian politics with the National Liberation Movement (NLM) mobilizing around Asante nationalism, while the Northerners also built their ethnic politics around their shared historical experience of colonial discriminatory development policies against them. An analysis is also offered on the extent to which Nkrumah deployed legislation and imprisonment to scuttle ethnocentrism in national politics. Nevertheless, the idea of "We are Ghanaians" failed even before Nkrumah was overthrown in 1966. By the late 1970s ethnic politics surfaced strongly on university campuses. The various ethnic groups formed home-based or ethnic associations, such as Asante Students Union (ASU). By the 1970s, the student front was badly polarized on ethnic lines.

Also by the 1990s, when democratization was coming to the fore, the re-tribalization of student politics was beginning to intensify. The New Patriotic Party (NPP) and the National Democratic Congress (NDC) had established their student wings on university campuses. The NPP formed their Tertiary Students Confederacy (TESCON) and the NDC formed the Tertiary Education Institutions Network (TEIN). These associations evinced ethnic elements, with the majority Akan believed to be members of both the NPP and TESCON, while the minority Akan perceived to be NDC and TEIN — the National Union of Ghana Students (NUGS) fractured along the pathways of ethnicity and their activities similarly became highly partisan. National political leaders would often financially sponsor a particular candidate to divide the students front or court support for students from a particular party.

By the time Ernesto Yeboah enrolled at the University of Ghana in 2003, student politics was very divided along ethnic and partisan lines. Also, given that he registered at the University of Ghana at a time when the NPP, a revitalized Danquah-Busia party was in power, Nkrumah's socialist idea was strictly under implicit surveillance. So, when as a fresher, he decided to mobilize students against the university's attempt at introducing a new residential policy that would marginalize students at one of the halls of residence — Jubilee Hall, under the guise of solving academic challenges on campus. But before he succeeded in mobilizing a significant number of students to protest against the university, a few students were disgruntled that a 'junior' fellow would lead them. Consequently, they subverted the protest by agitating against Ernesto Yeboah.

Later in 2005, the University of Ghana began showing signs of leadership failure in handling the organization of examination — leading to widespread examination scandals. Writing about the state of condition at the university at the time, Michael Whyte stated as follows:

> The University of Ghana [at Legon] has long been regarded as the Ivory Tower of not only Ghana but the West African Sub-region . . . Time was when the mere mention of Legon alone evokes envy and jealousy from other Ghanaians who never had the opportunity to study in this institution; time was when accepting an offer to attend University of Ghana was the biggest thing that could happen to any Ghanaian with ambition; time was when prospective students refused admission into any other universities except Legon giving Classics in Legon a priority over Bachelor of Commerce in the Cape Coast University (UCC) or Law in Kwame University of Science and Technology [KNUST]. Now the reverse is true. While other universities such as the KNUST and UCC are carefully studying global trends and responding to the demands of the modern world, the University of Ghana has gained another kind of reputation for the past few years. This time, it is a reputation in corruption, bribery, favoritism, nepotism, tribalism, personal vendetta, and above all, academic crimes with connivance and collaboration of the very authorities from whom much is expected and their family members.[54]

There were several leakages of university exams questions. As Ernesto said, the situation was so bad that students sometimes could read such leaked questions on public notice boards. Later, it was established that the son of the then Vice Chancellor of the University, Prof Kwadwo Asenso-Okyere, was the kingpin in such leakages. Ernesto and a few others raised concerns about the case, including Mr Samuel Okudzeto Ablakwa, now NDC Member of Parliament for the North Tongu Constituency in the Volta Region. Knowing what they considered as a complicit and compromised student union, Ernesto and his group formed the Concerned Students of the University of Ghana, Legon (CSL). They embarked on what they called a 'Peaceful Integrity March' to petition for the resignation of the Vice Chancellor Prof Kwadwo Asenso-Okyere as well as the Pro Vice-Chancellor, Prof

E. Ofori-Sarpong in order for restoration of integrity and dignity to the university. Other academics, including Whyte added his voice to why the Vice-Chancellor must go, on the ground that it would not help the marketability of graduates from the University of Ghana, and second, the scandal placed Ghanaian students in an awkward position in the competition for international scholarship awards and the drive to gain admission into the best universities in the world.[55]

But again, given that Asenso-Okyere was Akan and allegedly a member of the NPP, the Asante Students Union mobilized against Ernesto and his friends. As a resident member of the Commonwealth Hall (also known as 'Vandals' Hall), he secured the help of the traditional leadership, but to no avail. With nearly everyone disserting him, he and a few trusted friends led an mild street protest demonstration to present their petition to the University Council to investigate Asenso's son's case. Led by the traditional head of the Commonwealth Hall — the 'Chief Vandal,' Ernesto and his friends' 'Integrity Peace March' became the target of students ridicule, as only a few students joined the protest. Later in the year, the University Council asked Prof Asenso-Okyere to step aside temporarily until the Mfodwo Committee (that was set up to investigate the issue) submitted their report. The University Council eventually ratified the recommendations for appropriate disciplinary action to be taken.[56] On 6 May 2005, Prof Asenso-Okyere appealed against the university's decision, which did not go in his favour. The university still held that he was answerable for all the lapses identified by the Mfodwo Committee.[57]

Ernesto disclosed that as their petition yielded a positive response in the interest of students and integrity, the student community hailed him as a hero. Emerging as a selfless revolutionary student leader, he decided to contest the position of president of the Student Representative Council (SRC) in the 2006/2007 academic year. He appeared to have gained the support of his friends and colleagues at the Commonwealth Hall. He paired with a female Vice President from Akuafo Hall, and received university-wide support among the students. (Akuafo Hall was established as the second hall in 1953, after the University of Ghana was established in 1948. It was later renamed Akuafo Hall in 1954 to commemorate the generous gesture of the farmers of Ghana who offered financial assistance to the establishment of the University of Ghana.) Ernesto's preference for a Vice President from Akuafo Hall was informed by his interest in identifying with the farmers of Ghana who are hardly recognized for their service to the nation — even though agriculture constitutes the mainstay of the country's economy.

Meanwhile, the victory Ernesto won against Prof Asenso-Okyere had marked him for future marginalization. As he was emerging as the 'natural' leader of the Student Representative Council, the university authorities had also identified him as a potential troublemaker. Already, having embarassed a political science lecturer during lecture session for the professor's soiling of Nkrumah's integrity, Ernesto had become a subject of concern to some of the academics and fellow students. The opposition, in particular, came from students who leaned more towards the NPP government. Thus, during the vetting, the committee deliberately charged him for canvassing support before the ban on student politics was lifted. He denied this allegation and appealed to the Student Representative Council court for redress. But to his surprise, the Student Council upheld the university's decision. He attempted to appeal to the civil court for redress, but a few trusted friends advised otherwise. While Ernesto conceded to forgo any legal action against the university, he supported Lord Hammah who contested against Sammy Awuku, a member of the New Patriotic Party (NPP). Even though Lord Hammah won the contest over Sammy Awuku, Lord Hammah could not obtain the mandatory 50%+1 votes, and so the election had to go into a second round. At this point, the university issued a fiat disqualifying Lord Hammah from the race. The action of the university stirred agitation and uproar among the students, leading to the cancellation of the entire SRC executive elections in 2007.

Eventually, in 2007, Ernesto Yeboah completed and left the University of Ghana. Having practised his nascent Nkrumahist ideas at the university campus and knowing that the NDC and NPP would hardly foster Ghana's growth and development, he joined the Convention People's Party (CPP) — Nkrumaist party. He naively thought the CPP represented the true Nkrumah philosophy of governance and Pan-Africanism. Nevertheless, he was elected the

CPP's youth wing leader on 19 September 2015. As the leader, his aim was to ensure that the CPP regain its lost glory since Nkrumah was overthrown and the party proscribed from all national politics. (After the overthrow of Nkrumah, the CPP was banned from all political parties; Nkrumah's books were burned and some key stalwarts of the party were imprisoned. Also, CPP properties were confiscated and returned to the state.)[58]

When Rawlings successfully organized the 4 June 1979 coup, he restored the country to democratic governance. During this time, the CPP came back through erstwhile Nkrumah's members, including Imoro Igala, who formed the People's National Party (PNP). They appointed Dr Hilla Limann, a career diplomat to contest in the 19 June 1979 elections.[59] He won, which represented the miniature comeback of the CPP. Limann recuperated some of the industries Nkrumah and the leaders after him had started.[60] He also recorded some successes including completing and commissioning the Bamboi Bridge, which linked the south and north along the western boundary road of the country.[61] Nevertheless, for some reasons, including internal party wrangling, his party lost popularity with the Ghanaian public. And as economic hardship hit the nation, once again, despite all Limann's efforts at rebuilding Ghana's economy, Rawlings led another coup against the country on 31 December 1981.[62]

Rawlings banned partisan politics, forcing several of the country's elites who feared being haunted politically to go into exile. However, as the nation fell under both local and transnational pressures, Rawlings returned the country to democracy governance. Political parties, including the NPP re-mobilized as a refurbishment of the Danquah-Busia-Dombo tradition.[63] Conversely, the CPP could not stage a comeback until the 2000 elections, when Ghana's democratic experiment shifted significantly from Rawlings. But the return of the CPP did not have any major impact on Ghana's duo-politics. The CPP has been rocked by several internal challenges, including leadership crisis. The party has, therefore, not recorded any significant political presence by way of coming close to winning a presidential election — leading to one political scientist to refer to the party as those who run after the crumbs.[64] Another political scientist also said that the CPP has never been the third force in Ghana's politics, as the party has never scored 5 percent or more of the votes counted.[65] Against all this background, Ernesto assumes that the CPP was never formed to win any election; neither was it ever to represent Nkrumah. Ernesto confessed thus:

> The CPP, as we have it, is not Kwame Nkrumah's CPP. This CPP was constituted by a body of people who approached the court and the court said Okay, you can use the name CPP, use the colours of the CPP, you can use their cockerel and bla bla bla but take note that this CPP that you are going to constitute is not Kwame Nkrumah's CPP. The current 1992 Constitution forbids the existence of Nkrumah and anything that represented him. If you take the NLC Decree 23, it states that anybody who receives communication purported to have emanated from Nkrumah, the person is enjoined to report to the nearest police station or military barracks for Nkrumah's arrest. So, this is the truth of the history of our country.[66]

Between 2009 and 2014 Ernesto was a Deputy Director of Communications and Deputy National Youth Organizer of the CPP. As a youth leader, he was responsible for mobilizing the young men and women to bring the party close to clinching power from the NPP and NDC. He considered his role similar to that of Nkrumah, an effective youth organizer. In 2012, after the CPP was defeated in general elections, Ernesto organized the youth of the party to donate blood to Ghana's blood bank as a way of revitalizing the party's public image. Again, after 2016 elections, which saw the CPP losing miserably, leaving members disoriented, Ernesto (this time as the party's National Youth Organizer) decided to reorganize the party and reinvent its historic importance. He waded into a corruption charge against Mr John Dramani Mahama, the then president of Ghana. Since Mahama left office in 2016, allegations of corruption have been brought against him, one of which was the famous Airbus scandal. When John Mahama was the Vice President of Ghana and later took over as president in 2012 until 2016, he was alleged to have been involved in the Airbus scandal. He was tasked, as the Vice President under President J. E. A. Mills to mediate in the sale of Airbus military equipment to the country. He was alleged to have outsourced part of the contract to his brother, Samuel Adam Mahama.[67]

As usual, the issue was swarmed by partisan politics. At this point, the government, through the Office of the Special Prosecutor (OSP) — an omnibus office established in 2018, to fight corruption, inter alia) was tasked to investigate the issue. Martin Amidu, the former head of the OSP led the investigation. Like all politically charged scandals, the investigation did not yield any conclusive and satisfactory result. Beyond that, Mahama was struck by yet another allegation of corruption. This time, it involved being offered a Ford bus as a bribe by a Burkinabe road contractor. The nation appeared to have lost interest in the case. Reading the complicity of the elite in perpetually mainstreaming and structuring corruption, Ernesto petitioned the Commission for Human Rights and Administrative Justice (established in 1992 to fight corruption). At this point, the CPP leadership stepped in to berate Ernesto, for they considered the move as an ill-conceived initiative. The leadership also berated his role in organizing a blood donation campaign. In the end, the party leadership initiated Ernesto's removal from office in June 2016.

Consequently, he later issued the following statement in defiance against the party hierarchy:

I, Ernesto Yeboah, National Youth Organizer and Commnder-in-Chief of the Youth League of the Convention People's Party (CPP) have resolved to remain at post, despite my purported suspension by the Party's Central Committee in the evening of June 30th 2016. I shall ignore the so-called suspension and report to the party office in my capacity as Youth League leader to perform my official duties on Monday July 4, 2016; at exactly 10:00 am GMT. My decision above is based on a number of reasons. I'd want to make the point sufficiently clear that I did not immediately dismiss the reports of my suspension when I heard it on radio. I decided to give the so-called decision the benefit of the doubt, engage with the media (where I heard it from) in order to get the rationale behind it. Meanwhile, I have given the Central Committee (CC) ample time to do the right [thing], and administratively correct, thing (*sic)* by waiting for them to communicate their collective position properly. But it is interesting to note that until now, I have not received in writing, an official communication from the party's leadership on the said decision, not even a phone call. Their excuse cannot be the long holiday that followed their decision, for our service to the party is via volunteering; hence holidays actually presented them ample time to do the right thing. But they have ignored the administrative processes in the party. I, therefore will not be a party to such disorder and impropriety creeping into the CPP. One interesting development that our dear party members and Ghanaians must shift their attention to is this; since the allegation of the Ford gift broke, the CPP hasn't come out with what is supposed to be the official position. Is that position supposed to be different from that of the Youth League? Is that position supposed to agree with what the Flag bearer said? Curiously, the Central Committee could not tell Ghanaians this after several hours of their meeting. However, it seemed what was more important in that meeting was to suspend the General Secretary and I for "expressing a position that is consistent with the Party's ideology and beliefs. So, the question remains, what is the CPP's official position on the said Ford Gift to President John Dramani Mahama? All these developments point to a certain lack of clarity which does not bode well for the CPP. As a youth dedicated to my party and Ghana, I shall not allow myself to be dragged into indecision when the party's ideology and administrative systems are clear. It therefore becomes more expedient to join my fellow comrades to bring clarity to this Ford Scandal, while mobilizing votes for our party come November.

I shall therefore continue to work for our party as Leader of the Youth League.

The work continues.

Revolutionary regards[67]

But over time, he felt the CPP was beyond redemption, so he left to found the Economic Fighters League (EFL) — which will be discussed in the next chapter. Before then, however, we want to tease out a few things for reflection on youth political activism that makes it distinctively Ghanaian/African. First, the African worldview of non-binary cosmogony shapes young people's political activism, which unsettles extreme forms of capitalism and socialism — both largely about materialism. Second, the socio-political context of Ghana conditions the contours of young people's politics, such that it becomes the bastion from which they draw inspiration and criticism. Finally, young people who have heavily patronized political regimes in Ghana cut their political teeth from involvement in university campus politics. The Ernesto story is no exception, as we shall discuss in the next chapter.

NOTES/REFERENCES

[1.] Peter Sarpong, *Ghana in retrospect: Some aspects of Ghanaian culture* (Tema/Ghana: Ghana Publishing Corporation, 1974).

[2] Max Assimeng, *Social structure of Ghana: A study of persistence and change* (Tema/Ghana: Ghana Publishing Corporation, 1981).

[3] Busia, *The Challenge.*

[4] Kwame Gyekye, "Person and community in Akan thought," In Kwasi Wiredu and Kwame Gyekye (eds.), *Person and community: Ghana Philosophical Studies,* I, 101-122 (Washington: The Council for Research in Values and Philosophy, 1992).

[5] Michael Onybuchi Eze, "What is African communitarianism? Against consensus as a regulative ideal," *South African Journal of Philosophy,* 27, 4 (2008): 106-119.

[6] John Merriman, *A history of modern Europe: From the renaissance to the present* (3rd edition) (New York: W.W. Norton & Company, 2010).

[7] John Stuart Mill, *On liberty* (Ontario: Batoche Books Ltd., 2001); Jeremy Bentham, *An introduction to the principles of morals and legislation* (ed. J. H. Burns and H. L. A. Hart) (London: Athlone Press, 1970).

[8] Robert Bellah, Richard Madsen, William M. Sullivan, Ann Swidler and Steven M. Tipton, *Habits of the heart: Middle America observed* (California: The Regent of the University of California, 1985); Charles Taylor, *A secular age* (Cambridge, MA: The Belknap Press of Harvard University Press. 2007).

[9] Robert D. Putnam, *Bowling alone: The collapse and revival of American community* (New York: Simonn & Schuster, 2000).

[10] Pierre Bourdieu, *Language & symbolic power* (trans. Gino Raymond and Matthew Adamson). Cambridge: Polity Press, 1991.

[11] Ibn Khaldun, *The Muqaddimah: An introduction to history* (trans. Franz Rosenthal). London: Routledge & K. Paul, 1958.

[12] Francis B. Nyamnjoh, "Incompleteness: Frontier Africa and currency of conviviality," Journal of Asian and African Studies, 5, 3 (2015): 253-270.

[13] Prempeh, Nima-Maamobi.

[14] Charles Prempeh, "Re-imagining wasatiyyah as a socio-theological mediation of youth anger in Accra, Ghana," *Unisia,* 40, 1 (2022): 103-128.

[15] Interview with Ernesto, 5 March 2023.

[17] Ibid.

[18] Basil Davidson, *Black star: A view of the life and times of Kwame Nkrumah* (London: Allen Lane, 1973).

[19] Marika Sherwood, Kwame Nkrumah: The years abroad 1935-1947 (Legon/Ghana: Freedom Publications, 1996).

[20] David George Burnett, Charisma and community in a Ghanaian independent church (PhD thesis submitted to School of Oriental and African Studies, 1997).

[21] Komfo Ama Boakyewa, "Nana Oparebea," p. 56.

[22] Prempeh, Nima-Maamobi.

[23] Sigmund Freud, *The interpretation of dreams* (James Strachey) (London: Penguin, 1991).

[24] Birgit Meyer, Translating the devil: Religion and modernity among the Ewe in Ghana (Edinburgh: Edinburgh University Press, 1999).

[25] Ibid.

[26] Prempeh, "Christianity, culture."

[27] Ibid.

[28] Joseph Oduro-Frimpong, "'The fake is news': On popular visual media, fakery and legitimacy of contestation in charismatic Christianity in contemporary Ghana," Journal of African Cultural Studies, 325-343.

[29] Komfo Ama Boakyewa, Nana Oparebea and the Akonnedi shrine: Cultural, religious and global agents (PhD thesis submitted to the University of Graduate School, Indiana University, 2014), p. 56.

[30] Ghanaweb (4 July 2019), "Majority leader justifies construction of new parliament chamber," https://www.ghanaweb.com/ GhanaHomePage/NewsArchive/Majority-leader-justifies-construction-of-new-parliamentary-chamber-760572.

[31] Mike Oquaye, "The process of democratisation in contemporary Ghana," *Commonwealth & Comparative Politics*, 38, 3 (2000): 53-78.

[32] 2 Timothy 1:7.

[33] Interview with Ernesto 5 March 2023.

[34] George D. Chryssides, Historical dictionary of Jehovahs Witnesses (Lanham, Maryland: The Scarecrow Press, Inc., 2008).

[35] Karl Marx & Frederick Engels, *Manifesto of the communist party* (Peking: Foreign Languages Press, 1965), p. 48.

36 Kwame Nkrumah, "Movement for colonial freedom," Phylon, 16, 4 (1955): 397-409; George M. Bob-Milliar, Verandah Boys versus reactionary lawyers: Nationalist activism in Ghana, 1946-1956," *The International Journal of African Historical Studies*, 15, 1 (2014): 442-460.

37 Ebenezer Obiri Addo, Kwame Nkrumah: A case study of religion and politics in Ghana (New York: University Press of America, Inc., 1997).

38 Roger S. Gocking, *The history of Ghana* (Westport Connecticut: Greenwood Press, 2005), p. 101.

39 Ibid., 132.

40 Killick, *Development*, p. 266.

41 Kwame Nkrumah, *Class struggle in Africa* (London: Panaf Books Ltd., 1970).

42 Karl Marx, *Capital*. Vol. I (Moscow/Russia: Progress Publishers, 1887).

43 Francis Agbodeka, *A history of the University of Ghana: Half a century* of higher education (Accra: Woeli Publishing Services, 1998).

44 Charles Prempeh, "'Food before pressure': Food and food culture in Muslim inner-city in Maamobi-Accra since the 1980s," *African Journal of Social Sciences Education*, 2, 1 (2022): 1-21, p. 3.

45 Ibid., p. 3.

46 Ibid.

47 J. D. Finlay, "Students and politics in Ghana," *Daedalus*, 97, 1 (1968): 51-69, p. 59.

48 D. E. K. Amenumey, Ghana: A concise history from pre-colonial times to the 20th century (Accra: Woeli Publishing Services, 2018).

49 Baffour Agyeman-Duah, General Acheampong: The life and times of Ghana's head of state (Tema/Ghana: Digibooks Publishers, 2021).

50 Ibid.

51 BBC (12 November 2020), "Jerry John Rawlings, in his own words – BBC Africa," https://www.youtube.com/watch?v=ZxAVKXmHQOw.

52 Acquah, K. K. "A letter to Kantinka: A synopsis of socio-politico-economic situation in contemporary Ghana" (Kande-Accra: Dynamo Publishers, 2002).

53 Jesse Weaver Shipley, "Comedians, pastors, and the miraculous agency of charisma in Ghana," *Cultural Anthropology*, 24, 3 (2009): 523-552.

54 Michael Whyte (27 March 2005), "The Legon Vice-Chancellor must

[55] resign," https://www.modernghana.com/news/116504/the-legon-vice-chancellor-must-resign.html.

[55] Michael Kpessa Whyte, "The Legon Vice-Chancellor must resign," https://www.modernghana.com/news/116504/the-legon-vice-chancellor-must-resign.html.

[56] Ghanaweb (31 May 2005), "Vice-Chancellor asked to step aside until …," https://www.ghanaweb.com/GhanaHomePage/NewsArchive/Vice-Chancellor-asked-to-step-aside-until-82670.

[57] Modernghana (15 May 2005), "'Fired' Legon V-C appeals for review," https://www.modernghana.com/news/77837/fired-legon-v-c-appeals-for-review.html

[58] Eric Quaidoo, The United States and the overthrow of Kwame Nkrumah (MA thesis submitted to the Fort Hays State University, 2010).

[59] Agape Kanyiri Damwah, Dr Hilla Limann 1934-1998: His life and times (MPhil Thesis submitted to the University of Cape Coast, 2011).

[60] Ibid.

[61] Ibid.

[62] Ibid.

[63] Kwame Donkoh Fordwor, *The Danquah-Busia tradition in the politics of Ghana: The origins, mission, and achievements of the New Patriotic Party* (Accra: Unimax Macmillan, 2010).

[64] George M. Bob-Milliar, "'We run for the crumbs and not for office': The Nkrumahist minor parties and party patronage in Ghana," *Commonwealth & Comparative Politics*, 57, 4 (2019): 445-465.

[65] Ghanaweb (27 September 2022), "CPP has never been the 3rd force in Ghana's politics – Dr. Smart Sarpong," https://www.ghanaweb.com/GhanaHomePage/politics/CPP-has-never-been-the-3rd-force-in-Ghana-s-politics-Dr-Smart-Sarpong-1631264.

[66] Ghanaweb (20 June 2021), "Current CPP is not Kwame Nkrumah's CPP – Ernesto Yeboah," https://www.ghanaweb.com/GhanaHomePage/NewsArchive/Current-CPP-is-not-Kwame-Nkrumah-s-CPP-Ernesto-Yeboah-1291063.

[67] Oliver Holmey (11 May 2020), "Ghana: John Mahama splashed by Airbus corruption affair," https://www.theafricareport.com/27714/ghana-john-mahama-splashed-by-airbus-corruption-affair/

[68] Ernesto Yeboah shared document with author.

CHAPTER 5

The Economic Fighters League: A Youth Movement

The world sits on structures of multidimensional inequalities and marginalization. Some are very rich, and others are extremely poor. It appears this is an existential reality that unnerves persons who have both revolutionary ideas and a quest to contribute to human flourishing. For this purpose, public and academic discourses are filled with various diagnoses and prognoses about how to get around systemic inequalities. Incidentally, the causes of the inequalities in the world are hardly explained in a manner that everyone would appreciate. The Akan people of Ghana tersely explain existential inequality in a proverb that says, *"Nsa tia nyinaa ɛnyɛ pe"* — to wit, "All the fingers are not of the same length." This proverb helps to us understand whether the Akan is submitting to fatalism or otherwise. As stated in Chapter Four, the Akan considers human beings ontologically as earthly beings — which predisposes them to working hard to 'bring God on earth' instead of ascending to be with God in heaven. The Akan, therefore, does not easily submit to nature's dictates. Instead, the Akan philosophically attempts to ensure cosmic balance, appropriating the 'resources' God offers without unsettling the human quest for a meaningful existence.

The above context enables us to appreciate the significance of proverbs, in general. Among Africans, particularly the Akan, proverbs are idealistic statements that are not to be taken literally. They reflect 'truth' as ideal instead of just limiting themselves to 'facts' as a reality. At the same time, proverbs are part of communication devices that capture sublime 'truths' and aspirations. It is also a rhetorical device used in a persuasive speech. Proverbs are, therefore, highly fluid in terms of interpretation. Much as they have come about through observation of 'facts,' they tend to succinctly communicate a patina of 'truth.' As a quintessential expression of aspirations, proverbs have discursive relevance as the embodiment of the sages. Thus, the idea that "all the fingers are not of the same length," expresses a reality of inequality without condescending to doing nothing about it. For example, a popular proverb: "Though bent, but not broken is the quintessence of proverb." To the Akan, the gravamen of this proverb is that submitting to life's vicissitudes in despair is counter-human.

Instead of reading these proverbs as contradictory in nature, they must be read as complementary and structuring society towards working in complement other than a competition to foster communal benefits. It is against this background that the Akan have such practices as '*nnoboa*' (literally joining hands on the farm) — communally working together to support collective farming.[1] The point here is that, 'inequality' must be seen as a disorienting aspect of life. It causes justifiable anger, which is better channelled into a productive venture. Being angry at inequality is potentially a testimony that one is not willing to be part of it; submitting and responding to it in anger further destroys society. So, mainstreaming anger into building society, in Akan culture, fosters self-help and communally doing projects together. The self-help is routinized in the proverb, "It is the one who attempts climbing a good tree that deserves a push." This then sums up the communal ethos of the '*nnoboa*' system.

The Akan system is strictly neither capitalist nor socialist by nature. For example, several African leaders, including Nkrumah (Ghana) and Julius Nyerere (Tanzania), assumed that the African world was akin to the socialist philosophy. But academics such as Kwame Gyekye and Kwame Bediako have challenged this position.[2] These academics have argued that African leaders deployed the idea of socialism being indigenous to Africans to legitimize oppressive regimes.

Instead of socialism or capitalism, therefore, the Akan world was more about ensuring cosmic balance. The Akan society was also hardly fossilized in time. Cultural atavism is, therefore, not very necessary when discussing how the Akan addressed inequalities. Instead, the Akan world, like much of society, was highly amenable and fluid in adapting to changing trends in life. Akan social and political systems reformed accordingly through reflections on nature and inter-human and societal relations. For this reason, indigenous chieftaincy practice has recently (in 2015) accommodated Pentecostals who ordinarily were hostile to the ancestral cult as the foundation of the institution.[3] All said, the Akan system was a form of the economy of affection where individuals could accumulate, but the political elites ensured that wealth was also redistributed to help the poor. Among the Akan, a wealthy person, Ɔbrempɔn (or big man) must re-distribute his wealth as a patron to get clients who will support him.[4] It is the same philosophy of economy of affection that ensured that 'slaves' and persons in servitude (usually war captives) could rise through the ranks to occupy important positions in society.[5] Far from arguing that the Akan society was perfect; the Akan society was rather as human as every human society, struggling with dealing with life's existential inequalities. For this reason, the Akan society had several instances of unrest and agitations against leaders considered sadist and mean.

Judging from how other cultures have attempted to explain and respond to existential inequalities, the point could be made that two main philosophies cannot escape analysis. The first is socialism. The socialist philosophy to life assumes that the rise of capitalist ideology causes the world's inequalities. Considering the family as an entry point of analysis and etiological origin of inequalities, an insight could be gained from Friedrich Engels' late 19th century book, *The Origin of the Family, Private Property and the State*.[6] Engels wrote his book a couple of decades after Charles Darwin published his *Origin of the Species*, which is also about the etiological origins. But instead of focusing on God, Darwin explored the theory of evolution — a transition of an organism from simple to complex as the beginning of everything.[7] Deploying the same logic, Engels argued that until the agricultural revolution, families existed in a 'free-range' fashion. It was an egalitarian society where men as well as women could have as many sexual partners as possible without restriction. It was also a society where men and women had equal and unimpeded access to the resources that nature offered.

But the egalitarianism of the world (pre-agricultural world) was interrupted by the agricultural revolution, which Yuval Noah Harari, periodizing it around 9500-8500 BC, described as the 'biggest fraud,' given that "the average farmer worked harder than the average forager, and got worse diet in return."[8] For Engels, the agricultural revolution mainstreamed the marginalization of women as labourers who worked to fester the egos of men. The creation of surplus enhanced industrialization, which also supported the rise of the capitalist class, whose quest for profit structured class struggle between the working class and the capitalists who controlled the means of production. Engels and Marx overturned this structured economic equality in the Manifesto and recommended revolution from the working class — a revolution that would give them economic liberation other than their chains to the cog in the wheel of capitalism.[9]

Admirable as it is, the revolutionary zest and answer to the world of existential imperfection appears not to have yielded any lasting positive effect — at least not in the Ghanaian context. In Africa, in general, socialist ideas did not birth the needed economic prosperity other than repression of the rights of citizens who dissented along socialist ideas. George Orwell captures the problem of socialism in his *Animal Farm,* indicating how the socialist vision did not materialize in a politically liberated animal kingdom.[10] The point in all this is that Nkrumah's experimentation with a form of socialist ideology did not turn out well for several Ghanaians. Some of his own ministers became oligarchs; we have already mentioned Krobo Edusei, whose wife's capitalist taste resulted in the family's importation of a gold-plated bed from Britain, where the fault lines of industrialization presented discontent to Marx.

The socialist idea offers insight into economic inequality and potential responses, but it could arguably be concluded that Ghana's experiment with socialist ideas failed. The issues of self-aggrandizement that festered corruption was a major impediment. Emphasis is now placed on capitalism. The capitalist assumes that economic inequality may result from the state not giving enough freedom to its citizens to develop their skills. So, the capitalist world creates an imagined world of a 'free market,' where people must be free to create wealth. But taking a cue from Adam Smith's observation, "it is not from the benevolence of the butcher, the brewer, or the baker that we expect our dinner, but from their regard to their own self-interest."[11] It could be argued that capitalist is also not as free as alleged. The various facets of capitalism, neoliberalism have had the façade of ensuring free market for people to create wealth, but at least in the Ghanaian context, that has not been the case — just like Orwell's *Animal Farm,* Ngũgĩ wa Thiong'o's *Devil on the Cross* brings out the fault lines of capitalism — that makes a commodity of human beings.[12]

From the foregoing, it could be surmised, from the Ghanaian perspective, that the complex socialist experiment in the country created corrupt oligarchs, while the capitalist regime which has metastasized since the 1980s created a few wealthy people who lack the virtue to redistribute. In the end, it could be argued that whether Ghana practised the socialist or capitalist system, the result has nearly been the same — as true of the expression: "Value for money without value for human beings."

The question then comes back as to what causes inequality and how it could be dealt with. Much as Yuval Noah Harari considered the agricultural revolution to have set inequality in motion, he is not very convinced that both capitalism and socialism would solve the problem of inequality. Instead, holding a philosophy of scientism, he thinks that technological breakthroughs — largely advanced Artificial Intelligence (AI) — would help solve human challenges. In his book, *Homo Deus,* he demonstrated how AI research would help humans overcome life's main challenges: hunger, poverty, diseases and wars. He considers all these as technical problems that can be resolved through technological progress. In the end, after resolving all these challenges that birth inequality, human beings, according to Harari, would be *deus* — gods. The question then is what would human beings do with their time afterwards? Harari responded with his 21 lessons, thinking ethics/philosophy should be considered important.[13] Harari could be read as admitting, however tacitly, that the problem of humanity is not a technological breakthrough, as it is about poor human social skills. Using India as an example, Martha Nussbawm pointed out that even though India has advanced in technology, it has a huge economic imbalance among its populace — thus showing how economic and technological enrichment without development in the humanities (such as progress in social skills) never yields any significant result in overcoming inequalities.[14]

Will human beings ever overcome economic inequalities? The views of the major religions in Ghana are critical here. Economic inequality is admitted as an existential reality in Islam and Christianity, where Jesus is reported saying that the poor will always remain with mankind. One of the writers of the New Testament, James, said that all the troubles of the world that cause inequalities result from human ego, selfishness and self-serving tendencies — similar to Adam Smith's observation above. This means that much as Yuval Noah Harari ridiculed Jesus for not having enough foresight when he talked about the 'permanence presence' of the poor, the world's war on poverty has not yielded the desired result. The world has made significant progress in warding off poverty, but the pandemic scuttled almost all human efforts to end poverty during the last three decades. Similarly, the pandemic and the current Russian-Ukraine debacle undermined the vitality of Hararis' own theory. The overwhelming mortality rate resulting from the COVID-19 indicated that diseases are still real. The current political tension between Ukraine and Russia also shows that resources and nationalism, which Harari thought would be 'a thing of the past' because of resources being more about knowledge than material resources, remains strong in engineering wars in the 21st century — even if it is to nurse the ego of the political elites.

In Christianity, Jesus' response to poverty is for people to be generous and altruistic towards the poor, for the sake of Him (Jesus Christ). This was captured in his parable of the Good Samaritan in which the latter, after he had invested so much in taking care of the stranger (who had been attacked) told the inner-keeper to continue to take care of the sick person; and that when the Good Samaritan returns, he would pay for the cost incurred. This story is aptly imbued with both didactic and sociological significance because it brings about the other dimension of inequality — which is about how human beings should deal with strangers. Strangers/foreigners in a dominant culture, as could be elicited from the Economic Fighters League (EFL) activities, tend to be at the receiving end of structured inequalities. So, the fact that Jesus used the story of a Good Samaritan to define who one's neighbour should be indicates that inequalities could be significantly (not completely) overcome if human beings answer the question "Why should I do good to the *un*like?" — in light of doing good for the sake of Christ.

The Islamic response to the question of inequality is, *inter alia,* about being patient in enduring pain and doing good to all. This is an important entry point in ensuring that one's anger against inequality becomes productive, not destructive.[15] The Islamic concept of patience does not make human beings enslaved in the face of oppression, as it is to ensure that there is modesty in resisting evil. Nevertheless, Islam has deliberately put in place economic structures to deal with inequality. Islam is against excessive profit, which tends to commodify human beings — as Marx talked about in his theory of commodity fetishism. Similarly, Islam's deployment of fasting and *zakat* is an important channel of ensuring that the rich redistribute their wealth to support the poor.

In all this, while Marx may criticize religion as the opium of the masses, for religious people, patience and being altruistic for the sake of their God is an important way of dealing with inequalities. I next discuss the Economic Fighters League against all the above theoretical and historical contexts.

The Economic Fighters League

Since the millennium, several young people in Ghana have become more disillusioned about their future prospects. After a few have exercised their voting rights, including some members of the Economic Fighters League (Movement), many have concluded that both the New Patriotic Party (NPP) and the National Democracy Congress (NDC) have failed them. They have observed a structure such as the country's 1992 Constitution (which has held the country together for over three decades) has become complicit in festering elitists' interest. Coming from this perspective, the Movement is choreographing itself away from any of these two political parties. They are aware of the extent to which credible social movements lost their sting as advocates of human rights because a group has identified with one political or the other. The Movement is also very pragmatic in curating an apolitical identity for itself because of the disillusionment and discontentment that several Ghanaians have expressed about partisan politics. Cumulatively, the Movement maintains that shifting the country's economy from elitist control to mass-focused initiative would whet the country's quest for development. The Movement firmly believes that all the struggles of the country must coalesce in economic development. This is not very different from Nkrumah's promise of economic prosperity as the necessary outcome of political independence.

With the foregoing introduction, the Economic Fighters League argues that the battle for Ghana's youthful generation is the fight for economic freedom. The Movement claims that Ghana has been blessed with enough material and human resources to give everyone a decent life — high-quality education, health, shelter, food, etc. However, assessing the country's economic reality, the Movement concluded that it is a bleak reality in which agents of neo-colonialism amass the continent's wealth with insatiable greed, swimming in obscene luxury while the people wallow in abject poverty.[16] As they observed, this privileged few alternates between power and opposition in NDC and NPP. They assert that Ghanaians elect to change dysfunctional political parties, and the elected use their power to line up their pockets, while the masses remain poor. The Movement, therefore, assumes that they have people with the ideas, policies, and organization to defeat the neo-colonial economic system that favours the few at the expense of the majority. They believe that a new dispensation is possible — based on social justice, equality, and care for the environment. But this new way of doing things will not come about unless the youth fight for it. As a Pan-African Movement, it is growing out of local communities. They also remain committed to their "promise to speak and act on the issues and principles that have motivated us as Fighters; our voices will neither be stolen nor sold. We will continue to advocate for Economic Democracy, Pan-

Africanism, Peace and Justice."[17]

Posturing as a non-violent Nkrumaist Movement that had started in 2016 to build grassroots power towards socio-economic justice in Ghana, the Movement aims at fortifying the foundations of African unity and prosperity. The Movement is neither a political party nor an appendage of any political party. They also assert that they are not a group of jobless youth with nothing to do; that violence is not their tool, as the people unwittingly always become the unfortunate victims. According to the Movement, they are building a co-operative that would remain unnamed for security reasons. It has begun in the agricultural sector and would expand to other areas in due course to underpin their activism and existing advocacy initiatives with several sustainable projects designed to empower the people. The Movement has also been actively mobilizing on a number of fronts around basic needs that arise, hosting numerous blood donation drives, mobilizing relief for victims of catastrophes such as floods, and organizing workshops on topics ranging from entrepreneurship to security and new technology. They claim to have proved their credibility and built a robust urban presence.

The Movement's stated mission is to dismantle the system of economic exploitation plaguing Africa, challenging the neo-colonial structures that continue to deny the African people their economic freedom. They define a system as a combination of interconnected and interdependent parts working together to achieve a particular purpose. According to them, the way the system is set up ensures the functioning of the parts, which ultimately determines the outcomes. They further state that if a nation runs a bad system, the outcomes would also be bad; likewise if a nation operates a good system, the outcomes would also be good. The interconnection is such that happenings in one part would affect the other parts, which will also in turn affect others. The whole mechanism must operate organically.

As they opine, the present system is largely owned and controlled by foreigners, with only a few Ghanaians benefiting from the resources while the majority wallow in poverty. Governance is exclusionary as political participation is monetized beyond the reach of the ordinary people; the few who gain political power use it to steal from the national coffers, thus affecting the provision of essential services such as good quality health care. Meanwhile, the few privileged ones fly out for medical attention elsewhere. On the education front, the Movement concluded that education does reinforce their position as 'drawers of water and hewers of wood.' In this system, they stated that certain cultural tendencies limit the potential of the youth, while positive and relevant cultural forms are not given space to inform the country's development. Further, they maintained that certain religious practices reinforce the psychological battle against the people, thus creating a collective mind-set that perpetuates the undesirable system.

The Movement espouses economic democracy, Pan-Africanism, peace and justice. In doing so, they aim to continue the work of their socialist forefathers and mothers, to finally complete the liberation process and usher the continent into an era of sustainable peace and prosperity in a united Africa. They firmly believe they have the fighters, that the people (as ordinary as they are also) have the ideas, policies, energy and organization to dismantle the country's economic system that favours only some few at the top. The Movement grew out of local communities, and that is where, as they stated, their efforts are focused. As we have stated early on, they believe another world is possible — based on social justice, equality, and care for our environment. But they think it will not come about unless they fight for it. They believe that when they succeed, nobody would go to bed hungry, sleep on the street; truncate their education for lack of funds; no one would lack water and electricity; go to jail because they cannot afford legal fees; pregnant women would not give birth on the floor; young people would have jobs; nobody would be above the law — in essence, every Ghanaian would enjoy economic freedom in their lifetime because every Ghanaian all deserves it.[18] Their stated ideology is Nkrumaism, which they conceptualize as the comprehensive philosophical and ideological teachings and principles of Kwame Nkrumah, the first president of Ghana.

The Movement aimed to include the rural areas of Ghana and link them with urban people. Their focus would be on decentralization and the dissolution of the colonial borders. To achieve their goal of economic democracy, the Movement asserted a need for reclamation. For this reclamation, the Movement maintains that there must be a mass movement, to dismantle the current oppressive system and build a new, inclusive one instead. To achieve this, they plan to adopt a four-pronged approach. Over the years, the Movement's has organized, mobilized and expressed advocacy on several issues with considerable impact, accentuating their local and transnational ramifications of their vision.

In terms of administrative structure, the Movement operates with a central command and regional leadership that oversees their wards and community cells. Despite the vertical structure of the organization, they operate horizontally, giving primacy to the cell/people in the decision-making process. To this end, their wards and cells require support in solidifying their structures. They said they had engaged the middle class on Ghana's recent political and economic downturns. Through these alliances, the Movement said they have made the middle class more open to dialogue on radical change for Ghana, meaning it would now be easier to facilitate the building of class solidarity towards overhauling this divisive system and to ensure ideological alignment across the classes. Beyond the middle class, they are involved in training 'Agents of Change' to efficiently sensitize Ghanaians on their constitutional rights. The Movement reckons that it would need a large, nationwide team conversant on the current constitution to comfortably share knowledge with the grassroots in various languages and locations.

In 2017 the Movement organized a protest march outside Ghana's Parliament House, opposing plans to use Ghana as a US military base. This was in line with their mandate to fight neo-colonial structures that deprive the nation and its people of their sovereignty. While the Ghana Police threatened the demonstrators with violence, the protestors gallantly stood their ground and maintained a non-violent stand off. In the same year, the Movement extended its reach beyond Ghana to Sierra Leone and were able to mobilize the public in Ghana to donate relief items to deliver to the Sierra Leonean embassy after the devastation of the mudslides that year.

In July 2019, the Movement successfully halted Ghana's

planned expenditure of $200 million of borrowed funds on a new Parliament building. While Parliament was in session, the protestors drew attention to their cause from the Public Gallery. There had been widespread indignation over the plans to spend this money while Ghana was steeped in debt, and was in need of such necessary infrastructure as schools, hospitals and roads. The Movement's leader, Ernesto Yeboah, as well as two other members of the Fighters Leadership, were arrested and manhandled by the police. Charges were pressed but after public outcry, the demonstrators were released.

The Movement also supported and built solidarity with the National Association of Law Students and the Ghana School of Law Students' Representative Council to organize the first law students' protest in the history of Ghana, co-led by a member of the leadership, Commander Regina Amegah. This protest was a demand to open up access to legal education, which remains an exclusive space. This had the knock-on effect of making legal aid difficult for the majority of Ghanaians. The Movement's Fighter-General, Hardi Yakubu sustained injuries to his neck from rubber bullet fragments when the police fired teargas, hot water and rubber bullets at the unarmed protestors for lawfully exercising their rights.

Following the murder of African-American George Floyd on 25 May 2020, the Movement organized a lawful solidarity vigil dubbed #AccraBlackout in solidarity with #BlackLivesMatter. This action was in line with their Pan-African ideology — that all Black people are African, and that all Black people's struggles are the same everywhere, regardless of location. The Movement asserted that it was shameful for a number of state forces, including the Ghana Police, National Security and a Counter-Terrorism Unit to violently disperse the vigil and arrest the Movement's leader, Ernesto Yeboah, who was subjected to a ten-month trial, which was later dropped when, in an act of Pan-African solidarity, the All-African People Revolutionary Party (A-APRP), along with the 11 Black Lives Matter chapters and numerous other organizations released statements and petitions condemning the actions of the state.

Again, in 2019, the Economic Fighters League supported Ugandan liberation efforts, becoming the 'home' for the People

Power Ghana chapter. Over a period of two years, they actively engaged the media to sensitize the Ghanaian public; they organized demonstrations, released multiple joint statements condemning human rights violations, and put together various campaigns designed to put pressure on what they read as the oppressive regime in Uganda. The success of this campaign was evident as Ghanaians on social media took great interest in the 2021 elections and raised an outcry against the various human rights abuses suffered by Ugandans in that period.

Thereafter, the Movement argued that the malaise Ghana finds itself in emanated from deficiencies in its 1992 Constitution. From the lack of democratic accountability of the political leadership, to the neo-colonial interferences in Ghana's development, to the massive inflation and poverty, the Movement claimed that the fault lines could be traced to the constitution. Therefore, the Movement called for the abolition of this constitution in favour of a people-centred one. Years of advocacy around this goal of a constitutional change culminated in a targeted campaign — #NewConstitutionNOW, which would educate and mobilize the general public. In their #NewConstitutionNOW agenda, they stated that:

> #NewConstitutionNOW agenda, chosen because the current 1992 constitution underpins the oppressive system we face. Educating people on it allows us to link that system to our lived reality and educate them on how we can collectively create a system that serves the masses. Since our inception, we have condemned the 1992 Constitution as the cornerstone of the oppressive system we face. As such in order to dismantle the system the People of Ghana must demand and build a new Constitution. Fighters has undertaken to facilitate the mass movement around this goal, and seeks to mobilise 1.8 million people from all walks of life across the nation to this end.[19]

For almost a year, the Movement served as co-conveners of #FixTheCountry movement, using the hash tag to mobilize governance changes in Ghana. As co-conveners, they made their structures available to the advocacy of #FixTheCountry, organizing in Accra, Obuasi, Takoradi-Sekondi and their surrounds. They proposed the creation of a new constitution — creating a crusading cry around which Ghanaians could rally. All they were crying for was a move for inclusive governance where the youth (embracing men and women) are fairly represented in decision-making processes.

During the 2020 COVID lockdown, the Movement partnered with Food Bank Food for All Africa to distribute food to communities in Greater Accra and Central Regions of Ghana. Fighters assembled, packed and distributed food packages with the F4AA team. Consistently, they corroborated with various movements to fight for freedom across the African continent. For example, they organized a protest march in solidarity with the Sudanese Revolution, and engaged Nigeria's #EndSARS, among others. They said they were working to connect with their peers across the African continent and the Diaspora towards eventual African unity.

Assessing the Economic Fighters League (EFL)

The Economic Fighters Movement, so far, has embarked on a clearly articulated ideology and action designed to support human flourishing worldwide. Through the deployment of education and activism, the Movement has recorded significant successes in signalling the mass support they have received from Ghanaians and the African diaspora. The Movement's ideals are also very historic of Marxist and Nkrumaist paradigms, which has developed a form of political religion to whip up support for its activities. Much as the group claims to be apolitical, one finds nuances of politics in their activities — that is, generally taking politics to mean management of differences in the public sphere. Convincing people to rally behind a viable idea or vision is one way of marching toward economic prosperity. Taken in this context, the Movement is political, except that the leaders do not want the politics of the NPP and NDC to besmirch their identity.

Nevertheless, the Movement has been finding it hard to convince people to support their vision of changing the regimen of Ghana's systemic economic woes. That conviction goes beyond the realm of politics. In Ghana, mobilizing to give people hope needs to have a patina of religion, to succeed — since hope is immaterial. The Movement as an entity does not subscribe to a particular institutionalized religion, which it thinks may be part of the oppressive regime. The group also contests some cultural institutions, including chieftaincy's patriarchal and authoritative nature. Either way, both religion and chieftaincy tend to split people's loyalty. Religion redirects people's ultimate loyalty to a Being other than their human political leaders. Chieftaincy, which has surged in Ghana since the 1990s, also tends to divide people into ethnic alliances.

Both religion and chieftaincy, therefore, are significant impediments on the path of revolutionary ideas. It is against this background one could appreciate Nkrumah's selective and pragmatic engagement with both religion and chieftaincy. It is also the very same religion that Ghana's revolutionary leader of the 1980s disavowed chieftaincy and Christianity in favour of a revitalized indigenous religion — the Afrikania Movement. The point, however, remains that for Ghanaians to embrace any promise of hope, there necessarily needs to be a religious tinge to any political movement. Arguably, following promise made by the Movement, the people cannot hope for anything better than a utopian world, similar to that of Karl Marx:

> When we succeed, nobody will be forced to go hungry; sleep on the streets; truncate their education for lack of funds; lack water and electricity; go to jail because they can't afford legal fees; pregnant women will not give birth on the floor; no one will die because of bad roads; young people will have jobs; nobody will be above the law; in essence, every Ghanaian will enjoy economic freedom in their lifetime because we all deserve it.[20]

There are reasons for reading religious undertones in the Movement's promises: First, the promises cut across nearly everyone's aspiration. Second, the promises assume a world that appears to re-socialize and affirm the Ghanaian quest for meaning in the face of life's vicissitudes. Together, these promises mainstream the role of religion in uniting people for a common cause. Concurrently, instead of just the role of politics in managing differences, the Movement seeks to condense people's loyalty around the valve of an eschatological vision of an earthly bliss. Beyond the promises, as we will discuss in the next chapter, there is also the question of which legislative instruments and education can really turn people's interests towards the common good. From the history of Ghana, it appears that the 'I' — representing a particular ethnic group, political party or an established religion — has hardly surrendered to the imagined idea of "We are Ghanaians."

The Movement, as we have seen, went beyond the shores of Ghana to influence policies in Uganda; it mobilized support for the people of Sierra Leone in the hour of need; and also challenged South Africa's systemic marginalization of other African migrants in their country. All these interventions are refreshingly important for a group with an inclination towards Pan-Africanism. As to whether such a Pan-African agenda would succeed in the manner the Movement aspires is yet another issue altogether. Beginning from the early 20th century, the novel idea of the vision of uniting all Africans, including those in the diaspora, according to the dreams of such Pan-Africanists such as Marcus Garvey, W. E. B. Du Bois, Alfred Charles Sam (usually called Chief Sam), J. E. Casely Hayford, Edward Wilmot Blyden and Kwame Nkrumah, etc. — has hardly succeeded. The question we ask is whether the Movement has bitten more than it could chew, considering the large canvas it was operating from? Has it learnt any lesson from history at all?

NOTES/REFERENCES

[1] Kwasi Wiredu, "The moral foundation of an African culture," In David R. Morrow, *Moral reasoning: A text and reader on ethics and contemporary moral issues,* 216-225 (Oxford: Oxford University Press, 2018).

[2] Kwame Gyekye, *The unexamined life: Philosophy and the African experience* (Legon, Ghana: Sankofa Publishing Company Ltd., 2004/1996/1988); Kwame Bediako, "De-sacralization and democratization: Some theological reflections on the role of Christianity in nation-building in modern Africa," *Transformation: An International Evangelical Dialogue on Mission and Ethics,* 12, 1 (1998): 5-11.

[3] Charles Prempeh, "Religious innovations of chieftaincy in Ghana:

Pentecostal Christianity and the complex persistence and transformation of Akan chieftaincy" *Religion Compass*, (2021): 1-13, DOI: 10.1111/rec3.12426.

[4] Wilks, *Asante in the nineteenth century.*

[5] Perbi, A. *History of indigenous.*

[6] Friedrich Engels, *The origin of the family, private property and the state* (London: Penguin, 1986).

[7] Charles Darwin, *The origin of species* (edited with intro. Gillian Beer) (Oxford: Oxford University Press, 1996).

[8] Yuval Noah Harari, *Sapiens: A brief history of humankind* (London: Vintage Digital: 2016), pp. 86-87.

[9] Karl Marx & Frederick Engels, *Manifesto for the Communist Party* (Peking: Foreign Languages Press, 1965), p. 77.

[10] George Orwell, *Animal farm* (London: Secker and Warburg, 1946).

[11] Adam Smith, *An inquiry into the nature and causes of the wealth of nations,* Vol. I (Indianapolis: LibertyClassics, 1981), 27.

[12] Ngugi wa Thiong'o's *Devil on the cross* (London: Heinemann, 1987).

[13] Yuval Noah Harari, *21 lessons for the 21st century* (London: Vintage, 2018).

[14] Martha C. Nussbaum, *Women and human development: The capabilities approach* (Cambridge: Cambridge University Press, 2000).

[15] Prempeh, "Re-imagining."

[16] Interview with Ernesto 7 March 2023.

[17] Ibid.

[18] Interview with Ernesto 7 March 2023.

[19] https://fightersleague.org/main/issues/a-new-constitution/

[20] Economic Fighters League: Economic Democracy Now (Document shared with me by Ernesto Yeboah).

CHAPTER 6

#FixTheCountry — The Legacy of Nkrumah's *Consciencism* and Ghana's Post-COVID Development

Introduction

After a little over six decades of Ghana's independence, the country continues to struggle against the colonial legacies of underdevelopment. Postcolonial leadership and citizenship have collectively played roles in undermining the country's progress. Furthermore, neo-colonialism and the recent coronavirus pandemic have continued to reveal systemic inequalities in the country. In recent times, the youth poured their anger in street demonstrations and a few vociferous ones have called for a military takeover. In this chapter, we shall deploy a theoretical framework of Nkrumah's ideology of Consciencism to advance an argument for Ghana to invest in adaptive leadership to reorient citizens and those in authority to take charge of the country's quest for human flourishing. This chapter will further posit citizenship and nationalism as social constructs and emphasize the need for adaptive leadership to build postcolonial nations.

In May 2020, as Ghana and the world struggled to grapple with the debilitating effect of the novel coronavirus pandemic, a group of young men and women, with widespread national and global support, used social media to mobilize against Ghana's challenges. As the pandemic and its social distancing and safety protocols unveiled the systemic and structural challenges in Ghana, the youth identified with the sentiments expressed by the leaders of #FixTheCountry, leading to the formation of an online movement called #FixTheCountry Movement. This group started pressurizing the government to address issues relating to energy, education, infrastructure and corruption in the country. They also urged the government to address the slow economic growth, lack of accountability, high prices, and police brutality. The police, hiding behind the guise of the pandemic, attempted to frustrate this online youth mobilization. This ploy rather encouraged the Movement to intensify their use of social media, such that in the space of 10 days, there have been more than 6 million tweets, using the hashtag — #FixTheCountry.

We shall discuss the complex entanglements between social media and frustration — pointing out the extent to which Ghana's challenges could be addressed through a creative fusion of frustration and anger and adaptive leaders. Through critical reflections and use of online information and secondary data, this chapter will repudiate an overly simplistic designation of young men and women as simply irrational in their demands. It will also demonstrate how challenging the leadership of Ghana had become soon afterwards.

Street demonstrations were a major feature of 2020 as the pandemic took a heavy toll on human race. The coronavirus remains one of the most enduring challenges to human beings since the last century. Until the outbreak of the pandemic in March 2020, the basic conversation around the world was that human beings were on the brink of conquering the world. Certainly, as human beings, through science and technology, made advances in overcoming basic human challenges such as famine, wars, and diseases, TED Conference, an American media organization that posts talks online for free distribution under the banner of 'Ideas Worth Spreading,' had given the impression that human beings would soon unravel the puzzles of life. For example, Michio Kaku, an American theoretical physicist, futurist, and purveyor of scientific ideas, had, through his writings and conferences, popularized breakthroughs in science that address basic challenges of the human race. In one of his popular books, *Physics of the Impossible*, he raises high hope for the human race. As a physicist, he claims that in the past, technologies were deemed 'impossibilities' because the basic laws of physics and science were not well known. Consequently, as scientific knowledge advances, all technological 'impossibilities' had become possibilities, including death! He said robots and humanlike cyborgs might grant humanity a gift of immortality.[1]

Perhaps one person whose work highly raised the hope of human beings eradicating death is an Israeli public intellectual historian, Yuval Noah Harari. This Oxford-trained professor of history at the University of Jerusalem, wrote popular scientific books that indicated that death would be conquered. From his *Homo Sapiens*, to *Homo Deus*, and *21 Lessons for the 21st Century*, Harari posited that death would soon be neutralized. While his *Homo Sapiens* rolls out a detailed account of the evolution of human beings from ape to homo sapiens, his *Homo Deus* claims that the science of Artificial Intelligence (AI) would put an end to the nightmare of human death. Finally, his *21 Lessons* book answers the question as to what human beings would do when they become gods (*deus*). In this book, he advises what humans must do to avoid a relapse to one of the basic challenges of science — the absence of human community.

With such high hopes for a world on the precipice of total human domination — a world where death would be no more, a world where humanity would no more need a deity, it was a shock when the coronavirus struck and assumed epidemic proportions. Possibly, since the advent of modern science in the 18th century, nothing had come close to unsettling illusions about the power of science and technology like the coronavirus. As scientific breakdown came alongside the devastation of human community, the pandemic-induced lockdown and safety protocols of social distancing ran counter to human aspiration. Since the economic prosperity of the 1960s, human beings have become more individualistic in their lifestyle. As indicated already, this led to sociologists, including Robert Bellah, who referred to the social condition of the 1960s as 'expressive individualism.' Charles Taylor also referred to the creeping individualism as the 'age of authenticity.' These scholars used these expressions to highlight how human beings have moved from communal life to becoming more self-oriented. The 14th century Arab philosopher, Ibn Khaldun, referred to humans discarding communalism as the death of *Asabiyya* — which he gave as the reason for the collapse of human civilization.

Much as economic prosperity has engendered the world of 'selfie' (self-centredness), human beings are ontological social beings with a natural quest for gregariousness.[2] This implies that as social beings oriented towards sociogenic activities, human beings have accessed the internet, particularly social media, to build human community. It also means that the internet-mediated migration of human activities from offline to online did not necessarily result in the total deconstruction of human sociality. What the internet world has done is that it has transformed offline communities into online virtual communities.

An online community may have its challenges, including the complexity of loneliness, but the coronavirus-induced lockdown rules and social distancing and safety protocols have, perhaps, been more devastating than anything human beings could have imagined. The pandemic-induced face covering, social distancing, and intensification of human 'transmogrification' to virtual beings, the pandemic deconstructed all illusions about human progress as a movement from the primitive to civility. The virus reduced social distancing to some form of physical distancing, accentuating a complex of human loneliness. This loneliness unsettled the human desire for touch and social interaction.

But more specifically, the pandemic has rendered more visible the structured and systemic economic, social, and political inequalities globally. As a result of the pandemic, the visibility of commodity fetishism, where late capitalist ideology has reduced social relation to monetary relation, where partisan politics has been reduced to oligarchy, and where racism remains an enduring major challenge that outdates Du Bois' projection of it as a challenge of the 20th century.[3] Consequently, not only has the pandemic deconstructed the high hopes human beings invested in science and technology, but it has weaponized and monetized pandemic-related vaccines globally. This has reversed the progressive march of rationalism as a break from a primitive past of superstitions and myth to the world of superstitions and conspiracy. This unsettlement of 'modernity' as total irreversible progression has resulted in some people tagging the pandemic as plandemic.

Global agitations against the visibility of structural injustice, exemplified in the murder of George Floyd, an African-American who was grotesquely murdered by a police officer (Derek Chauvin) in Minneapolis, Minnesota (USA), led hundreds of people to street demonstrations. As part of the pent-up frustration and anger with a world of injustice, the demonstrators pulled down statues of famous persons whose activities and inactions the demonstrators read as having set the world on a trajectory of injustice and human collapse.

In this global context, Ghana's enduring challenges of poor sanitation and squalid living conditions, graduate unemployment, erratic power supply (known locally as *dumsor*), corruption, partisan politics, and institutional challenges in addressing these basic challenges morphed into the teaser #FixTheCountry — the Movement, which was one of the creative ways young people in Ghana have galvanized social media to perceive partisan politics as gerontocratic and oligarchic. As the political elites grappled with youth-accumulated frustration and fought against the pandemic, the social Movement had to embark on street demonstrations nationally, with Ghanaians in the diaspora joining the fray. Some young men and women, including Kalyjay (Joshua Boye-Doe), Efia Odo (Andrea Owusu), Captain Smart (Blessed Godsbrain Smart), and Ernesto Yeboah, who through the Economic Fighters League, provided institutional support for the #FixTheCountry Movement. The #FixTheCountry Movement wanted the government to address energy, education, infrastructure and corruption issues. They also called on the state to resolve issues of slow economic growth, lack of accountability, high prices, and police brutality.

The police attempted to frustrate this online mobilization — using the pandemic as an excuse. This made the Movement intensify their use of social media, such that in a space of ten days, more than 6 million tweets appeared using the hashtag. The goal of this chapter is to discuss the complex entanglements between social media and frustration, pointing out the extent to which Ghana's challenges could be addressed through a creative fusion of anger and adaptive leadership.

Eventually, the Movement succeeded in getting approval to embark on street demonstrations in August 2021.[5] Having secured approval, its international convener, Oliver Mawuse Barker-Vormawor mobilized both local and trans-local supporters to embark on a street demonstration, and submitted a petition to the political elite. Oliver is a doctoral researcher in International Law at the

University of Cambridge in the United Kingdom. He holds Master degrees in Law from Harvard Law School and Université Hassan II in Casablanca, Morocco. He is an experienced diplomat and lawyer with varied professional experiences in international law. He has worked as an Assistant Director at the Legal Department of the Ministry of Foreign Affairs of Ghana; Law Clerk to the Vice-President (and later President) of the International Court of Justice; and Legal Officer at the United Nations Office of Legal Affairs.

During the street demonstrations that began in Accra, young men and women carried such placards as encapsulate their concerns: "Give the youth a chance to be responsible"; "Bring back Nkrumah State farms"; "The youth are jobless and crying"; "The country needs equality"; "Ghana is the most corrupt religious country"; "A new constitution now"; "Ghana is the only country we have"; "Mr Prez! Stop the corruption and save Ghana from civil war"; "President Nana Addo should be the last Oldman president in Ghana"; Tribal politics is backwardness"; "Stop suppressing freedom," etc.

The major demand of the Movement boils down to a demand for a new constitution, as the old one has failed to achieve the aspirations of 'Freedom and Justice' embedded in Ghana's motto. The Movement's petition to this end reads thus:

On 28th April 1992, the people of Ghana went to a referendum to adopt a new constitutional document. The Constitution was supposed to provide a rebirth for a beaten and tired nation. It was supposed to celebrate our resilience as a people and our commitment to building a democratic society. The document carried the Hopes and Aspirations of people with a sense of belief. A belief that the new Constitution will offer Justice. A belief that the New Document will set Ghana on the rails for shared prosperity, liberation and true democracy. A belief that abuse of power, corruption, inequality and immoral elite politics will give way to freedom! Nearly 30 years on; those dreams have remained still-born. The Constitution has failed in its assumptions and in its design. It has become the most prominent face of a Republic that has entrenched vile corruption; institutional disregard for Ghanaian lives; human rights abuses; and economic exclusion. Its provisions have been instrumentalized to shield immorality and provide immunity for the corruption of a decrepit political class. Its ethos has been infested with greed, inhumanity and criminal insensitivity. Over the past few months, #FixTheCountry has created a platform that has mobilized Ghanaian civic conscience to reclaim our society; and build a new path that leads to justice. We are asking questions that show the depth of the Republic's moral corruption. In a society where all civic institutions and administrative bodies have been corrupted from within by the political class and its enablers and corrupt appendages, #FixTheCountry is mobilizing citizens to become the last piece of resistance. We are demanding a new society founded on justice. We are refusing to play by the rules of a political class that is so disinterested in the Ghana project. We are asking for a reset in the direction and the assumptions that pervasive immorality thrives on in our body politic. For Ghana to work, we will need to reset to rebuild! For our democracy to work again and to deliver on its promises, we must urgently redesign the rules of engagement based on what past experiences have thought us. We need a Constitution for a New Generation that understands the urgency of justice.[6]

#FixTheCountry Movement and Social Media

Since independence, Ghana has had several civil society and pressure groups calling on the political elites to fix the country's challenges. Because the Ghanaian public often tags civil society groups as partisan in their motive, the leadership of the #FixTheCountry Movement decided (or so it appears) to see themselves as apolitical. Oliver defined the objectives and aims as follows:

Many people have asked me and some others what the whole FixTheCountry protest is about. And I have always been hesitant to define for anybody what it should mean to them . . . FixTheCountry resonates with so many of us because we know, deep down within us that this country can do better. I want everyone to find their reason and purpose for showing up on the day of the protest. For some people, it's about the pain of losing relatives through a dysfunctional healthcare system. For others, it is about more than that. It's about a political system that has no consequences. One that allows certain people to get away with just about anything, as long as they wield a party card.[7]

But given that the public or politicians like to label pressure groups as partisan in orientation, Oliver expressed the non-partisan nature of the Movement as follows:

1. No political party has put me, or any of the other Convenors, up to this.
2. No one, not myself or anyone I know, has received any money or demanded anything from any political party.
3. This is not and cannot be about regime change. Our problem is not about one party or the other. It's the entire system that is not working.
4. We need solutions that transform the structure of our governance and how we hold leaders to account.[8]

After listening to comments Ghanaians were making, Oliver and other leaders of the Movement summed up three main demands of the Movement thus:

1. A new constitution or, at the very worst, a review of the current one. This must be done in a framework that actually leads to results; if not, we will hit a dead end as the Constitution Review Commission's report.
2. An enforceable Economic Recovery Programme that involves every sector of the economy and makes a comprehensive development plan.
3. A testimonial and reconciliation process that allows every Ghanaian who had suffered wrongs and injustices to get the chance to tell their story. "People need to heal from the pain of this democracy. We need to build people's faith again. We need to give them a reason to make them believe that Ghana can work again.[9]

It is clear that the leadership of the Movement was largely pressing for an adaptive answer to Ghana's challenges. As part of their resolutions, they stated, "We are asking for a reset in the direction and the assumptions that pervasive immorality thrives on in our body politic."[10] The issue of immorality is important, as it resonates with the inclinations of several southern Gold Coast intellectuals, including J. E. Casely-Hayford and John Mensah Sarbah, who among the early political elites, admitted that Ghana was in need of more adaptive answers than technical ones. Even so, the demands of the Movement easily circulated on social media, thus indicating the critical role of social media in local and global mobilization against discontent. Social media has been an important breakthrough in broadening the channels of communication; it has also amplified local conflicts unto the global canvas. As an online communication, social media has also subverted the rules of temperate communication and amplified anger and frustrations beyond reasonable levels.

With state institutions struggling to protect the complex demarcation between freedom of expression and freedom of responsible expression, Prof Joy Henrietta Mensa-Bonsu bemoaned the challenge of 'reckless' speech on social media as the death of the "era of book no lie."[11] While it is not entirely true that a book, after going through rigorous editorial scrutiny, is purged of blatant falsehood, it is equally true that it can project political propaganda and untruths. This is why the older and conservative generation are sceptical of young people's use of social media. The mixed responses to social media and responsible speech have not diminished the use to which young men and women use the medium to communicate. During the last decade or so, the youth have leveraged Facebook, WhatsApp, Instagram, and other social media handles to mobilize against injustice.[12]

Some academics have identified the hybridity of the communication technologies that the Movement resorted to, especially social media, to fuel their activities in Ghana and the diaspora.[13] But social media was not enough to guarantee the relative success of the Movement. Other academics have identified the Movement's ability to mirror the broader concerns of the Ghanaian society at large.

The Movement adopted three main strategies:

1. Depicting the Ghanaian government as irresponsible.
2. Portraying the Ghanaian people as victims.
3. Issuing a clarion call to action.

Accordingly, these strategies were framed with linguistic resources, and they enabled the protestors to recruit support for their objectives, as well as rally the masses for offline demonstration.[14] Others have also argued that the Movement expanded the frontiers for youth activists and other dissident groups within the political system to demand democratic accountability from members of the political class.[15] For example, before 2019, some young men and women demonstrated their enthusiasm and exuberance by forming pressure groups to challenge the state. While online mobilization transformed into offline street demonstrations and possibly inspired other 'marginalized' groups to assert themselves, such demonstrations have not always yielded the desired results. In effect, youth mobilization might have startled the political elite to address some national issues, but this, so far, left the youth dissatisfied.

Moreover, the political elites tended to succeed in politicizing the pressure groups, and in the process, fragmenting the youth front in challenging what might be considered as regime incompetence. Furthermore, politicians have tried without much success to influence the youth in the low-income bracket, especially, to become 'foot soldiers' of their parties.[16] The elite tended to view such foot soldiers with apprehension, considering their activities as potentially explosive and subversive of Ghana's burgeoning democracy. Thus, after the Ayawaso Wuogon incident, the state passed a law that banned the activities of foot soldiers.

With offline mobilization nearly curtailed, the youth considered social media as a necessary communication channel to carry on the fight. Through social media, the youth have launched protests against issues such as the government's proposal in 2018 to expand the parliament of Ghana. The agitation of hashtag #DropTheChamber combined with civil society to 'force' the government to 'drop' the idea of expanding the country's parliament.[17]

Social media has proved to be an important avenue for communication and for the fact that #FixTheCountry Movement resorted to using this medium resonated with several Ghanaians and its diaspora. Just a few days after the social media campaign began in the early days of May 2021, the Movement assuredly received widespread support from Ghanaians in the country and globally. Supporters included celebrities, civilians, politicians, religious leaders, chiefs, and other civil organization groups. The Movement leveraged the country's celebration of the controversial Founders' Day and took to the street to demonstrate against what they considered as poor and failed leadership. As a form of counter-hegemony to a celebration that limits the decolonization struggles to a few Ghanaian families, a rival group that appeared pro-government and styled itself as #Fixyourself also emerged. This group argued that Ghana's problem is attitudinal — as citizens have not demonstrated enough goodwill and responsibility to fix the country. The two groups have similarly received support from the Ghanaian populace.

As the #FixTheCountry polarized the country into different groups, not least political parties, several social media discourses highlighted the possibility of the government being 'forced' into action to address the structural challenges that the nation was facing. Indeed, as the Movement rallied support to demonstrate on the streets of Accra and other major cities in the country, the government's representative called them for a meeting. The meeting was to assure the young men and women that the government was doing everything possible to address the country's challenges. The Finance Minister, Ken Ofori-Atta and other government high-ranking officials admitted that the country certainly faced challenges, but they were confident they could fix them all.

The second reason for the meeting was to persuade the Movement's leadership to avoid demonstrating on the streets. This was because, while the coronavirus pandemic had unsettled the lives of several Ghanaians, many young men and women were ready to 'risk' their lives for a better Ghana. The danger about COVID-19 was that the virus did not only spread fast but could be highly infectious. Given this reality, the government passionately appealed to the young men and women to desist from their street demonstrations.

The police were also invited to reason with the leadership of the Movement.

Despite the meeting, the leadership of the Movement decided to continue with the street demonstrations. Two main reasons account for this. First, the government and its party leaders openly ignored the safety protocols against the pandemic. For example, they thronged the funeral of their former General Secretary, Kwadwo Owusu Afriyie (popularly known as 'Sir John'), which was held on 3 June 2021. But given the importance of funerals in Ghana in expressing sympathy, the president and several of the leading members of the New Patriotic Party (NPP) did not set a good example in obeying safety protocols, especially the one about avoiding large gatherings. The behaviour of the NPP leadership received condemnation from several Ghanaians who took to social media to vent their disappointment.

The second reason was the inspiration drawn from demonstrations in Western countries. At the time, hundreds of people had massed up on the streets in the USA and other European countries to protest against the grotesque murder of an African-American, George Floyd, on 25 May 2020. This incident took place at the peak of the pandemic. It was worth noting that Western leaders did not use violence to stop people from venting their anger, even when the demonstrators pulled down statues of some persons suspected to have inspired racism in recent history. Consequently, the leadership of the Movement in Ghana, determined to go ahead with their protestations, gave the police assurances to the police that they would observe the necessary COVID-19 safety protocols during the street demonstration in Accra. The authorities, however, were not convinced.

Instead, the police went to the High Court for an injunction to prevent the Movement's street demonstration. The court granted an ex-parte motion against the protest on 6 May 2021. Not satisfied, the leadership of the Movement appealed to the Supreme Court, which subsequently nullified the injunction. Justice Srem Sai, the lawyer for the #FixTheCountry Movement argued convincingly.[18] Meanwhile the Movement had drawn the support of several older Ghanaians, including religious leaders and traditional authorities, including the Dormaahene.[19]

Counter-Force: #FixYourAttitude Movement

In the midst of all these goings-on, a not too strong counter-Movement — the #FixingTheCounry Movement had emerged, led by Ernest Owusu Bempah, NPP government appointee who was the head of the Corporate Communications for Ghana. This new force defined their *raison d'etre* as being "an amalgamated umbrella body of all right-thinking Ghana — first activists, patriots of political divide and other progressive forces. We are proud to state without any sentiler [sic] of doubt that [their] toils . . . led to the landmark 2016 victory of the NPP government."[20] Because #FixingTheCounry Movement declared itself as sympathisers of the NPP, the group held a conference and harped the achievement of the NPP government since 2016. Bempah said stated the achievements of the NPP as follows:

> The Free Senior High School, One-District-One-Factory, Digitalization, Free Technical Vocational Education, the Planting for food and jobs, Restoration of Allowances for Teachers and Nursing Trainees, Reviving Scholarship Secretariat, the Nation Builders Corps, Youth in Afforestation, NEIP, the Amplified Projects and the Ghana Enterprises Agency are all youth-driven.[21]

Owusu Bempah and his pro-NPP members were strategic in the name of their movement. Named #FixingTheCountry Movement, the pro-NPP group appeared reconciliatory. Earlier, Frank Annoh-Dompreh, the member of Parliament Nsawam Adoagyir was alleged to have castigated the #FixTheCountry members as lazy people.[22] Annor Dompreh's comments received robust backlash from the Ghanaian populace, including some sympathizers of the NPP. Perceptibly pro-NPP celebrities, including Afia Schwarzenegger (formally known as Valentina Nana Agyeiwaa), used the hashtag #FixYourAttitude to amplify the response of the NPP leadership. Consequently, the #FixYourAttitude readily resonated with Ghanaians who had held a contrary position to the #FixTheCountry Movement.

Afia Schwarzenegger expressed the #FixYourAttitude position as follows:

Go to the passport office, if you don't have money, you can't have a passport. Go to DVLA, people are taking huge sums of monies for driver's licenses without passing through the correct channels. Corruption has hit every part of the Ghanaian system. Ghana Police, Ghana Immigration, Ghana Army. Is it the president who takes the bribe? You are the same people taking the bribe, but you want the government to fix the country. Is it the president who takes bribes at the Passport Office? Ghanaians are too corrupt. It is you and I who become politicians. So, fix your attitude first before pushing the #FixTheCountry Agenda.[23]

The foregoing discussion indicates that while the youthful constituency of Ghana is polarized over Ghana's challenges, both camps are frustrated over the same challenges that undermine human flourishing. The difference is the perspective from which they examine the complexities of the issue. All this implies that it is simplistic to profile the youthful constituency as lazy and lacking industrious attitude. Instead, the conversation demonstrates how the youth is determined to contribute to shaping Ghana's development. They are ready to be part of the solution. The critical issue, which the two camps admit, is the prevailing attitude of 'blame culture' that Ghanaians often evince — where they blame everyone, but themselves for the country's predicaments.

Taking a Second Look at the #FixTheCountry Movement

In order to formulate a theoretical understanding of the #FixTheCountry Movement, data was gathered from the website of the #FixTheCountry Movement (https://fixthecountrygh.com). The data was identified and compiled from the public page of vocal members of both camps. Online news articles from media houses such as Ghanaweb; CitiNews, and Myjoyonline) were gathered. In all, a total of 50 texts that focused on the social, political and economic discussions on how Ghana needed to be fixed were gathered. These were analyzed through grouping them into broad categories to clearly demarcate the views of the two camps. Copying and saving recurring phrases, images, concepts, and axioms into a special computer-related folder was undertaken. Phrases like, "Our leaders are corrupt"; "We're all corrupt" and "Ghana must be fixed" were collected. Employing critical reflections and contextual analysis of these phrases enabled the repudiation of an overly simplistic designation of young men and women as simply irrational in their demands and the leadership of Ghana as irredeemably incompetent. Instead, this perspective points out the nuanced interactions that take place between multiple local and global forces in shaping Ghana's economic progress. Also, the usual tagging of the youth as #FixYourAttitude; or the leaders as #FixTheCountry; and Nkrumah's *Consciencism* as a theory, could serve as an entry point in discussing Ron Heifetz's contemporary adaptive theory of leadership.

The point is not to cow the youth into passive acceptance of injustice, but instead, it is to argue for government to invest in adaptive answers to Ghana's challenges. Moving away from reading Ghana's challenges as technical and offering technical answers, there is a need for social and philosophical interventions. Concurrently, while constitutional reform, as a major demand of both camps, may help resolve some of the human-induced imbalances, it might render inequality in society. This recalls Thomas Jefferson's declaration that:

> We hold these truths to be self-evident, that all men are created equal, that their Creator endows them with certain inalienable rights, that among these are life, liberty and the pursuit of happiness.[24]

The frustrations of the Ghanaian youth are also part of pandemic-induced global concern against systemic multidimensional disequilibrium. Further, there is also a need to consider the worldview of street demonstrations for their own sake. For example, one placard read: "Give the youth a chance to be responsible." This could be assumed to mean the Ghanaian youth want to contribute their quota to advancing Ghana's flourishing — that the youth wanted to be listened to. The question was whether they wanted the chance for the whole country, or in furtherance of their own self-interest? For example, in Ghana, a graduate who sells bread makes headlines on social media — usually depicting the status of the graduate as some kind of self-debasement. There appears, therefore, a disconnection between a university degree and the selling of bread. But if responsibility is the issue, why should it be circulated on social media in derogatory terms?

Furthermore, Ghanaian society tends to generate antinomies. For example, when one visits the 'bush canteen' (an apology of an eatery) on the campus of University of Ghana, one would find students eating in ways that one associated with 'illiterates' (in other words, those who have had no Western education). One finds students eating weird combinations of food, for example, mixing boiled beans, fried plantain, eggs, and avocado. Or students eating *fufu* and hot light soup and sipping chilled assorted soft drinks at the same time. In contrast, a typical denizen of Maamobi slum, for example, might have for breakfast porridge and *koose*, all made from millet — a better combination than the ordinary university student (presumably coming from the middle class), living in a gated community, who eats a melange of junk food for breakfast. The reason for the antinomies is not necessarily technical, a situation that demands the provision of more schools and hospitals. The issue is more about people reorienting their lives to appreciate changes in society. This calls for an adaptive leadership that cannot be taken for granted.

Adaptive Leadership

The argument implies the need for adaptive leadership from the political elite. This leads to a discussion of the theory of adaptive leadership. Several academics and politicians (including Barack Obama, the former president of the United States of America), hold the view that leadership and development are entwined when one attempts to make sense of Africa's predicament.[25] Africa is held out as the scar on the conscience of the world. Ironically, she is the richest but poorest. It is the place where weak institutions hold sway, thus deepening the African predicament. Therefore, Africans and their leaders are urged to build strong institutions. Barack Obama, for example, in his speech to the people of Ghana when he visited the country's Parliament, urged Ghanaians to build strong institutions to minimize corruption for development. Corruption of all shades has been flagged as a major challenge. It appears that corruption and leadership are considered Siamese twin concepts in discussing leadership, particularly in Ghana and in Africa, as a whole. Several youths charge the political leadership in Africa of corruption. Interestingly, politicians whose party is in government see no corruption — talk no corruption and do no corruption. The party in Opposition, however, see otherwise.

While admitting the complexities of the leadership in Ghana, one could argue that the country's challenges are technical and adaptive. Since the technical responses have been responded to (however insufficiently) since independence, one could focus one's interest on the adaptive aspect. Nearly all the political elites from Nkrumah to the current Nana Akufo-Addo's government, have invested in building schools, hospitals/clinics, and roads; expanded the police service intake; upgraded the training of the police; democratized to allow for more civic society participation, and economic restructuring.

Ghanaians may justifiably see these technical responses as insufficient, but it is also true that the attitude of Ghanaian citizens towards nation-building has not been encouraging. This means that much as the political elites may not have inspired leadership to promote human flourishing, liberal governance has had its own aporia. Since the Fourth Republic Ghanaians often compare their leadership with that of Paul Kagame of Rwanda. Certainly, it would be simplistic to dismiss the achievements of Kagame. However, there is a need to contextualize the comparison. Rwanda is a country that shares a common memory of genocide and is fortunate to have a leader who has enjoyed security of tenure for a little over two decades. In comparison, Ghanaian political elites have often struggled with issues of security of tenure. Obviously, President Kagame has leadership skills that encourage growth and development, but the political regime of 'benevolent' dictatorship can hardly be compared to Ghana's burgeoning liberal democracy.[26]

The dynamics may not be the same if we compare Kagame with Museveni, Rwanda's immediate neighbour who has had security of tenure. Kagame has benefited from the genocide to lead his people, as the threat of a relapse into the status quo ante would not auger well for his citizens and the international community. Consequently, scholars in the international community did what they could to ensure that peace and development prevailed in Rwanda. Museveni had a different experience. As the 'strongman' of the Great Lakes Region, Museveni has a strong army that benefits from the West, who allegedly channels money to Uganda. But, unlike Rwanda, much of the resources in Uganda benefit Museveni and enriches his military more than human capital development.

The above does not justify Museveni nor necessarily encourage any form of an authoritarian regime. Instead, it points to the complexity of the leadership challenge in Ghana/Africa. As Assensoh aptly argued, the colonial and neo-colonial realities complicate leadership in Africa.[27] Overcoming such a challenge cannot only be done with the emphasis placed on technical answers. For example, the issue of corruption can hardly be significantly overcome if the Ghanaian people do not see it more as an adaptive challenge. It is for this reason that one may agree with Kwame Gyekye that the issue of political corruption is fundamentally a moral problem, which implies a need for what he referred to as, 'commitmental moral revolution.'[28] This involves a change in attitude and responses of the individual members of society to the moral values, principles, and ideals cherished by society.[29] He concluded, "therefore, we must pay serious attention to personal integrity and character matters."[30]

By emphasizing individual integrity as key in leadership and the complex issues of corruption in Africa, Gyekye reminds his audience of the need for them to see the state as a social construct. This provides an important watershed for the call for adaptive leadership and answers because Ghana, as a social construct, must appeal to shared moral philosophy (which will soon be discussed along with Nkrumah's *Consciencism*, to advance the argument). Suffice it to say that indigenous societies were equally socially constructed. The chiefs and clan heads were leaders in the case of centralized societies such as the Asante and Mole-Dagbani. In the case of non-centralized (or acephalous societies) such as the Tallensi, the earth priests (*Tendaana*) were the leaders.

Nevertheless, as has already been stated, in both centralized and acephalous societies, social constructions and myths were invoked to enforce social cohesion as well as enforce individual and collective responsibility. For example, the largest Akan group, the Asante, deployed the sacralization of the Golden Stool as the soul of Asante and the non-disclosure of the other's ancestral background to firm Asante imagined unity. Therefore, the traditional political leaders appeal to sociogenic activities such as those that involve the lifecycle — marriage, birth, death, and the rituals of reincarnation — to help people develop adaptive capacities. Also, essential oral cultures, cultural symbols, songs, and other folklore were used to ensure adaptability and amenability in governance, leadership and development. The sense of amenability imbued in indigenous societies partly explains the survival of chieftaincy as the enduring pre-colonial legacy — albeit with some changes — among the various ethnic groups in Ghana.

In pre-colonial history, the social construction of society and the quest for adaptive culture were embedded in the Akan proverb that, "The clan is like the forest if one watches from afar, the trees appear standing together, but when one gets closer, one realizes that each tree is standing on its own." That society is socially constructed places responsibility on both the leadership and the followers to reinforce each other in warding off life's existential challenges — making the individual a constitutive member of society than just being a shadow of it.[31]

Towards the end of the 20th century, the issue of adaptive leadership has been masterly undertaken by Ronald Heifetz, founding director of the Centre for Public Leadership at the John F. Kennedy School of Government, Harvard University, USA. As a clinical psychologist, he deploys evolution theory and cultural evolution to focus on adaptive leadership as critical in building societies, businesses and non-governmental institutions. He advanced his theory in his three seminal books.[32] Heifetz summarised and expanded his theory since the 1990s in his book, *The Practice* published in 2009. The theory has been around and studied for nearly decades, so it will not be very necessary to go into great length with it. Suffice it to summarize the key argument of his adaptive theory. Heifetz defines adaptive leadership as the practice of mobilizing people to tackle tough challenges and thrive.[33] Based on this, he argued that several of the challenges of the world are adaptive challenge, which requires people to reorient themselves, culturally and socially, to thrive.

He argued that whether the causes of human challenges are externally or internally induced, human beings have the cultural-DNA to adapt. But he also argued that in difficult situations, human beings tend to want a quick fix, which makes them rely more on technical answers. The technical responses have a transient result. Consequently, the technical issues of racism and other forms of structured disequilibrium have not yielded the much-desired result. The challenge for the recurrence of social challenges, which often result in systematic inequality and exclusion of minority groups, is the human tendency to abnegate responsibility and hold on to conservative values that have outlived their use.

All this means is that adaptive leadership is critical. According to him, adaptive leadership is important in resolving much of the world's challenges because,

> To build a sustainable world in an era of profound economic and environmental interdependence, each person, each country, and each organization is challenged to sift through the wisdom and know-how of their heritage, to take the best from their histories, leave behind lessons that no longer serve them, and innovate, not for the change's sake, but for the sake of conserving and preserving the values and competence they find most essential and precious.[34]

One could tease out a few issues in the above succinct application of adaptive leadership as follows: First, adaptive leadership must build on existing cultural realities and worldviews by being creative in choosing and leaving behind what is relevant and which one is not. Second, adaptive leadership involves individual responsibility in the comity of other people. Third, individuals can change but are often reluctant to give up worldviews and traditions that are hardly relevant. It could be added that adaptive leadership is about how individuals can build their adaptive capacity to answer the existential questions of life.

Concurrently, it is could be argued that if individuals answer the following questions well, they will deploy their anger against systemic injustice in a more constructive way: Who am I? Why am I here? And is there life after death? These socio-philosophical questions will help the youth and the older generations to reflect soberly on their actions and inactions that perpetuate injustices of all kinds.

Since the responses to these questions may not be derived from the technical answers of life, society — as socially constructed — provides an important context for individuals to develop adaptive capacity.

#FixTheCountry and Ghana's Citizenship: A Reconsideration

This section begins with the assertion that Ghana is a social construct based on socio-religious philosophy, which calls for adaptive leadership to help its citizens to deal with structured challenges. It also argues that the British imposition of 'formal' colonial rule in the late 19th century, did not curtail the practice of religion in the public sphere.[35] Further, it is maintained that the documentation of citizenship, through biometric cards and legislation, are technical issues to reaffirm Ghana's social construction as an imagined community of one people.

In all this, it could be contended that Ghanaian citizenship is more socially constructed than it is technically construed.[36] For the above reasons, Ghana's secular status is not the absence of religion in the public sphere, as it is about religious plurality that allows for equal religious expression. This understanding chimes with the genealogical history of the concept, which never meant the absence of religion in the public sphere. Historically, in Western history, particularly in England until the second half of the 19th century, the concept was used to designate the transfer of church property, particularly land lay ownership.[37] In the middle of the 19th century, the terms 'secularism' and 'secularists' were introduced into English by freethinkers to avoid the charge of their being 'atheists' and 'infidels.'[38]

The struggle against colonialism was largely anchored on what the nationalist profiled as Ghana's common experience of oppression. This articulation of identity entwined with a common experience of pain was also part of the construction of the idea of 'Africans.'[39] By *othering* Europeans, an imagined African common identity was established. As established in Chapter One, Nkrumah poignantly articulated this when he inverted Jesus' words, "Seek ye first the political kingdom and all shall be added."

Nkrumah's inversion of the Bible and his engagement with religion incurred the discontent of Christians.[40] Nevertheless, Nkrumah's appropriation of the Bible had several reasons. The first was to use religion as a counter-hegemonic force for nationalism. The second was to reinvest in the ancient practice of constructing a society based on religion or religious rituals.[41] However, Nkrumah's appropriation of religion is explained. What appears trite is that he understood the role religion plays in the social construction of human society. However, the critical question that Nkrumah and several of the postcolonial leaders of Africa faced was similarly about how to form a nation out of a people whose history of pluralities has been made complex with additional enduring layers — Islam and Christianity.

Whether through mystifying narratives of birth or sacralizing Ghana's political symbols, Nkrumah often resorted to the indigenous of non-binary worldview to build Ghana. By incorporating the past religious reality and the colonial and postcolonial reality of complex pluralities, Nkrumah was involved in what could be referred to as creative eclecticism and the logic of cultural hybridity — choosing examples from the past to comment on possible futures.[42] This creative eclecticism involved his creation and reconstruction of Ghana's history as an intermeshing of three forces — the indigenous traditions, Islam and Christianity. Nkrumah put these strands together to develop his idea of *Consciencism*, which is designed to provide answers to the complex issues of postcolonial development.

Before discussing *Consciencism* in the next section, suffice it here to discuss the measures Nkrumah took to build an imagined Ghana as a country of one people with a common destiny. It has already been stated that Ghana's nationalism was anchored on the sentiment of othering the colonisers. Beyond that Nkrumah and the nationalists had to convince the Asante and the Ewe to join in the country's independence as a unitary state.[43] Ghana could have had independence in 1956, but for the Asante and Ewe contestations. With independence, finally attained in 1957, Nkrumah and his supporters took up the task of constructing Ghana as an imagined nation of oneness. Through legislative means, that is, passing a law to outlaw the formation of political parties on religious, ethnic lines, and deportation of those he considered a threat to Ghana's unity, Nkrumah hoped to unite Ghana.

At the same time, he constructed and profiled Ghana to the African diaspora as the ideal country for their ancestral home. This is partly because of the colour synchrony between the flag of Ghana and those of the Rastafarian movement due to a shared pan-African history. The colours are originally Ethiopian. Ethiopia and pan-Africanist movements adopted them in light of Ethiopia's independence, and Rastafarianism drew on this identification (see also their worship of Haile Selassie). When designing the Ghanaian flag, Theodosia Okoh drew on the same pan-African colour symbolism. The star also clearly indicates this — coming from Marcus Garvey's Black Star Line.[44] Additionally, Nkrumah relied on symbolic nationalism to construct an imagined national identity for Ghanaian citizens. He, therefore, embarked on the agenda of symbolizing Ghanaian money, postage, stamps, museum exhibits, monuments, national anthem, emblems, the national flag, and political flags.[45]

Consciencism: **Nkrumah's Dilemmas**

While several of Nkrumah's books have been widely read and severally cited, *Consciencism* appears not to have a similar appeal. *Consciencism* has not been one of the recommended reading texts in Ghanaian universities. Many scholars read it as an academic exercise. Several reasons account for this. First, as a philosophy, the text is difficult to read. Second, could be that by the time Nkrumah published *Consciencism*, he had become more aware of the challenges of Ghana's quest for human development, beyond his usual rhetoric in his book, *Africa Must Unite*, which he published a year before *Consciencism* and his primary political slogan, "Seek ye first the political kingdom and all other things shall be added."[46]

In his foreword to Fuller's monograph, the Ghanaian professor, A. B. Assensoh, one of the few African journalists to have interviewed Nkrumah during Nkrumah's exile in Conakry in the late 1960s, wrote the implication of Nkrumah's symbolic nationalism as follows:

> Symbolic slogans created a firestorm of accusations levelled at Nkrumah by foreign and domestic critics, who viewed them as evidence of Nkrumah's insatiable appetite for acquiring and maintaining political powers. Always cognizant of his public image, Nkrumah used the international and domestic media to defend the minting of his likeness of Ghana's new coins, currency, and postage stamps. He argued that he was forced to take these actions given Ghana's high rate of illiteracy, which compelled him to use visual signs and symbols to convince the people that the country was really free, and that he, and not Queen Elizabeth II, was now the ruler in charge of Ghana.[47]

In all of this, Nkrumah incorporated the precolonial idea of sacralizing mundane elements to forge social cohesion and conviviality. For this reason, in particular, Nkrumah's *Consciencism* is very important for this study. *Consciencism*, as Ali Mazrui described it in his series: 'Africa's Triple Heritage' or 'Africa's Trinity of Cultures,' is very nuanced in Nkrumah's capturing of human nature and nation-building. Merging Marxism and Ghana's religious heritage,[48] Nkrumah reflected on the role philosophy, ideology, and faith could play in human sublimation of self-centredness to eschew corruption and also promote human flourishing. Nkrumah's dialectical moments were his own efforts at reconciling the existential internal contradictions in the colonial enterprise. The theory of dialectic moment helped Nkrumah to reconcile the reality that Africans were both the oppressors and agents of oppression. This was part of his reading of colonialism as both metaphysical (based on an entrenched philosophy) and geographical. Africans who inhabited the philosophy of colonialism, through colonial education, as well as the infested colonial geographical space, were capable of reliving the colonial moment by both aping and becoming a comprador for colonialism.

Concomitant with the above, Nkrumah aimed to deploy Africa's religious and cultural heritage to promote unity and focus on how individuals could engage in self-sublation for nation-building. From an understanding of Nkrumah and the fact that he published his *Consciencism* in 1964 (a year after Fanon's *Wretched of the Earth*), it may be surmised that Nkrumah was not unaware of Fanon's critique of the impotence of postcolonial African elites. Fanon had concluded in 1963 that the working class in Africa were more reactionaries and privileged groups who could hardly be entrusted with the odious postcolonial task of advancing the interest of Africans without often falling into the colonial era to mimic the antics and oppression of the colonizers.

Certainly, Fanon had to also contend with his subscription to violence as a force to overturn colonialism without violence becoming a reality in postcolonial Africa.[49] More importantly, while the ideas of Nkrumah and Fanon cannot be reduced to simplistic and superficial analysis, it could, nevertheless, be argued that the two political figures shared the idea that the colonial enterprise exerted impact on Africans that had both material and philosophical ramifications. Fanon, for example, admitted that the colonial enterprise was a complex entanglement of "economic substructure and superstructure."[50]

Fanon, as recounted by Nigel, observed the dilemmas in colonialism and postcolonial reality in terms of the strategy of violence:

> Fanon had already glimpsed these dilemmas in countries that had achieved independence and were well aware of the symptoms exhibited by his patients. He clearly foresaw various aspects of postcolonialism: the upheavals and fratricidal conflicts; the hypocrisies and hucksterism of national elites; and above all, the sufferings of the men and women, and indeed of entire communities and generations, who have been indelibly marked by the violence to which they have been subjected, and whose very future is compromised.[51]

As Nkrumah reflected on the internal tensions in the human ontological self-centredness, he was not far from the earlier European social thinkers who had undertaken a similar exercise in the logic of social contract. To mainstream his understanding of complex human nature, before 1964, Nkrumah had appealed to academics to use education to refine the human spirit for selfless service to humanity. At the opening of the Institute of African Studies on the campus of University of Ghana, in 1963, he defined true education as:

> True academic freedom — the intellectual freedom of the university — is everywhere fully compatible with service to the community: for the university is and must always remain, a living, thinking and serving part of the community to which it belongs.[52]

Nkrumah's Ideological Institute at Winneba and Young Pioneer Movement were part of his efforts to counter the complex impact of colonialism, foreseeable neocolonialism, and the counter-productivity of Ghanaians. Since independence, several of the country's postcolonial leaders have emphasized the need for cultural recuperation to assert an imagined Ghanaian identity that is productive.

The next section discusses how African liberation theorists, Ghanaian leaders, and Nkrumah have examined the issue of adaptability. They all argue, however, from the different perspective that the Ghanaian/African predicament needs social and mental reorienting instead of just focusing on technical issues.

Adaptive Leadership and Fixing Ghana's Challenges

It could be deducted from the forgoing that while the challenges of postcolonial Ghana are technical, they are more adaptive in orientation. Citizens, therefore, need to develop adaptive capacities as coping strategies. It is largely the need for adaptive capacity that Nkrumah, as part of the independence declaration, said the following about adaptive capacities:

> And, as I pointed out at our Party conference at Saltpond, I made it quite clear that from now on, today, we must change our attitudes and minds; we must realize that from now on, we are no more a colonial but free and independent people! But also, as I pointed out, that entails hard work. I depend upon the millions of the country, the chiefs and people, to help me reshape the destiny of this countrreshape

this country. We are prepared to build it up and make it a nation that every other nation in the world will respect! We know we are going to have a difficult beginning, but again, I am relying upon your support. I am relying upon your hard work. Seeing you in these thousands, it doesn't matter how far my eye goes, I can see that you are here in your millions, and my last warning to you is that you are to stand firm behind us so that we can prove to the world, that when the African is given a chance, he can show to the world that he is somebody.[53]

Nkrumah was very prescient in observing that a major challenge to bringing about the economic prosperity of the political kingdom was not necessarily technical but the adaptive capacity of the people he would lead. This was important because colonialism as both philosophical and geographical underpinnings, had left enduring imprints on the people of Ghana. Colonialism had produced what the Ghanaian historian, Adu Boahen referred to as 'colonial mentality,' which Akurang-Parry expanded as Ghanaians being:

So taken in by foreign things to the detriment of our culture and development as a nation. As a result, Ghana is now a petri dish in which the nurturing of one of the debilitating viruses of our time occurs: a tide of sustained self-fulfilling marginalisation of Ghanaians and, by extension, Africans as a whole.[54]

As colonialism incapacitated both the physical and creative capacities of the colonized, Nigel Gibson expanded on Fanon's analysis of the African dilemma as more psychological and adaptive from the perspective of the entanglement between decentralization and development as follows:

Decentralisation is not simply an administrative or technical issue; it is a social issue attached to the goal of deepening national consciousness into humanism and connected with the work of involving the masses of people in the day-to-day running of their lives.[55]

Also, reflecting on Fanon, he said:

Given this context, radical intellectuals must eschew political power and concentrate all their philosophical work on convincing the formerly excluded but newly politicised people that the future belongs to them and that they cannot rely on imaginary or iconic leaders, prophets or anyone else.[56]

The post-Nkrumah political elites also observed the need for adaptive answers to Ghana's developmental challenges. By calling for socio-cultural adaptability among Ghanaians to advance human flourishing, Busia observed that:

> Physical enslavement is tragic enough, but the mental and spiritual bondage that makes people despise their own culture is much worse, for it makes them lose their self-respect and faith in themselves.[57]

Given that colonial education was partly responsible for subjecting Africans to mental enslavement, Kofi Asare Opoku aptly argued that "What makes a people truly free is their independence of mind." He considered this a truism because,

> The fact that in almost every aspect of national endeavour our first impulse is to go outside the borders of our country to seek help is evidence of a lack of sufficient faith in ourselves which betrays a mind not yet free, for we do not show that we have laid our hands on the greatness which lies in our cultural heritage.[58]

Concluding Thought

Ghana's fight against underdevelopment remains a complex issue. It largely remains a battle between those out of government (who claim to fix the country) and those in government (who think the citizens are quite impatient). But as pointed out, Ghana's developmental challenges cannot be limited to just the country's internal affairs. It is a complex mixture of colonial legacies of underdevelopment, elite state capture, corruption among the citizenry, and contemporary realities of neo-colonialism. By comparing Ghana with other developed economies, the country continues to register street demonstrations, some citizens' call for violence, divisive partisan politics, and media sensationalism. Undoubtedly, the challenges confronting the country are overwhelming. But given its complexities, this chapter has argued that the elite should invest in adaptive leadership by inviting the various institutions of socialization, including religious bodies, schools and civil societies to reorient leadership and citizens to develop adaptive capacities as part of building Ghana as a social construct.

REFERENCES/NOTES

[1] Michio Kaku, Physics of the impossible: A scientific exploration into the world of phases, forces field, teleportation and the time of travel (New York: Doubledy, 2008).

[2] Berger, The sacred.

[3] W. E. B. Du Bois, *The souls of black folk* (edited and intro by Brent Hayes Edwards) (Oxford: Oxford University Press, 2007).

[4] Matthew D. Kearney, Shawn C. Chiang and Philip M. Massey (9 October 2020), "The twitter origins and evolution of the COVID-19 'plandemic' conspiracy theory," httpsmisinforeview.hks.harvard.edu/article/the-twitterorigins- and-evolution-of-the-covid-19-plandemic-conspiracytheory/ https://www.google.com/search?q=%.

[5] Wilberforce Asare (8 June 2021), '#FixTheCountry demonstration: Supreme court sets high court order aside,' https://www.asaaseradio.com/supreme-cout-okays-fixthecountry-demonstration.

[6] https://fixthecountry.com/petition/new-constitution-for-a-new-generation/(Accessed: 18 January 2022).

[7] Ibid

[8] Ibid.

[9] Ibid.

[10] Ibid.

[11] Univers TV (14 May 2020), "Vetting of Supreme court justice nominee, Prof. Henrietta J.A.N. Mensa Bonsu," https://www.youtbue.com/watch?v=NBuV WnXPlcY.

[12] Agana and Prempeh, "Of farms."

[13] Collins Adu-Bempah Brobbery, Caroline Aboagye Da-Costa, and Ephraim Nana Apeakoran, "The communicative ecology of social media in the Organization of Social Movement for collective action in Ghana: The case of# fixthecountry," *Information Impact: Journal*

of Information and Knowledge Management 12, no. 2 (2021): 73-86.

14 Mark Nartey and Yating Yu., "A discourse analytic study of #FixTheCountry on Ghanaian Twitter," Social Media + Society 9, no. 1 (2023): 1-11.

15 Abdul Hakim Ahmed, "Ghana's rebellious civil society and democratic consolidation: A critical assessment of #fixthecountry movement," *African Journal of Social Sciences Education* 2, no. 1 (2022): 50-72.

16 George M. Bob-Milliar, "Party youth activists and low-intensity electoral violence in Ghana: A qualitative study of party foot soldiers' activism," *African Studies Quarterly,* 15, 1 (2014): 125-152; Justice R. K. Owusu Kyei and Lidewyde H. Berkmoes, "Political vigilante groups in Ghana: Violence or democracy," Africa Spectrum, 55, 3 (2020): 321-338; Isaac Owusu Nsiah, "'Who said we are politically inactive?: Areappraisal of the youth and political activism in Ghana 2004-2012," *Journal of Asian and African Studies,* 54, 1 (2019): 138-135.

17 Abdur Rahman Alfa Shaban (10 July 2019), "Ghana parliament drops$200m chamber idea citing public opposition," https://www.africanews.com/2019/07/10/ghana-parliament-drops-200m-chamber-idea-citing-public-opposition//.

18 Nii Larte Lartey (June 8, 2021), "We're grateful for Supreme Court's ruling; we'll ensure Ghana is fixed – #FixTheCountry conveners"; Accessed: January 14, 2022; https://citinewsroom.com/2021/06/ were-grateful-for-supreme-courts-ruling-well-ensure-ghana-is-fixedfixthecountry-conveners/.

19 Ghanaweb (9 January 2022), "Dormaahene lauds 'Fix The Country Movement," https://www.ghanaweb.com/GhanaHomePage/NewsArchive/Dormaahene-lauds-Fix-The-Country-Movement-1440439.

20 Graphic Online TV (August 16, 2021), "'Fixing The Country Movement to embark on a nationwide campaign," Accessed: December 12, 2021, https://www.youtube.com/watch?v=jDZ0hARqQ8w.

21 Riddimsghana (August 5, 2021), "Ernest Kofi Owusu Bempah Speaks On Fixing The Country Movement"; Accessed: December 10, 2021, https://riddimsghana.com/general-news/ernest-kofi-owusu-bempah-speaks-on-fixing-the-country-movement/.

22 Myjoyonline.com (4 May 2021), 'Annoh-Dompreh apologies for #FixYourself comment," https://www.myjoyonline.com/annoh-dompreh-apologises-for-fixyourself-comment/

[23] Accra Mail (May 9, 2021), "Fix The Country: Afia Schwarzenegger Slams Ghanaians to Fix Their Attitude", Accessed: July 5, 2021, https://accramail.com/fix-the-country-afia-schwarzenegger-slamsghanaians-to-fix-their-attitude/

[24] Paul John, *A History of the American People* (London: HarperCollins Publishers, 1997), 110.

[25] Ebenezer Obadare and Wale Adebanwi (eds.), *Governance and the crisis in contemporary Africa: Leadership in transformation* (Basingstoke, Hampshire: Palgrave Macmillan, 2016); Ike Okonta, The failure of leadership in Africa's development (Lanham: Lexington Books, 2020).

[26] Shawn Russell, "The benevolent dictatorship in Rwanda: Negative government, positive outcome?" *The Applied Anthropologist*, 32, 1 (2012):12-22.

[27] A. B. Assensoh and Yvette M. Alex-Assenson, *African military history and politics: Coups and ideological incursions, 1900–Present* (Basingstoke, Hampshire: Palgrave Macmillan, 2001).

[28] Kwame Gyekye, *Tradition and modernity: Philosophical reflections on the African experience* (Oxford: Oxford University Press, 1997), xi.

[29] Ibid

[30] Ibid.

[31] Michael Onybuchi Eze, "What is African communitarianism? Against consensus as a regulative ideal," *South African Journal of Philosophy*, 27, 4 (2008): 106-119.

[32] Ronald A. Heifetz, *Leadership without easy answers* (Belknap: Harvard University Press, 1994); *Leadership on the line: Staying alive through the dangers of leading* (Harvard: Harvard Business School Press, (2002); and *The practice of adaptive leadership: Tools and tactics for changing your organization* (Cambridge, MA.: Harvard University Press, 2009).

[33] Ibid

[34] Ibid., 16

[35] John Dunn and A. F. Robertson, *Dependence and opportunity: Political change in Ahafo* (Cambridge: Cambridge University Press, 1973).

[36] Francis B. Nyamnjoh, "From bounded to flexible citizenship: Lessons from Africa," Citizenship Studies, 11, 1 (2007): 73-82.

[37] Hugh McLeod, "Secularization", *The Oxford Companion to Christian*

Thought (Oxford: Oxford University Press 2000), 653.

[38] Talal Asad, *Formation of the secular: Christianity, Islam, modernity* (California: Stanford University Press 2003), 23.

[39] Ali A. Mazrui, "On the concept of 'We are all Africans,'" *American Political Science Review*, 57, 1 (1963): 88-97.

[40] Kwame Arhin (ed), *The life and works of Kwame Nkrumah* (Accra: Sedco Publishing Ltd., 1991).

[41] Adrian Hastings, *The construction of nationhood: Ethnicity, religion and nationalism* (Cambridge: Cambridge University Press, 1997).

[42] Peter Burke, *Cultural hybridity* (Cambridge: Polity Press, 2009), 102.

[43] Kwame Botwe-Asamoah, Ewe nationalism; a historical perspective (MA thesis submitted to the Southern Connecticut State College, 1977).

[44] Charles Prempeh, "Dreadlocks in the Church of Pentecost: Rasta or Ras tafarianism," *PentecoStudies* 2.1 (2021): 36-55, pp. 41-42.

[45] Fuller, *Building the Ghanaian nation-state.*

[46] Kwame Nkrumah, *Africa must unite* (New York: Frederick A. Praeger, 1963).

[47] Kwame Kwame Nkrumah, *Ghana: The autobiography of Kwame Nkrumah* (London: Thomas Nelsons and Sons Ltd., 1957), 164.

[48] Ali A. Mazrui, "African Islam and comparative religion: Between revivalism and expansion," *Third World Quarterly*, 10, 2 (1988): 499-518, 503.

[49] Adam Branch and Zachariah Mampilly, *Africa uprising: Popular protest and political change* (London: Zed Books, 2015), p. 19.

[50] Frantz Fanon, *The wretched of the earth* (trans. C. Farrington) (New York: Grove Press, 1963), 40.

[51] Nigel C. Gibson and Roberto Beneduce, *Frantz Fanon, psychiatry and politics* (London/New York: Rowman & Littlefield, 2017), 13.

[52] Speech made at the University of Ghana, Legon February 24, 1963, cited in Kwame Nkrumah, *Axioms of Kwame Nkrumah* (London: Hertford, 1965), 59.

[53] Kwame Nkrumah, "Independence Speech," In Kwasi Konadu and Clifford C. Campbell The Ghana reader: History, culture, and politics, 301-302 (Durham/London: Duke University Press, 2016).

[54] Kwabena Akurang-Parry, "Obama's visit as a signifier of Ghanaian's 'colonial mentality'" in Kwasi Konadu and Clifford C. Campbell, The Ghana reader: History, culture and politics, 440-447 (Durham/

London: Duke University Press, 2016), 441.

[55] Nigel C. Gibson, Fanonian practices in South Africa: From Steve Biko to Abahlali baseMjondolo (Scottsville: University of KwaZulu-Natal Press, 2011), 13.

[56] Ibid.

[57] K. A. Busia, *The challenge of Africa* (New York: Frederick A. Praeger, 1962), 7.

[58] Kofi Asare Opoku, "Independence of the mind," *Journal of Black Studies* 1, 2 (1970): 179-186, 180.

CHAPTER 7

ZongoVation and the Youth in the Zongo Communities

Introduction

It was mentioned in the introductory chapter that the various challenges that some analysts often identify the Ghanaian youth with could also be found among the Muslim communities. In this chapter, we shall look at youth participation in development within an organization called ZongoVation. The spotlight will be on Mahmoud Jajah, the founder, who established this youth non-governmental organization to encourage tech-entrepreneurship among the youth. We shall make the point that activism and politics are not always about street demonstration, but also taking self-help initiatives. This is not to denigrate other youth movements, which were premised on holding street demonstrations and elevate the activities of ZongoVation. All these various movements play complementary roles to each other in advancing the cause of the youth.[1]

The Zongos in Context

Historically, the Muslim communities, also known as Zongos (meaning "strangers' quarters") has often been stigmatized within public discourses as the hub of criminal activities. Already, tagged as Zongos or 'stranger's quarters,' the term has evolved over the decades to denote multi-dimensional marginalization of certain residents. Historically, this negative profiling partly came about due to the colonial strategy of deploying Hausa people from Northern Nigeria into the security services to subdue and subvert nationalist tendencies in the late 19th century Gold Coast. Similarly, as already stated, while the British claimed to have abolished slavery at the turn of the 19th century, by 1874 when the British established the Hausa

Gold Coast Constabulary, they enlisted slaves into it.[2] With the British stationing the soldiers among some Akan areas in the coastal part of the colony, the coastal people cultivated a condescending attitude towards the Hausa.[3] Not only that, the British imposed Hausa as the lingua franca on the lower-rank officers of the Constabulary, and the Hausa language readily became associated with nearly all those who enlisted in the colonial security service.[4] Over time, the British came to look at the Northern Territories as a source of labour supply and began enlisting several Hausas into the Constabulary.

The conflation of Hausa language as the identity of everyone who enlisted in the British security establishment marked the beginning of the Zongo identity. During the late colonial era of the 19th century when the British decided to annex Asante and incorporate it into colonial governance, the British established Zongos in Kumasi, which then has been the heartland of Asante political and spiritual hub. (The Golden Stool, the soul of the Asante people, resides there.) By the 18th century, the Asante had already established contact with Muslim clerics and scribes who provided both spiritual and administrative assistance to the Asante Kingdom. Nevertheless, by 1896, the British established the first constituted Zongo in Kumasi, which was headed by headsmen. Much as the Zongos have been ethnically plural from its establishment, Islam and Hausa language became major characteristics of the Zongos.

Furthermore, the British strategy of divide and rule coupled with the loyalty of the Hausa ensured that the Hausa were often selected as headsmen of the Zongos. As previously mentioned, by the 1830s, a few Muslims had registered their presence in Accra. For various reasons, including the environment and health, the British relocated the colonial capital from Cape Coast to Accra in 1877, by which time, the British had extended the Zongo experiment into the city. Accra's elevation as the business and administrative capital drew more migrants, including those from the Northern Territories, into the city. By the late 19th century, therefore, Zongos started springing up in the city. To foster the smooth governance of the Zongos into migrant communities, the British awarded loyal and enterprising Hausa soldiers with leadership positions. Some were made Zongo leaders.

By the turn of the 20th century and by the end of World War II in 1945, several new Zongos had emerged, which included Accra New Town, Nima and Maamobi.[5] Madina, also a Zongo community, became a major enclave for the Kotokoli etnic group who were asserting their freedom from the Hausa in the 1950s. The various layers of internal fragmentation, indexed by religion and ethnicity, affected the trajectories of Zongo communities. The new Zongo communities, subsisting away from the direct control of the colonial governor, until the 1950s, implied that they were not privy to the 'crumbs' of developmental service that fell from the table of the colonial governor. Until the 1950s, therefore, the new Zongos had to embark on their own development agenda — usually under the leadership and guidance of religious figures and headsmen of the various ethnic groups.

The self-help initiatives of the Zongos did not help much, as the pace of modernity appears to overturn the adaptability of the religious and traditional authority figures. Much as the new Zongos had started asserting their ethnic and religious identities away from Hausa dominance, they also made sured that Western education did intrude upon their freedom. Already, by the 19th century, the Christian missionaries had started prosetalyzing through the building of schools. This discouraged several Muslims from sending their children to school for Western education. In similar vein, the Ahmadiyya Muslims who had begun Western education in the 1920s had not been readily accepted as Muslims by the so-called orthodox Muslims. Be that as it may, many parents in the new Zongos made up their mind to exclude their children from going to school.

At the beginning of the 1950s Ghana's first president, Kwame Nkrumah, made several attempts at reconstructing the Zongos. He even promised to upgrade Nima and Maamobi into inner cities within Accra. This promise boosted the population numbers of other outlier Zongo communities, such as Ashaiman (in the Greater Accra Region) and Kasoa (in the Central Region). However, lack of political will and the eventual overthrow of Nkrumah in 1966 ended the upgrading of the Zongos. General Ignatius Kutu Acheampong's government, in the 1970s, constructed roads that further opened up the new Zongos, especially Maamobi and Nima. In time, the

Zongos exhibited all the indexes of underdevelopment. Frustration and personal choices compelled some of its youthful constituency to sink into 'ghettos' (or enclaves) with a sub-culture of marijuana smoking.

Conditions in the Zongos worsened in the 1980s with the IMF and World Bank imposing neo-liberal economic policies on Ghana. At that time, several young men and women in the Zongos made every effort to foster social services as *conditio sine qua non* in defining Islam. Apart from national politics that stagnated Zongo development, the internal fragmentations created conflicts, crystallizing in the 1990s when two Muslim groups, the Sufi (Tijaniyya) and the Sunni (Ahlu Suna) clashed over which group had the right teaching of Allah's Prophet Mohammed. The politicians exploited the status and vulnerability of youth to further sink the Zongos. We have already mentioned how state sponsorship of Arabic language became complex, if not problematic — given the plurality of the Zongos and the limited use of Arabic in Ghana and the West African sub-region.

Consequently, at the turn of the millennium, the Zongos had not registered much change in their quest for human flourishing. Again, the situation was compounded by some politicians from Ghana's two dominant political parties — the New Patriotic Party (NPP) and the National Democratic (NDC) — who easily instigated the already frustrated youth called 'foot soldiers' and 'vigilantes' to indulge in political violence. With the proliferation of mobile communication, which began with using phone credit cards in the early 2000s, one observed several young men dabbling in credit card fraud. Usually, these young men used credit cards to purchase goods, often clothes from abroad. By 2003, Nima and Maamobi, for example, were flooded with jerseys and other European clothes. The practice of using credit cards to purchase goods online came to be known as '*Sakawa*,' a Hausa word whose etimology '*Ka na sa kawa*' meant "You're putting in." Another version of the origin of the word had it that Sakawa came from the corruption of the Hausa expression, "*Mallam Isa kawa*," meaning "Mallam Isa's ring," — apparently, a Moslem spiritual man gave his young clients a spiritual ring, which facilitated anonymity to the youth who practised *Sakawa* in the Zongo communities.

Subsequently, *Sakawa* spread beyond the Zongos into other areas such as Swedru in the Central Region of Ghana. Academics gave *Sakawa* extensive attention. Broadly speaking, *Sakawa* represents internet fraud.[6]

Sakawa, however, redefined several socio-cultural and political lives in the Zongos. First, the cost of dowry, which included *leife* (contingent prestation) went up. Some afluent *Sakawa* boys presented car as their *leife*. One of them, nicknamed Duster, even purchased mini-buses (known in Ghana as *Trotro*) for some Zongo youth to use as part of economic empowerment. In Maamobi, a few of the *Sakawa* boys revived old and struggling football clubs and formed new ones to boost sporting activities in the community.

By 2010, Ghana attained notoriety and bad image for internet fraud globally. Some Euro-American countries blacklisted the country. The government made efforts to combat *Sakawa*. Working with western stakeholders, Ghana secured sophisticated technology to fight internet fraud. The government established several youth initiatives such as the National Youth and Employment Programmes to re-orient the youth into worthwhile ventures. The country recorded modest success.[7]

For the most part, the country's youth remained frustrated. Meanwhile, more ghettos have sprung up in the Zongos. Research conducted in 2001 revealed a persistent marijuana culture.[8] Religiously inspired violence in the West African sub-region gave rise to rapacious spread of ISIS and Boko Haram in the sub-region, threatening the security of Ghana. It was reported that some of these extreme religious organizations were recruiting youths from these hot spots. The Zongos continued to witness increased violence, including a recent one at Ashaiman, where two criminals murdered a 21 year-old military officer, Imoro Sheriff in March 2023.[9] It is against such a turbulent background that we shall now discuss Mahmoud Jajah and his ZongoVation efforts to rally the youth in the Zongo.

Mahmoud Jajah and His ZongoVation

Tracing his ancestry to Bole in the Savannah Region of Ghana, Mahmoud Jajah was born in Tema, in the Greater Accra Region of

Ghana. In order to harness hydro-electric power for use in smelting aluminum,[10] the colonial governor considered Tema as far back as 1949 for this contingency. An aluminum-smelting industry required a harbour that would connect the colony to the rest of the world. By 1951, the governor conceived Tema as suitable for a harbour.[11] This was because Tema already was a fishing village, only 15 miles east of Accra, the capital. It had physical advantages such as deep water close to the shore; a steep rocky sea bed; and it provided potential for industrial and urban development, since Shai Hills,[12] a quarry site lay only 20 miles to the north. By 1960, the harbour was almost completed; however, it opened for restricted commercial operations in January 1961. By 1962, full-time commercial operation began.[13] In the 1960s, Kwame Nkrumah set up the Tema Development Council to plan and construct Tema as a city.[14] Since then, the area has attracted migrants across Ghana and from other West African countries.

Among those migrants who moved to Maamobi and Tema included Jajah's maternal grandparents. Jajah's grandfather and mother, Alhaji Issaka Jajah and Hajia Fati Issaka Jajah, respectively, were among the earliest settlers in Maamobi in the 1950s. Coming from Bole in the Northern Region, in the 1940s, the family first settled at Adabraka, and thereafter moved to Maamobi at the time the community was evolving. At Maamobi, Jajah's maternal grandparents emerged as key stakeholders, contributing to the construction of the community's central mosque.

When the community needed an Imam, Alhaji Issaka Jajah was proposed, but for personal reasons, he turned it down. Currently, his brother (Mahmoud Jajah's uncle), Sheikh Nuhu Mohammed Karmogdey Jajah is now the Chief Imam of the Ayawaso North Municipality. In addition to intellectually supporting the growth of Islam, Alhaji Issaka Jajah focused his attention on providing social services, out of which he built Darul Hijra Islamic School on 4 January 1977. The name, Darul Hijra means, "the place of refuge" in Islamic history. Alhaji Issaka Jajah built the school to reinforce Islam education since Prophet Mohammed, the founder of Islam, enjoined Muslims to "seek knowledge even if it meant going to China."

Given that the late 1970s marked a major downturn in Ghana's economy, under the military leader, General Ignatius Kutu

Acheampong, Alhaji Issaka Jajah's school was patronized by members of his own family and other families in the Zongo community. The fact that the school had been established by a Muslim helped in deconstructing an earlier perception that some Muslims parents had about the 'corrupting' effect of missionary education.

According to Mahmoud Jajah, his father first worked with a predominantly Christian dry dock company in Tema in the 1980s. His father and mother hardly resided together at Tema. The marriage arrangement was akin to a duolocal system where the man and the woman, after marriage, stayed separated and only met when necessary. This practice was very common among the Ga people of Accra. But in the case of Mahmoud Jajah's parents, whose Islamic social structure required that the woman moved to stay with her husband, his parents sporadically only stayed together. Three children were born, including Mahmoud Jajah, being the last born. He was born on 20 April 1984. Mahmoud Jajah retained his maternal grandfather's surname, 'Jajah,' which also runs at odds with the paternal social structure of both Islam and the Gonja people of Northern Ghana.

When Mahmoud Jajah was about five years old, his father decided that he and his two other siblings (Haruna Jajah and sister, Mamata Jajah) had to relocate to Maamobi to stay with Mahmoud Jajah's maternal grandfather's house. Since the late 1980s, Mahmoud Jajah had lived in Maamobi; had all his basic school education there until later in the 2000s when he travelled overseas to work and also pursue further education.

According to Mahmoud Jajah, his childhood experiences were fraught with challenges. Growing up, he did not have role models or mentors. The Zongo community was also reeling under social challenges such as increasing consumption of marijuana. As already mentioned, his mother, a businesswoman, spent much of her time in Abidjan, the largest commercial city of Côte d'Ivoire. During the 1980s, when the Western imposition of neoliberal economic policies impoverished several urban dwellers, women were among those who were severely impacted.[15] Several households were either headed by women or manned by grandparents in the 1980s.[16] Not only did Mahmoud spend much of his time with his grandparents, his mother, unfortunately, passed away when he was still young. By the time his mother died, Mahmoud Jajah had enrolled at his grandfather's school, Darul Hijra Islamic School and was in Primary 4.

Mahmoud Jajah said that growing up with other kids from deprived backgrounds was very difficult for him. Unlike the other kids who appeared enthusiastic about their future profession, Mahmoud did not know exactly what he wanted to do in future. He summed up his confusion when he said, "So I will say there was nothing directing or influencing my life choices. Everything was on autopilot for me."

After his Primary education, his uncle Alhaji Abubakar Jajah (Babamma), to whom he remains grateful, decided to send him to a private school for his junior secondary education at F'Eden Mission Preparatory School in Kokomlemle. According to him, there 'my real education' started. The school was established by Mr Charles Yaw Yeboa-Korie, one of the trailblazers of Pentecostalism in the 1960s.[17] As an enterprising educationist, Rev. Yeboa-Korie founded several schools, including F'Eden Mission School in the 1970s.[18]

An evangelistic-driven Christian leader, Yeboa-Korie founded the school, and ensured that the school's curriculum reflected the secular, non-religious aspirations of Ghana. He extended to all students religious liberties. Mahmoud Jajah narrated his experiences at F'Eden thus:

> I didn't know much about Christianity until I went to F'Eden. At Darul Hijra Islamic, we were all Muslims, and mostly speak Hausa even in class. I started learning to speak English at F'Eden." I was one of the top students, especially in General Science. And because of my performance, I was advised to read General Science at the Senior High School.

After his junior secondary school education in 2000, Mahmoud did a brief stint at the La Presbyterian Secondary School, but later applied for transfer to join the West Africa Secondary School (WASS) where he read General Science. At WASS, he was elected Vice President of the Ghana Muslim Students Association (GMSA), a para-religious organization for Muslim students that was established on 29 October 1972 to promote solidarity among Muslims as well as deepen their faith in Islam on school campuses. He played a major role in the activities of GMSA until he completed his secondary school education in 2002. On hindsight, he admitted he should not have pursued Science:

> Because I turned out to be an average student, I couldn't even pass my SSCE examination. So after secondary school, I decided to study on my own for two years before passing as a private candidate in Business Management. I took Business Management because I realized that my strength lies there and I could study this subject on my own.

Having eventually passed the Business Management exam, Mahmoud Jajah applied to the Central University in 2006 and graduated in 2010 with a BSc in Management Studies. Pastor Mensa Otabil, a charismatic preacher, founded the International Central Gospel Church (ICGC) and the Central University, initially to train pastors in 1988.[19] In 1991, it was incorporated under a new name, Central Bible College. By 1993, the name became Central Christian College. Then in 1998, the institution was converted to a private university. In 2016, the university received a presidential charter, and became an autonomous, fully-fledged university under the name, Central University.[20] At the university, Mahmoud Jajah became more exposed to religious plurality, which fostered respect and religious tolerance.

After his university education, Mahmoud Jajah undertook a one-year mandatory national service at the Central Administration of the University for Development Studies in Tamale — a university that Ghana's former president, Jerry John Rawlings established as the first public university in Northern Ghana in 1992.[21] During his national service, his uncle Yussif Jajah, who was doing his masters at the University of Dundee in Scotland, United Kingdom advised him to do a masters course in oil and gas management. He applied and gained admission. He won a scholarship from the Ghana Education Trust Fund (GETFund), which was established in 2000 to assist students nationwide with funding opportunities.[22] Unfortunately, Mahmoud Jajah could not complete his Masters studies:

> I noticed that I struggle with academic studies, although I am a voracious reader. I don't like being in the classroom and I don't

like academic work. Along the way I lost interest in the study of oil and gas management. Unfortunately, I couldn't complete my programme, although the university gave me ample opportunities to try to finish the programme, I just lost the interest. So I dropped out!

Eventually, he decided to study Law. He enrolled at a private Law School — the Mountcrest University College in Accra, which was established by Mr Kwaku Ansa-Asare and Mrs Helena Ansa-Asare in 2008 "to train and prepare a new generation of graduates in body, mind and spirit, for the transformation of society,"[23] in 2013, but dropped out after a year. Meanwhile, Mahmoud Jajah realized that his passion for community development was rather growing — having cultivated the passion and worked as a social worker after his secondary school education. He chanced upon, David Schwartz's book, *The Magic of Thinking Big*, which as he said, "changed my worldview completely." The book made him to realize his potential and what he could do with his life to touch the lives of others. As a voracious reader and student of the Quran, Mahmoud Jajah picked most of his inspirations from the Quran, and also from business books such Schwartz's. He admired entrepreneurs who set up businesses to create jobs for the youth.

Somewhere in March 2003, he mobilized some friends to start AVERT Youth Foundation, a community-based youth group aimed at creating awareness about the importance of education among the youth of Maamobi and Nima. At its peak, the organization had more than 300 members. It was at AVERT Youth Foundation that he learnt more about leadership and community service. He had the opportunity to organize community many activities. It was through AVERT that he applied and got selected by the British Council in Accra as one of only two Ghanaians (the other being a lady) to represent Ghana at the Pan African Youth Conference in Cape Town, South Africa in August 2005. These events gave him exposure and experience on global youth activities. Mahmoud Jajah also realized that he was a 'builder' in the sense that he liked to build organizations. In other words, he considered him as an entrepreneur. He co-founded Mahlid Communications Limited with his friend,

Alhassan Khalid to publish a national student newspaper called, *The Student Observer*. He was the Chief Executive Officer, Publisher and Editor of the newspaper. He said:

> It was really a tough and ambitious project. We didn't have the money, but we were full of ambition and determination. We launched the newspaper at the British Council Hall in Accra. We had reporters from tertiary institutions across the country. Unfortunately, we couldn't sustain the newspaper because students were not paying for it and we were not getting the sponsorship to sustain it. But the experience and the exposure it gave us cannot be quantified. I used my experiences in running *The Student Observer* to win an international essay competition organized by the US-based Think Tank, the Center for International Private Enterprise (CIPE).[24]

Mahmoud Jajah also started *Fortune Investment Club* with some friends to educate themselves on business and investment issues as young people. After he returned from his studies in the UK in 2012, he helped to found *Zongo for Mahama*, a political group that mobilized voters for the 2012 Presidential aspirant of National Democratic Congress (NDC), John Mahama, who eventually won and served for a term. Mahmoud Jajah was also the founding General Secretary of the group. He did a stint with the NDC and became the personal assistant to His Excellency Alhaji Said Sinare, who was then Ghana's ambassador to Egypt. In 2014, Ambassador Sinare became Ghana's ambassador to the Kindgom of Saudi Arabia, so Jajah joined him in Riyadh as his Personal Assistant. In Riyadh, Mahmoud Jajah was also in charge of undocumented Ghanaians in the Gulf Cooperation Council (GCC) countries. He returned home from Riyadh in August 2017 when his political party, the NDC, lost power to the New Patriotic Party (NPP).

Before that, Mahmoud Jajah registered the Initiative for Youth Development (IYD) to help empower young people in marginalized communities, especially in the Zongos. So when he returned home from Riyadh, he started organizing empowerment programmes for the youth. In 2018, he organized the Young Zongo Women Empowerment Programme at the Accra International Conference

Centre. He also organized the Young Zongo Women Leadership Programme, with his friends.

Mahmoud Jajah also started a solar energy startup called Amanah Energy Limited aimed at providing decentralized renewable energy to schools and small businesses in Ghana. Although the business collapsed, he won in 2015 a $5000 grant from the Tony Elumelu Entrepreneurship Programme. Since 2016, he has embarked on a few trips to the Arab world. During one such trip to Dubai in 2017, he got to know about the One Million Arab Coders Initiative, so he started reading more about technology and how it could impact society.

Upon his return to Ghana, he concluded that tech innovation and entrepreneurship would be the best way to lift the people of the Zongo out of poverty. So he started the ZongoVation Hub. He started this in May 2018 and hoped to become one of the leading tech hubs in Africa. His vision for ZongoVation Hub "is to make the Zongo communities in Ghana the leading tech hub in Africa by 2030, *Insha Allah*."

Zongovation Hub is a non-profit organization established and incorporated on 2 May 2018 as a community technology innovation hub dedicated to the development and growth of young entrepreneurs and start-ups in the Zongo communities across Ghana. The hub supports young people with ideas to become entrepreneurs by providing them with all the necessary tools, resources and networks they require in order to succeed. ZongoVation Hub does not directly take equity, invest or impose time limit on membership start-ups. The Hub, however, provides seed grants and connect members with venture capital funds and investors. The Hub works exclusively with young entrepreneurs, especially tech-inclined ones, by understanding the process they go through and their needs at each stage of their entrepreneurial journey. The Zongo communities benefit from the flexibility and freedom to build their own businesses and develop products. The Hub organizes training workshops and offers consulting services, and is committed to building a viable tech-ecosystem, including conversations around democracy and governance, human rights, corruption, gender, and economic rights in the Zongo communities.

The ZongoVation Hub runs the Zongo Kids Coding Boot camp. This is an initiative targeted at the youth between the ages of 10 and 15 years (usually Junior High School leavers) to equip them with digital skills. They take the kids through topics such as basic Microsoft office (Word, Excel and PowerPoint), basic UI/UX design and introduction to HTML and CSS. The training lasts seven weeks. A total of twenty-three students have so far graduated. The Hub also runs a boot camp for young adults too. Topics covered span the construction of e-commerce website, software development, event management system, cyber security, etc. Their Zongo Shark Tank Business Reality Show is interesting. This is a reality TV show that identifies, encourages, and supports young people with business ideas that can help create jobs. The maiden edition of this reality show, launched in 2022, saw about 22 businesses present their ideas to a panel of judges. At the end of the seventh episode, ten finalists competed for the grand prize. The first three winners were given Gh¢10,000 each as seed capital to run their businesses. On graduation day the trainees display their projects to attract funding. Mahmoud Jajah summed up his experience thus:

> I believe strongly that with the power of digital technology, we can transform the Zongos in our lifetime. I want the kind of Zongo where every young person has the opportunity to live their dreams, and become whoever they want to become in this world.[25]

He recounted a major challenge with running his organization:

> Our peculiar challenge for me is that our youth do not have opportunities available to other youth in non-Zongo communities such as scholarship programs and job opportunities.[26]

On challenges hindering Ghana's development, he observed:

> Our lack of visionary and selfless leaders is affecting our progress. Internationally, we used to be non-alligned. But now the country shifts more towards the West than the East. And this is affecting our historical image as a non-alligned nation.

Finally, Mahmoud Jajah is also a humanitarian. In April 2019, he joined the International Committee of the Red Cross as a humanitarian worker, providing humanitarian assistance to victims of armed violence in the north-eastern part of Nigeria.

NOTES/REFERENCES

1   The author has been a resident of Maamobi for nearly 4 decades, having lived in the community since 1984 when he was 2 years.

2   Balakrishnan, "Of debt and bondage."

3   Ibid.

4   Akosua Anyidoho and Esther E.K. Dakubu, "Ghana: Indigenous languages, English and an emerging national identity," in Anderson Simpson (ed), *Language and national identity in Africa*, 141-157 (Oxford: Oxford University Press, 2008).

5   Prempeh, *Nima-Maamobi*.

6   Joseph Oduro-Frimpong, "Sakawa rituals and cyberfraud in Ghanaian popular video movies," *African Studies Review*, 57, 2 (2014): 131-147; Alice Armstrong, 'Sakawa' rumours: Occult internet fraud and Ghanaian identity, *Working Paper*, No. 08/2011.

7   Emmanuel Tetteh Jumpah, Johnny Owusu-Arthur and Richard Ampadu-Ameyaw, "More youth employment programmes, less youth in work: A relook of youth employment initiatives," *Cogent Social Sciences*, 8 (2022): 1-15.

8   Charles Prempeh, Islamic and drugs: A study of the use of marijuana among Muslim youth in Maamobi community, Accra (MPhil unpublished thesis submitted to the Institute of African Studies, University of Ghana, 2011).

9   Myjoyonline (13 March 2023) "Ashaiman: Police give a blow-by-blow account of how soldier was killed; 6 suspected nabbed," https://www.myjoyonline.com/ashaiman-police-give-blow-by-blow-account-of-how-soldier-was-killed/.

10 David Hilling, "Tema – The geography of a new port," *Geography*, 51, 2 (1966): 111-125.

11 Ibid.

12 Ibid., 115.

13 Ibid., 116.

14 Iain Jackson, "Development visions in Ghana: From design schools and building research to Tema new town," *Architectural History*, 65 (2022): 293-326.

15 Akua Kuenyehia, "The impact of structural adjustment programs on women's international human rights: The example of Ghana," in Rebecca J. Cook (ed), *Human rights of women: National and*

international perspectives, 422-436 (Philadelphia: University of Pennsylvania Press, 1994).

[16] S. D. Barwa, *Structural adjustment programmes and the urban informal sector in Ghana* (Geneva: Development and Technical Cooperation Department, International Labour Office, Geneva, 1995).

[17] Charles Yaw Yeboa-Korie, https://dacb.org/stories/ghana/yeboa-korie-cy/.

[18] Ibid.

[19] https://www.central.edu.gh/74.

[20] Ibid.

[21] https://www.uds.edu.gh/about/history/.

[22] https://gra.gov.gh/wp-content/uploads/2020/09/ge_trust_fund_act.pdf.

[23] https://mountcrestuniversity.edu.gh/.

[24] The link to his essay could be found here: https://www.cipe.org/blog/2009/09/15/the-2009-cipe-international-youth-essay-winners-part-two-of-three/.

[25] Africanews (2019), "Mahmoud Jajah sets to transform Ghana's deprived inner cities using digital technology," https://espact.com/mahmoud-jajah-sets-to-transform-ghanas-deprived-inner-cities-using-digital-technology/.

[26] Ibid.

CHAPTER 8

The Man Behind the Mask: The New Force

The tapestry of Ghana's history is made up of many things, including the country's production of its own philosopher kings and talented tenth — at least, from the perspective of Plato and W. E. B. Du Bois, respectively.[1] Ghana has blazed the trail in many areas of life on the African continent. The most commonly known is that it was the first to gain political independence in Sub-Saharan Africa, thus paving the way for other African countries to follow suit. Ghana (formerly known as the Gold Coast) has produced several enigmatic figures, whose achievement rather baffled the world. For example, during the colonial era, the Gold Coast produced Anton Wilhelm Amo, one of the foremost and greatest thinkers of German Enlightenment and first black African to successfully and publicly defend a doctorate in philosophy and letters from a German university. His thesis was on the impassivity of the human mind (*De Humanae Mentis Apatheia*). He also taught philosophy at Wittenberg and later at the University of Halle and supervised his own doctoral students.[2] K. A. Busia became the first Gold Coaster to have earned a doctoral degree in Sociology from the University of Oxford in 1947. He is considered one of the brilliant minds Africa has ever produced, and the letters in his name, 'Busia' (on the lighter side!) stood for "Best University Scholar In Africa."

Ghana also produced Kwame Nkrumah, a colossus in the annals of Pan-Africanism, who in December 1999 was adjudged by BBC's programme, "Focus on Africa" as the 'Man of the Millennium.'[3] Other charismatic personalities surfaced in Ghana. One was Flt Lt Jerry John Rawlings, who in 1979, caused an upheaval in the governance of Ghana and ushered the country from military rule into the present constitutional dispensation. In recent times, an enigmatic young man began to emerge during the build up to the general elections billed for December 2024. He erected billboards across Ghana, displaying a masked man calling for a change from the hitherto duopoly relay race between two political parties, namely the National Patriotic

Party (NPP) and the National Democratic Party (NDC), which dominated the political landscape since 1992. The man in the mask later revealed himself as Nana Kwame Bediako, a relatively young self-made businessman who held himself out as speaking for the youth.

The Man, Nana Kwame Bediako

Born to Akan parents from both Asante and Bono regions in the southern part of Ghana, Nana Kwame Bediako Cheddar (variously nicknamed as 'Cheddar,' and 'Freedom Jacob Caesar'), has come from humble beginnings. He started running his own business at the age of eight years, rearing his two fouls to produce eggs, which he sold for profit at that tender age. He attended Apam Secondary School in Ghana, and attempted, but could not complete his undergraduate education in Business Studies at Waltham Forest College, in the United Kingdom. While in college, he dabbled in the less-fancied scrap metal business. This made the whole difference in his fortunes. His success in business thereafter has been meteoric.

The transition between business and politics needs some explaining. From what anyone can glean online, his views are very eclectic, and less consistent — possibly indexing the complexity of life's knowledge as existentially incomplete. In other words, his religious and political views are hardly systematized in all of his interviews given online.

His Ideas on Religion

His religious and political views are hardly part of what one may consider conventional — which is what he desires to be known for. For example, religiously, he is ambiguous about whether he is a Christian with a personal faith in Jesus Christ. He considers himself to have been born to a mother who is deeply 'spiritual' and vegetarian. Obviously, her mother was from an austere religious disposition, but we are not told which strand of religion she belongs to.

Considering himself as a spiritual person (rather than a Christian, because he is never explicit in his talks), 'Cheddar' shares a general belief in the existential reality of God who gives gifts to His creation. He also sometimes refers to this God as 'the universe who gives' and whose providence must be treated with tenderness and care.

'Cheddar' claims he pays his tithe and lives a righteous life. While we are aware of the centrality of tithing in some strands of Christianity, including the Adventists who have made it an article of faith, we are not sure about what he meant by living a righteous life, except to say that, he loves to treat everyone and all of God's creation with justice and love. He has visited and spoken at Christian gatherings, inspiring young men and women to aspire for greatness in life.

But his emphasis in these youthful forums is rather at odds with the Christian notion of salvation by grace, through faith and resting in Christ alone. He nevertheless considers himself ordained; therefore he uses words like 'anointed by God' to bring his idea of 3Rs, namely revolution, reformation and redemption in the 'realms of the universe.' Whatever he meant by 'realms in the universe,' this has not been very clearly articulated — partly signifying his lack of systematization in thought.

His Politics

Politically, 'Cheddar' considers himself a 'leader,' not a politician. (This leaves one wondering whether a politician is not some kind of leader too.) He labels himself a Pan-Africanist, who does not align with any political party or shares a restricted vision of a localized citizen. From the interviews he granted, it appears 'Cheddar' has grander designs beyond his country, Ghana. Like Kwame Nkrumah, who preceded him, 'Cheddar' nurtures Pan-Africanist dreams, anchored on a Messianic ethos of having been 'chosen,' or 'ordained.' 'Cheddar' believes he could move Africa away from wobbling along on the clutches of underdevelopment and despondency. He hopes to harmonize the resources of the continent and those of the rest of the world to achieve that purpose. He is far less enamoured about aid, which he considers rather enslaving the continent to a perpetual economic and political servitude to foreign powers. 'Cheddar' ultimately hopes to convert African resources into wealth for all Africans, but the launch pad of his ambition would start from his becoming head of state of Ghana first.

Like the Hebrew, Moses in the Old Testament, 'Cheddar' cherishes the hope of leading Africa to 'the promised land.' But the challenge, to which he has hardly given enough attention, is how all his grandiose ambitions would be achieved. For example, whereas Nkrumah led the new postcolonial nation, Ghana, into heavy industrialization, the question is how 'Cheddar' would navigate through the labyrinth of a politically savvy but disparate citizenry, holding various degrees of loyalty, comprising clinging family members, fawning friends and political chicanery. How would he hammer this motley array of metals into an amalgam, malleable enough to buy into his vision of national unity, which will transform Africa into a united states within a continent we call Africa? Dr Kwame Nkrumah, 'Cheddar's' predecessor, has trodden this path early on. He started with knocking down the border posts between his country, Ghana and Upper Volta (now known as Burkina Faso). Then he moved on to form a union of sorts with Guinea and Mali in what was known as Ghana-Guinea-Mali Union. What became of this sentimental union of states? History is full of lessons. Has 'Cheddar' really understood these lessons from history? The answer is blowing in the wind.

Cheddar's Incursion into Politics

In 2023, several cities in Ghana, particularly Accra, was besieged with billboards that carried an intriguing figure wearing a mask, flanked on both sides by other masked figures. This set tongues wagging with speculation. Wild guesses were made as to the identity of the person wearing the mask in the foreground. Some questioned the gimmick behind the billboards. Traditionally, in African societies, the mask plays significant roles. We recall the *egungun* in Ibo culture, captured vividly in Chinua Achebe's widely read novel, *Things Fall Apart*. To disguise and obscure one's social identity or status, it was customary to wear a mask. The deities manifest themselves to humans by wearing masks. Therefore, if humans assume the role of ancestral spirits or deities (which belong to a different realm), they can only do this though disguising their earthiness through the medium of masks. The mask is the bridge that enables the transition from the mundane realm of human limitations to the boundless dimension of the other-worldliness.

Socio-linguistically, therefore, masks, as artefacts of material culture, communicate power, aesthetic qualities of a people, and fosters the structuring of an ordered society. It was among these reasons that the afore-mentioned masked figures, visibly shown on public billboards, excited much curiosity among Ghanaians. True, several people might not have ascribed any ill intention to the masks, because the billboards had been authorized by appropriate state agencies. The masks kept everyone in suspense. For as long as they remained Ghanaians were mystified. It was not until the beginning of January 2024 that the figure behind the mask was revealed — under dramatic circumstances!

The date was 7 January 2024 and the occasion was a convention in Accra to which some key (if controversial) public and political personalities across Africa were invited to speak. Among those invited to speak were Julius Malema, the leader of South Africa's leftist political movement, the Economic Fighters Party (whose participation was virtual); Ambassador Arikana Chihombori-Quao, former African Union representative to the United States of America; and Peter Obi, who made several political waves in Nigeria's presidential elections, having placed third as an independent candidate. There was also Prof P. L. O. Lumumba, a well-known Pan-African activist and intellectual from Kenya. Apparently, this potpourri of speakers did not sit well with the political authorities in Ghana. For example, Peter Obi's political ideology appears to deconstruct gerontocracy (Many African leaders were octogenarians, including Ghana's president at the time); Prof P. L. O. Lumumba in 2023 stirred controversy when he reprimanded the democratic government of the USA for imposing vacuous and needless same-sex agenda on Africa; Julius Malema's rhetoric of economic and political redemption for Africans had favourably predisposed him to several of Ghana's leftist-ideological constituency, his open declaration support for minority sexual rights ditched his fame before Ghana's religious constituency. As for Ambassador Chihombori-Quao, her charge against the Western world for fostering neo-colonial tendencies has entangled her and her audience into a complex web of transnational politics. The tension in Accra was high. So were the stakes. Against all this background was the looming shadow that the year 2024 was for Ghana's elections.

The government was jittery. And it moved in quickly to stop the event from taking place, citing national 'security risk' as the reason.

The speakers had been invited under the auspices of Cheddar's new Movement for change, also known as the New Force. The Movement appointed a Belgian working as a media person in Ghana, Shalimar Abbiusi, as its spokesperson.[4] The Ghana government was suspicious about a non-Ghanaian citizen allied to a potential presidential candidate in the person of 'Cheddar.' This was all it took to set the coercive instrument of the state in motion against 'Cheddar's Movement.

Already citizenship is a major politicized subject in Ghana. Two Ghanaian nationals had early on been convicted having dual citizenship, dividing the loyalty between Ghana and European countries where they were domiciled, at the time they were elected into Parliament. One of them of Mr Adamu Dramani Sakande who had won as the Member of Parliament for Bawku Central on the ticket of the NPP in 2008, was convicted of having dual citizenship at the time he filed his nomination. He was subsequently jailed for two years — technically on charges of perjury and deceit in 2012.[5]

There was also the case of James Gyakye Quayson, an elected Member of Parliament for the Assin North Constituency, whose case had hit a *cul de sac* in court.[6] Anchored on what we have already discussed as the socially constituted nature of citizenship, the politicians had a ready reason to nip the new Movement in the bud. Arresting and holding Shalimar Abbiusi to a legal battle against the state, the cracks on the Movement had a nationwide and transnational coverage. But the melée of trouble also helped the Movement come to a limelight among Ghanaians. Drawing sympathy from an already fractured political environment, the hitherto mysterious — the man behind the mask finally took his mask off on the occasion of the international speaking engagement of 7 February 2024 in Accra. By unmasking himself as Nana Kwame Bediako (alias 'Cheddar,') the battle lines for the presidency at the 2024 polls in Ghana has been firmly drawn.

What Is in a Name?

In the several interviews that Nana Kwame Bediako granted journalists, he indicated that his names are divinely pre-ordained to make him the appointed leader of Ghana. First, 'Cheddar' makes himself appear older than his name, which is critical in competing in a country's election where gerontocracy is key. Among the Akan, 'Nana' is the default title of all chiefs, precisely because it marks out the bearer as a direct representative of the ancestors. Meanwhile, to be an ancestor, one must live a life worthy of emulation, devoid of avoidable moral and ethical infractions. So, to represent an ancestor in secular and mundane affairs is to be clothed in ancestral wisdom and experience — all of which earns one the authority to govern. That is the main reason why chiefs serve as mediators between the ancestors and the living on earth — based on a non-binary world that is fluid in enabling interpenetration of movements between the spirits and the ritual experts.

The second name, 'Kwame' is also very important. Again, among the Akan, the name *Kwame* has a theophoric signification. It is one of the names the Akan ascribe to God as *Twereduampon* Kwame. Some Christians, particularly the Seventh-Day Adventists misconceive this title or name of God. It is misinterpreted to mean that the Akan worship God on Saturdays. In the past, the Akan did not worship God directly, nor set aside any particular day for congregational worship in the manner that Adventists do. As a day/natal name, which is the default name of any Akan male child born on a Saturday, Kwame's appellation is "*ɔte nanka ɛduro,*" which translates roughly as "he who has an antidote against a poisonous snake bite is simply a healer." As healer, God is the ultimate antidote against death.[7]

Ghana's first president also bore the name, 'Kwame.' Coincidentally, 'Cheddar' who is a namesake, considers himself as continuing from where Kwame Nkrumah left off. He regards Ghana's first president as the source of his inspiration. It is significant that 'Cheddar,' in an attempt to consolidate and push forward his presidential agenda chose the Old Polo grounds where Kwame Nkrumah announced Ghana's independence to the world, to launch his unmasking event!

Finally, the 'Bediako,' his surname is also of significance. One of Ghana's foremost researchers on Akan names, Kweku Darko Ankrah, who has been studying Akan names (onomastics) for decades, shares the following insight on the name, 'Bediako':

> [The name means] he who has come to fight; The Born-Fighter. (*Bediako*, lit: 'he came to fight' is an anglicisation of the Akan honourific name, *Bɛdiako*. Bediako is the by-name of the Akan name, *Asare*. This explains why most Asares use the compound name, Asare-Bediako. Bediako is also given to child who was born during war or on the battlefield. Ghanaian Christians use the name Bediako 'the warrior who has come to fight for us', as one of the powerful appellations to venerate *Ewurade Nyankopɔn*, 'The Lord God'. Bediako is a strong invincible warrior and a hero who nothing can stop. He has solid stamina, rough-skin and strength. On sight, Bediako looks calm, but he is not calm person; in fact, he is a dormant lethal time-bomb waiting to explode. You dare Bediako at your own peril.

Kweku Darko Ankrah further explains the appellation for the 'Bediako' name as follows:

> *Bediako Brempɔn; Efiri tete; onipa pɛ ko a, kɔ ne nko. Ayebiagyae, Osereboɔ Sakyi a ɔwɛ dade amono; kusukusu a ɔma okunafo didi anopa tutu. Me ne wo ka ɔse me nne wo ka ntira. Yaw Ahwinti Bediako. Wo na wohwinti ma mmofra ti bo boo soɔ.*

> (Bediako the Noble man, from the ancient days; anyone who wishes a fight, fight him. The accomplisher; Sakyi the whetstone who eats fresh iron; The fog that forced a widow to eat at dawn. I am cool with you; he says it is just because I am cool with you. Yaw Bediako the Stumbler. It's you who stumbles for heads of children to go crashing against the stone).[8]

We could discern clearly that 'Cheddar,' the man behind the

mask, has carefully plotted out his entry into Ghana's politics! Bearing nicknames such as 'Freedom Jacob Caesar' mark him out as a careful and calculating man. Annexing 'Jacob' into his identity imbues him with some kind of religious aura, potentially Christian; and 'Caesar,' invests an empire building trait, reminiscent of Caesar of the Roman Empire. Since money is important in politics, the relatively young Bediako also calls himself 'Cheddar,' a slang name for money. As a mogul in real estate business, his name 'Cheddar' is significant.

The New Force Movement: Search for the Message, Not the Messenger

We have argued that there are major financial and socially constructed matters that obstruct the efforts young people investing in politics. Unfortunately, in the minds of several Ghanaians, politics has increasingly been identified with corruption. Some even say, "politics is a dirty game." To distance himself from this tag, 'Cheddar' constantly asserts he is not a politician; that he does not know how to do politics. This admission reveals his naivety and overly simplistic understanding of politics as coterminous with corruption. He insists he is a 'leader' and not a politician.

However, 'Cheddar' cannot easily wriggle away from any disclaimer's note that he is not a politician. By his own admission, he brought four distinguished African speakers, who as we have established, represent pluralities of ideas on the African continent to (as it turned out) prop up his presidential ambition. He also succeeded in launching his Movement under the atmosphere of glitz and entertainment — having invited some of Ghana's top musicians such as Efya (Afia Boafowaa Awindor), Stonebwoy (Livingstone Etse Satekla), and Wiyaala (Noella Wiyaala Nwadei) to perform at the event. It was his idea to bring together these relatively high profile entertainers to his launch event dubbed 'The Convention,' scheduled for 7 January 2024. As to be expected, the Convention attracted not only the Ghanaian youth, but also young people from neighbouring countries, including Côte d'Ivoire, Togo and Nigeria.

It was not for nothing that he chose as his Personal Assistant a Belgian, ostensibly to demonstrate how the Movement cuts across 'racial' lines and shows international credentials. His astuteness is shown in creating a mystique around a masked personality on the billboards, setting tongues wagging for days. Then the mask was dramatically 'removed' in full public glare, in the presence of a constellation of august motivational dignitaries from across the continent of Africa. With the cover blown, a young man of 44 years appeared, boldly announcing himself as the mystery man behind the mask. The stupefied audience began to wonder what message lay behind the masked messenger. This echoes an Akan wise saying, which stipulates that *"Ɔnipa ɛne ni din sɛ,"* to wit, "One is no different from the name one bears."

The political authorities acted swiftly, perhaps on the intelligence they gathered. The government hurriedly wrote a letter to stop the event for reasons of state security. The grammatical and factual inaccuracies in the letter only revealed the haste and desperation. This was in spite of the fact that the Convention had duly booked and paid for the venue well in advance. Besides, early on 'Cheddar's Convention or New Movement had applied to Ghana's Electoral Commission to have their Movement registered as new political party, but the Commission had yet to respond. Further, the New Movement had also established offices in all sixteen regions in Ghana, in fulfillment of a constitutional requirement. They presented themselves as apolitical Movement, involved in charity work. They granted interviews to gain nationwide attention. The internet became saturated with several of these interviews in which 'Cheddar' presented himself as the one to lead Ghana's industrial renaissance. However, 'Cheddar' had his fair share of detractors. Some held that he was a 'pondzi schemer' seeking to deceive Ghanaians; others considered him a disillusioned demagogue. Only time would tell.

Conclusion

Undoubtedly, the New Force Movement is a major addition to what may be arguably considered a populist movement in Ghana. As we have discussed, 'Cheddar' utilized social media and social services, to secure an anchor in the Ghanaian psyche. As an accomplished businessman his ambition is to secure his place among Ghana's millennials. However, he swims against the tide of sceptics and virulent critics, who attack his personality rather than analyze his policies. Be that as it may, 'Cheddar' is consumed with the determination (like other Ghanaian leaders preceding him) to redefine the destiny of Ghana. His frailty appears to be his inability to clearly articulate in a convincing way the new things he brings on board and how he hopes to accomplish them. His brilliant rhetoric tends to be rather diversionary, as he keeps digressing to talk about things that are hardly related. He comes across as a passionate dreamer, who is yet to 'walk the talk,' so to speak. For example, when asked about how he would build Ghana to be at par with the so-called developed countries, he took refuge in his castle of rhetorical confabulations.

No doubt, 'Cheddar' certainly has impacted the youth and has put pressure on Ghanaian politicians to re-negotiate with the electorate in making Ghana's politics more policy and implementation focused. Indeed, 'Cheddar' needs to ground his passion by incorporating the services of political strategists, communicators, and key stakeholders in Ghana's politics. If he could persuade traditional chiefs, religious leaders, business moguls and respected personalities in society as well as in the entertainment industry to buy into his programme, he might emerge in Ghanaian politics to be a force to reckon with in future.

NOTES/REFERENCES

[1] Plato, The republic (eds. G. R. F. Ferrari, Trans. Tom Griffith)
  (Cambridge: Cambridge University Press, 2000); W. E. B. Du Bois,
"The talented tenth," In W. E. B. Du Bois, *The essential works of Du Bois.*

[2] Dot Price (2021), "Rethinking the Enlightenment: Anton Wilhelm
  Amo (c. 1703 to c. 1753)," https://www.bristol.ac.uk/history/
  public-engagement/blackhistory/snapshots/
  nzimaantoniuswilhelmamoafer/.

[3] Woeli Dekutsey, *Kwame Nkrumah, the Great African* (Accra: Woeli
Publishing Services, 2021)

[4] Adomonline (11 January 2024), "How Shalimar Abbiusi became New
  Force Spokesperson. Cheddar," https://www.adomonline.com/
  how-shalimar-abbuisi-became-new-force-spokesperson-cheddar/

5 Ghanaweb (27 July 2012), "Bawku Central MP Adamu Sakande convicted; jailed two years," https://www.ghanaweb.com/ GhanaHomePage/NewsArchive/Bawku-Central-MP-Adamu-Sakande-convicted-jailed-two-years-246093.

6 Modernghana (8 February 2024), "No error in High Court orders on James Gyakye Quayson's trial — Judge," https://www.modern ghana.com/news/1291188/no-error-in-high-court-orders-on-james-gyakye-quay.html.

7 The Asante methodology admits that not even the famous Komfo Anokye, the talismanic figure behind the formation of the Asante Empire, survived in his search for an antidote to death. He could not be the Twereduampon Kwame — the dependable healer over the fortress of death. We must also mention that whereas death among the Akan is not an extinction, but a transition, death is not desirable as it painfully disrupts all forms of social ties, simply stated in dirge as, "ɔwuo sɛi fie" — to wit, "Death breaks the home." All of this is better expressed in Kofi Awoonor's "Songs of sorrow."

8 Kweku Darko Ankrah, *Sweet names of Africa* (unpublished manuscript), p. 300.

9 Ibid., p. 300.

Chapter 9

Conclusion

The place of young people in the politics of Ghana and Africa has received extensive research attention. In both academic and popular discourses, emphases have been placed on the extent to which young men and women deploy media and other forms of digital technologies to upset the structures of gerontocratic and highly commodified politics. Technological capabilities in contemporary politics have similarly taken the conversation away from young people's deployment of militaristic approach to addressing their grievances via the channels of transactional politics, which allow young people to mobilize online; apply the exuberance of youthful hopefulness to embark on offline street protests and demonstrations against the political elites. The combination of both online and offline political activism often compels the political establishment to find a way of dialoguing with young people, instead of just applying the legitimate use of coercion available to the modern state. Mostly such approaches are just dialogues for transactional politics.

In an attempt to broaden the frontiers of participatory politics as part of international relations, young people readily align with their contemporaries across the world to push for local reforms. At the same time, the increasing ideological globalism, fashioned around revitalized Marx's metanarrative of the oppressed and oppressor binary draws public sympathies towards young people's disenchantment. Meanwhile, framing the challenges of young people and the nation-state in a dualistic rigidity hardly goes far in revising the structures of governors. It does not also touch on some of the critical issues such as the constitutionality of the state as socially constructed and the nature of the human person, as deeply self-centred. It is here that scholarship on youth and politics tended also to dangle around the subject, holding a superficial analysis, without incorporating the multi-layered complexities of public governance and personal interests.

It is against the above that this study has concentrated on specific case studies of individual young men whose worldviews are shaping their political discourses and activism. Ernesto Yeboah, Oliver Mawuse Barker-Vormawor, Mahmoud Jajah, and Nana Kwame Bediako are all Ghanaians offering answers to some of the major questions about Ghana's underdevelopment. They have gone beyond mere rhetoric to investing in activism in the form of providing social services for their respective constituencies. Also, much as they may have different political philosophies, they are all involved in both direct and indirect appeal to the transcendental as a means of legitimizing their vision for Ghana, thus indexing Ghana's enchantment with the public sphere. Meanwhile, with the exception of Mahmoud Jajah, the rest have fallen short of applying a realist perspective of politics to their itinerary. They tend to romanticize the answers they have for young people, idealizing the metanarrative of the oppressed and oppressor, all of which cause them much pain and ultimate disappointment when those they seek to 'save' rebuff them. Arguably, their simplistic conceptualization of the modern state and citizens, as though these elements are naturally constituted, remains fault lines in their politics.

Consequently, these impassioned young leaders finally become discouraged and disillusioned. At the time of writing, Ernesto Yeboah had gone very quiet, his voice is hardly heard on national issues; Oliver Barker draws consolation for being the former lead organizer of the #FixTheCountry Movement, while Nana Bediako ('Cheddar') is already courting public ridicule for some outlandish promises. Cheddar's campaign narrative of deploying technology to dredge a river to enable ships sail inland to Kumasi, the heart of Asanteland is considered not just a locus classicus of science fiction, but an index of a dreamer. Mahmoud Jajah is also confronted with apathetic young people, who after receiving skilled training at different levels of technology, expect to be provided with funding to start their careers. Jajah has consequently used social media, including his pervasive presence on Facebook, to drive home the importance of business acuity needed by young people to thrive in the competitive digital world. But all this comes against a reality of inadequate supply of economic and physical infrastructure to enable young people carry through their vision. There is also the reciprocal social expectation, where parents look up to their older children as a source of both social and economic resources. Compounding this challenge is societal expectation of young people to marry and have children. Considering marriage as *ibadah* (an act of worship) and sacrament/covenant among Ghana's major religions, Islam and Christianity, respectively, marriage offers social capital; while the absence of it reinforces marginalization of adult-singles. The importance of marriage particularly constitutes a nemesis for young women who make forays into digital technology. Apart from all the aforementioned issues young people face, there are also complex forms of digital dictatorship, which could be more pernicious than pre-industrial stifling of political freedom.

In the end, the stakes are high for young people and their participation in public governance, all of which requires the need to balance the 'why' and 'how' philosophies of life. This means that instead of young people migrating in search of 'greener pastures,' which are illusory, they ought to consider the wisdom in the adage of 'a bird in hand is worth two in the bush.' Our point is that a well-informed worldview that allows the youth to think of life as a privilege; they should consider themselves as needed at home rather than becoming needy in someone else's homeland. This would make the whole difference.

The discourse around critical theory, which is driving the metanarrative of the oppressed and oppressor, fosters blame culture, instead of a culture of penitence. Blame culture allows young people to exclude themselves from the possible role they play in complicating their challenges. For example, several Ghanaian young men and women would look down on a graduate who sells bread for subsistence. This is because these young people equate high education with an opportunity to work in an air-conditioned office. This is a poor understanding of work culture. Nana Kwame Bediako, the businessman, seemed to take a different view. He made his first million bucks selling scrap metal! Therefore, the Ghanaian youth need to revise their notes. There is dignity in labour, no matter what labour. Young people must find creative ways of resolving their own challenges.

In conclusion, this study seeks to incorporate a philosophy of life, which would include state and public governance. It makes the case for creating an interface where the ruling elite and young people would appreciate adaptive leadership. When the education system is rigidly choreographed on neo-liberal and skill-starved education, young people would be less prepared to see life as purposeful. The youth would see life only as a quest for money and chasing after materials things. It is against this perspective that we have underscored the importance of Nkrumah's Consciencism, which regrettably is the least read of Nkrumah's published works. The charge that Nkrumah's book is seen as complex is only an apology. Who says life is not complex, anyway? In the final analysis, no one should elevate the much vaunted Science, Technology, Engineering and Mathematics (STEM) education to the detriment of the humanities. Ghana needs to keep a fine balance between these fine strands of life-long education. Education must sustain human dignity while fostering human flourishing in philosophical imperatives at all levels of public and private schooling.

Bibliography

Ababio, E. F. Conflict, identity and co-operation – The relations of the Christian church with the traditional, colonial and national state in Ghana with special reference to period 1916-1966 (PhD thesis submitted to the University of Edinburg, 1991).

Abiola, I. *The negritude moment: Explorations in francophone Africa and Caribbean literature and thought* (Trenton, N.J.: Africa World Press, 2011); Aimé Fernand David Césaire, *Discourse on colonialism* (trans. Joan Pinkham) (New York: Monthly Review Press, 1955).

Abrahamsen, R. and Bareebe, G. "Uganda's 2016 elections: Not even faking it anymore," *African Affairs,*115, 461 (2016): 1-15.

Accra Mail (May 9, 2021), "Fix The Country: Afia Schwarzenegger Slams Ghanaians to Fix Their Attitude," Accessed: July 5, 2021, https://accramail.com/fix-the-country-afia-schwarzenegger-slams-ghanaians-to-fix-their-attitude/.

Acquah, K. K. "A letter to Kantinka: A synopsis of socio-politico-economic situation in contemporary Ghana (Kande-Accra: Dynamo Publishers, 2002).

Addo, E. O. "Religion and politics in Africa: An assessment of Kwame Nkrumah's legacy for Ghana," in Nimi Wariboko and Toyin Falola (eds), *The Palgrave handbook of African social ethics*, 185-201 (Cham: Palgrave Macmillan, 2020).

Adotey, E. "'9th may 2017 is our day': The homeland study group foundation and contested national imaginaries in postindependence Ghana," *Nations and Nationalism*, 28, 2 (2022): 662-679.

Adotey, E. "'Operation eagle eye': Border citizenship and cross-border voting in Ghana's fourth republic," *Journal of Borderlands Studies*, 38, 1 (2023): 21-38.

Adotey, E. "A matter of apostrophe? Founder's day, founders' day, and holiday politics in contemporary Ghana," *Journal of West African Studies*, 5, 2 (2019): 113-139.

Adjaye, J. K. "Asantehene Agyeman Prempe I and British colonization of Asante: A reassessment," *The International Journal of African Historical Studies*, 22, 2 (1989): 223-249.

Adzimah-Alade, S.; Akotia, C. S. and Annor, F. "Vigilantism in Ghana: Trends, Victim Characteristics, and Reported Reasons," *The Howard Journal of Crime and Justice*, 59, 2

(2020): 194-213.

Africanews (2019), "Mahmoud Jajah sets to transform Ghana's deprived inner cities using digital technology," https://espact.com/mahmoud-jajah-sets-to-transform-ghanas-deprived-inner-cities-using-digital-technology/.

Agana, A. and Prempeh, C. "Of farms, legends, and fools: Re-engaging Ghana's development narrative through social media," *Media, Culture & Society* (2022): 1-17.

Agbodeka, F. *A history of the University of Ghana: Half a century of higher education* (Accra: Woeli Publishing Services, 1998).

Agboka, G. Y. "Ghana: Letter to the Speaker – Curbing religious imperialism in our nation," https://allafrica.com/stories/200803311320.html.

Agyeman-Duah, B. "Ghana, 1982-6: The politics of the PNDC." *Journal of Modern African Studies* 25, 4 (1987): 613-642.

Agyeman-Duah, B. *General Acheampong: The life and times of Ghana's head of state* (Tema/Ghana: Digibooks Publishers, 2021).

Agovi, K. E. "Words, music, dance and parody in confusion: The performance of Nzema Avudwene songs," *Research Review*, 6, 2 (1990): 1-7.

Ahmed-Rufai, M. "The Muslim Association Party: A test of religious politics in Ghana," *Transactions of the Historical Society of Ghana*, NS, 6 (2002): 99-114.

Ahmed, A. H. "Ghana's rebellious civil society and democratic consolidation: A critical assessment of #fixthecountry movement," *African Journal of Social Sciences Education* 2, no. 1 (2022): 50-72.

Aidoo, A. A. "Order and conflict in the Asante empire: A study in interest group relations," *African Studies Review*, 20, 1 (1977): 1-36.

Ajana, B. *Governing through biometrics: The biopolitics of identity* (Basingstoke, Hampshire: Palgrave Macmillan, 2013).

Ajayi, J. F. A. "The place of African history and culture in the process of nation-building in Africa south of the Sahara," *Journal of Negro Education*, 30, 3 (1961): 206-207.

Akon-Mensah, M. Citizenship in Ghana: Understanding its cultural and political construction (PhD Diss., Universidade do Minho (Portugal), 2019).

Akonor, K. *Africa and IMF conditionality: The uniqueness of compliance, 1983-2000* (New York: London: Routledge, 2006).

Akurang-Parry, K. "Obama's visit as a signifier of Ghanaian's 'colonial mentality' in Kwasi Konadu and Clifford C. Campbell, *The Ghana reader: History, culture and politics,* 440-447 (Durham/London: Duke University Press, 2016), p. 441.

Akyeampong, E. "African socialism; or, the search for an indigenous model of economic development?" *Economic History of Developing Regions,* 33, 1 (2018): 67-87.

Akyeampong, E. "Christianity, modernity and the weight of tradition in the life of 'Asantehene' Agyeman Prempeh I, c.1888-1931," *Journal of International African Institute,* 69, 2 (1999): 279-311;

Akyeampong, E. and Obeng, P. "Spirituality, gender, and power in Asante history," *The International Journal of African Historical Studies,* 28, 3 (1995): 481-508.

Aldrich, R. *Banished potentates: Dethroning and exiling indigenous monarchs under British and French colonial rule, 1815-1955* (Manchester: Manchester University Press, 2018).

Allman, A. "Rounding up spinsters: Gender chaos and unmarried women in colonial Asante," *The Journal of African History,* 37, 2 (1996): 195-214.

Allman, J. M. "'Hewers of wood, carriers of water': Islam, class, and politics on the eve of Ghana's independence," *African Studies Review,* 34, 2 (1991): 1-26.

Allman, J. M. *The quills of the porcupine: Asante nationalism in an emergent Ghana* (Wisconsin: The University of Wisconsin Press, 1993).

Amenumey, D. E. K. *Ghana: A concise history from pre-colonial times to the 20th century* (Accra: Woeli Publishing Services, 2018).

Anderson, A. B. *Imagined Communities: Reflections on the Origin and Spread of Nationalism* (London: Verso, 1991).

Ankrah, E. (13 March 2023), "We have been mistreated on our own land for far too long – Ga Mantse fumes," https://www.myjoyonline.com/we-have-been-mistreated-and-sidelined-on-our-own-land-ga-mantse-fumes/.

Anshan L. "Asafo and destoolment in colonial southern Ghana, 1900-1953," *The International Journal of African Historical Studies,* 28, 2 (1995): 327-357.

Anyidoho, A. and Dakubu, E.E.K. "Ghana: Indigenous languages, English and an emerging national identity," in Anderson Simpson (ed), *Language and national identity in Africa,* 141-157 (Oxford: Oxford University Press, 2008).

Aouragh, A. and Alexander, A. "The Arab Spring: The Egyptian Experience:

Sense and Nonsense of the Internet Revolution." *International Journal of Communication* 5 (2011), 1344-58.

Arhin, A. (ed), *The life and works of Kwame Nkrumah* (Accra: Sedco Publishing Ltd., 1991).

Arhin, A. *West African traders in Ghana in the nineteenth and twentieth century* (London: Longman, 1979).

Arhin, K. "The Asante praise poems: The ideology of patrimonialism," *Paideuma* (32 (1986): 163-197.

Armstrong, A. 'Sakawa' rumours: Occult internet fraud and Ghanaian identity, Working Paper, No. 08/2011.

Asad, T. *Formation of the Secular: Christianity, Islam, Modernity* (California: Stanford University Press 2003), 23.

Asante, S.K.B. "The neglected aspects of the activities of the Gold Coast Aborigines Rights Protection Society," Phylon, 36, 1 (1975): 32-45.

Asare, W. (8 June 2021), "//FixTheCountry demonstration: Supreme court sets high court order aside," https://www.asaaseradio.com/ supreme-court-okays-fixthecountry-demonstration.

Asiwaju, A.I. Artificial boundaries (An inaugural lecture delivered at the University of Lagos on Wednesday 12 December 1984).

Assensoh, A. B., and Alex-Assenson, Y. M. *African military history and politics: Coups and ideological incursions, 1900 – Present* (Basingstoke, Hampshire: Palgrave Macmillan, 2001).

Assimeng, M. *Social structure of Ghana: A study of persistence and change.* (Tema/Ghana: Ghana Publishing Corporation, 1981).

Atiemo, A.O. "International human rights, religious pluralism and the future of chieftaincy in Ghana," Exchange, 35, 4 (2006): 360-382.

Babu, A. R. M. African socialism or socialist Africa? (Dar es Salaam/ Tanzania: Tanzania Publishing House; London: Zed Press, 1981).

Balakrishnan, S. "Building the ancestral republic: Cemeteries and the necropolitics of properties in colonial Ghana," *Journal of Social History* (2022): 1-25.

Balakrishnan, S. "Of debt and bondage: From slavery to prison in the Gold Coast, c. 1807-1957," Journal of African History, 61, 1 (2020): 3-21.

Barwa, S. D. Structural adjustment programmes and the urban informal sector in Ghana (Geneva: Development and Technical Cooperation Department, International Labour Office, Geneva, 1995).

BBC (12 November 2020), Jerry John Rawlings, in his own words – BBC

Africa," https://www.youtube.com/watch?v=ZxAVKXmHQOw.

Bediako, K. "De-sacralization and democratization: Some theological reflections on the role of Christianity in nation-building in modern Africa," Transformation: An International Evangelical Dialogue on Mission and Ethics, 12, 1 (1998): 5-11.

Bellah, B.; Madsen, R.;. Sullivan, W. M.; Swidler, A. and Tipton, S. M. Hab its of the heart: Middle America observed (California: The Regent of the University of California, 1985).

Belley, H. K. "Advances in social media and political campaigns in elections: An assessment of the 2016 general elections in Ghana," *Asian Journal of Education and Social Studies,* 12, 1 (2020): 20-28.

Bentham, J. An introduction to the principles of morals and legislation (ed. J. H. Burns and H. L. A. Hart) (London: Athlone Press, 1970).

Berger, P. L. *The sacred canopy: Elements of a sociological theory of religion* (New York: Anchor Books, 1967).

Bergère, C. "'Don't tax my megabytes:' Digital infrastructure and the regulation on citizenship in Africa," *International Journal of Communication,* 13 (2019): 4309-4326.

Berman, E. H. "African responses to Christian mission education," *African Studies Review,* 17, 3 (1974): 527-540.

Bernal, M. *Black Athena: The Afroasiatic roots of classical civilization: The fabrication of ancient Greece, 1785-1985,* Vol. 1 (New Brunswick: Rutgers University Press, 1987).

Bernal, M. *Black Athena: The Afroasiatic roots of classical civilization: The archaeological and documentary evidence,* Vol. II (New Brunswick: Rutgers University Press, 1991)

Bernal, M. *Black Athena: The Afroasiatic roots of classical civilization: The linguistic evidence,* Vol. III (New Brunswick: Rutgers University Press, 2006).

Boadi, D. (17 August 2021), "Akufu-Addo-Bawumia-led government is fixing the country as promised – Ernest Owusu Bempah," https://www.ghanaweb.com/GhanaHomePage/NewsArchive/Akufo-Addo-Bawumia-led-government-is-fixing-the-country-as-promised-Ernest-Owusu-Bempah-1335061.

Boafo-Arthur, K. (ed.), *Ghana: One decade of liberal democracy* (London: Zed Books, 2007).

Boahen, A. A. *African perspective on colonialism* (Baltimore: Johns Hopkins University Press, 1987).

Boahen, A. A. *General History of Africa: Africa under colonial domination,*

1880-1935, Vol. 7 (London: Heinemann, 1985).

Boahen, A. A. *Topics in West African history* (Harlow: Longman, 1986).

Boakye, E. A. (25 March 2022), "US Court throws out Kennedy Agyapong's $9.5M defamation suit against Kevin Taylor," https://citinewsroom.com/2022/03/us-court-throws-out-kennedy-agyapongs-9-5m-defamation-suit-against-kevin-taylor/.

Boakyewa, K. A. Nana Oparebea and the Akonnedi shrine: Cultural, religious and global agents (PhD thesis submitted to the Indiana University, 2014).

Boateng, C. A. *The political legacy of Kwame Nkrumah of Ghana* (Ontario: The Edwin Mellen Press, 2003).

Boateng, E. A. *Government and the People: Outlook for Democracy in Ghana* (Accra: Institute of Economic Affairs, 1996).

Bob-Milliar, G. M. "Party youth activists and low-intensity electoral violence in Ghana: A qualitative study of party foot soldiers' activism," *African Studies Quarterly*, 15, 1 (2014): 125-152;

Bob-Milliar, G. M. "'We run for the crumbs and not for office': The Nkrumahist minor parties and party patronage in Ghana," *Commonwealth & Comparative Politics*, 57, 4 (2019): 445-465.

Bob-Milliar, G. M. Verandah Boys versus reactionary lawyers: Nationalist activism in Ghana, 1946-1956," *The International Journal of African Historical Studies*, 15, 1 (2014): 442-460.

Bosch, T. "Twitter activism and youth in South Africa: The case of #RhodesMustFall," *Information, Communication & Society*, Vol. 20, no. 2 (2017), pp. 221-232.

Botwe-Asamoah, K. Ewe nationalism; a historical perspective (MA thesis submitted to the Southern Connecticut State College, 1977).

Bourdieu, P. *Language & symbolic power* (trans. Gino Raymond and Matthew Adamson) (Cambridge: Polity Press, 1991).

Boyd, J. B. Jr., "African boundary conflict: An empirical study," *African Studies Review*, 22, 3 (1979): 1-14.

Branch, B. and Mampilly, Z. *Africa uprising: Popular protest and political change* (London: Zed Books, 2015).

Brik, A. B. "Introduction: Facing the wave: A journey in the shadow of the pandemic," in Brik, A.B. (ed), *The Covid-19 pandemic in the Middle East and North Africa*, 1-20 (New York: Routledge, 2023).

Brobbery, C.A.; Da-Costa, C.A. and Apeakoran, E.N. "The communicative ecology of social media in the Organization of Social Movement for collective action in Ghana: The case of #fixthecountry," *Information Impact: Journal of Information and Knowledge Management* 12, no. 2 (2021): 73-86.

Brukum, N. J. K. Northern territories of the Gold Coast under British colonial rule, 1897-1956: A study in political change (PhD thesis submitted to the University of Toronto, 1997).

Burke, P. *Cultural hybridity* (Cambridge: Polity Press, 2009).

Burnett, D. G. Charisma and community in a Ghanaian independent church (PhD thesis submitted to School of Oriental and African Studies, 1997).

Busia, K. A. *The challenge of Africa* (New York: Frederick A. Praeger,1962).

Busia, K.A. *The position of the chief in the modern political system of Ashanti: A study of the influence of contemporary social changes on Ashanti political institutions* (Oxford: Institute of Social and Cultural Anthropology, 1951).

CBS News (8 March 2023), "What we know about Tyre Nichols' death and the Memphis officers charged with murder," https://www.cbsnews.com/news/tyre-nichols-death-investigation-memphis-police-officers-charges-what-we-know/.

Césaire, A. *Discourse on colonialism* (trans. Joan Pinkham) (New York: Monthly Review Press, 1972).

Chazan, N. "Ethnicity and politics in Ghana," *Political Science Quarterly*, 97, 3 (1982): 461-485.

Chryssides, G.D. *Historical dictionary of Jehovahs Witnesses* (Lanham, Maryland: The Scarecrow Press, Inc., 2008).

Clifford, J. "Travelling cultures," in Lawrence Grossberg, Carl Nelson and Paula A. Treichler, *Cultural Studies*, 96-116 (London: Routledge, 1992).

Cook, J. (14 February 2023), "Future-proofing careers and business in the changing world of work," https://www.businessleader.co.uk/future-proofing-careers-and-business-in-the-changing-world-of-work/.

Cox, I. *Socialist ideas in Africa* (London: Lawrence & Wishart, 1966)

Dalberto, S. A. and Banégas, R. (eds). *Identification and citizenship in Africa: Biometrics, the documentary state and bureaucratic writings of self* (London: Routledge, 2021).

Damwah, A. K. Dr Hilla Limann 1934-1998: His life and times (MPhil Thesis submitted to the University of Cape Coast, 2011).

Dankwah, J. S. and Mensah, K. "Political marketing and social media influence on young voters," *SN Social Sciences*, 152 (2021): 1-19.

Danquah, J. B. "The historical significance of the Bond of 1844."

Transactions of the Historical Society of Ghana, 3, 1 (1957): 3-29.

Darby, P. "'Let us rally behind the flag': Football, nation-building, and Pan-Africanism in Kwame Nkrumah's Ghana," *Journal of African History*, 54, 2 (2013): 221-246.

Darko, S.P. "Ghana's law on publication of false news is vague and easily abused," https://eprints.lse.ac.uk/113932/1/africaatlse_2022_02_25_ghana_law_publication_of_fake_news_vague.pdf.

Darwin, C. *The origin of species* (edited with intro. Gillian Beer) (Oxford: Oxford University Press, 1996).

Davidson, B. *Black star: A view of the life and times of Kwame Nkrumah* (London: Allen Lane, 1973).

de Witte, M. "Afrikania's dilemma: Reframing African authenticity in a Christian public sphere," *Etnofoor*, 17, ½ (2004): 133-155.

Deshpande, A. *The grammar of caste: Economic discrimination in contemporary India* (Oxford: Oxford University Press, 2011).

Diop, C. A. *The African origin of civilization: Myth or reality* (trans. Mercer Cook) (Westport: Lawrence Hill, 1974).

Du Bois, W. E. B. *The souls of black folk* (edited and intro by Brent Hayes Edwards) (Oxford: Oxford University Press, 2007).

Dumbe, Y. "Islamic polarisation and the politics of exclusion in Ghana," *Islamic Africa*, 10, 1-2 (2019): 153-180.

Dumbe, Y. "Islamic polarisation and the politics of exclusion in Ghana: Tijaniyya and Salafist struggles over Muslim orthodoxy," *Islamic Africa* 10 (2019): 153-180.

Dumbe, Y. "Islamic polarisation and the politics of exclusion in Ghana," *Islamic Africa*, 10, 1-2 (2019): 153-180.

Dumbe, Y. Islamic revivalism in contemporary Ghana (Södertörns högskola, 2013), p. 38.

Dunn, J. and Robertson, A. F. *Dependence and opportunity: Political change in Ahafo* (Cambridge: Cambridge University Press, 1973).

Duodu, C. (8 February 2015), "Mahama's Guantanamo deal angers Ghanaians," https://newafricanmagazine.com/11610/.

Dzisah, W. S. "Social media and elections in Ghana: Enhancing democratic participation," *African Journalism Studies*, 39, 1 (2018): 27-47.

Ebrahimji, A. (7 June 2020), "These controversial statues have been re moved following protests over George Floyd's death," https://edition.cnn.com/2020/06/03/us/statues-removed-george-floyd-trnd/index.html.

Engels, F. *The origin of the family, private property and the state* (London: Penguin, 1986).

Eze, M. O. "What is African communitarianism? Against consensus as a regulative ideal," *South African Journal of Philosophy*, 27, 4 (2008): 106-119.

Faanu, P. and Graham, E. "The politics of ethnocentrism: A viability test of Ghana's democracy?" *Insight on Africa*, 9, 2 (2017): 1-18.

Falola, T. and Jennings, C. (eds.), *Sources and methods in African history: Spoken, written, unearthed* (Rochester, NY.: University of Rochester Press, 2003).

Fanon, F. *The wretched of the earth* (trans. C. Farrington) (New York: Grove Press, 1963).

Finlay, J. D. "Students and politics in Ghana," *Daedalus*, 97, 1 (1968): 51-69.

Fordwor, K.D. *The Danquah-Busia tradition in the politics of Ghana: The origins, mission, and achievements of the New Patriotic Party* (Accra: Unimax Macmillan, 2010).

Fortes, M. "The political system of the Tallensi of the Northern territories of the Gold Coast," in Meyer Fortes and E. E. Evans-Pritchard (eds), *African political systems*, 239-271 (London: Oxford University Press for International African Institute, 1970).

Foucault, M. *Discipline & punish: The birth of the prison* (trans. Alan Sheridan) (New York: Vintage Books, 1977).

Freud, S. *The interpretation of dreams* (James Strachey) (London: Penguin, 1991).

Freyburg, T. and Garbe, L. "Blocking the bottleneck: Internet shutdowns and ownership at election times in Sub-Saharan Africa," *InternationalJournal of Communication*, 12 (2018): 3896-3916.

Fuller, H. *Building the Ghanaian nation-state: Kwame Nkrumah's symbolic nationalism* (New York: Palgrave Macmillan, 2014).

Gadjanova, E.; Lynch, G.; Reifler, J. and Saibu, G.*Social media, cyber battalions, and political mobilisation in Ghana* (Exeter: University of Exeter, 2019).

Gellner, E. *Nations and nationalism* (Oxford: Blackwell, 1986).

Gelvin, J. L. *The Arab Uprisings: What everybody needs to know* (Oxford: Oxford University Press, 2012).

Ghanaweb (1 September 2022), "Why KNUST and UG were cited for running unaccredited courses in A-G's report," https://www.ghanaweb.com/Ghana-HomePage/NewsArchive/Why-KNUST-and-UG-were-cited-for-running-unaccredited-courses-in-A-G-s-report-1614827.

Ghanaweb (2 February 2019), "Ayawaso West Wuogon by-election: Violent acts frightening, worrisome. CSOs," https://www.ghanaweb.com/GhanaHomePage/NewsArchive/Ayawaso-West-Wuogon-by-election-Violent-acts-frightening-worrisome-CSOs-720226.

Ghanaweb (20 June 2021), "Current CPP is not Kwame Nkrumah's CPP – Ernesto Yeboah," https://www.ghanaweb.com/GhanaHome Page/NewsArchive/Current-CPP-is-not-Kwame-Nkrumah-s-CPP-Ernesto-Yeboah-1291063.

Ghanaweb (27 July 2012), "Bawku Central MP Adamu Sakande convicted; jailed two years," https://www.ghanaweb.com/GhanaHomePage/NewsArchive/Bawku-Central-MP-Adamu-Sakande-convicted-jailed-two-years-246093.

Ghanaweb (27 September 2022), "CPP has never been the 3rd force in Ghana's politics – Dr. Smart Sarpong," https://www.ghanaweb.com/GhanaHomePage/politics/CPP-has-never-been-the-3rd-force-in-Ghana-s-politics-Dr-Smart-Sarpong-1631264.

Ghanaweb (29 October 2022), "Oliver-Barker Vormawor faces two court rulings on felony charges November 11," https://www.ghanaweb.com/GhanaHomePage/NewsArchive/Oliver-Barker-Vormawor-faces-two-court-rulings-on-felony-charges-November-11-1652387.

Ghanaweb (31 May 2005), "Vice-Chancellor asked to step aside until …," https://www.ghanaweb.com/GhanaHomePage/NewsArchive/Vice-Chancellor-asked-to-step-aside-until-82670.

Ghanaweb (4 July 2019), "Majority leader justifies construction of new parliament chamber," https://www.ghanaweb.com/Ghana HomePage/NewsArchive/Majority-leader-justifies-construction-of-new-parliamentary-chamber-760572.

Ghanaweb (9 January 2022), "Dormaahene lauds 'Fix The Country Movement," https://www.ghanaweb.com/GhanaHomePage/NewsArchive/Dormaahene-lauds-Fix-The-Country-Movement-1440439.

Gibson, N. C. *Fanonian practices in South Africa: From Steve Biko to Abahlali baseMjondolo* (Scottsville: University of KwZulu-Natal Press, 2011).

Gibson, N. C., and Beneduce, R. *Frantz Fanon, psychiatry and politics* (London/New York: Rowman & Littlefield, 2017).

Giddens, A. and. Sutton, P.W. *Essential concepts in sociology*. Cambridge: Polity Press, 2014, p. 56;

Anthony Giddens. *The Constitution of Society: Outline of the Theory of Structuration*. Cambridge: Polity Press, 1984, pp. 16-40.

Gocking, R. *The history of Ghana* (Westport, Conn.: Greenwood Press, 2005).

Gopaldas, R. "Digital dictatorship versus digital democracy in Africa,"

South African Institute of International Affairs (2019): 1-18.

Graham, C.K. *The history of education in Ghana: From the earliest times to the declaration of independence* (London: Frank Cass, 1971).

Graphic Online TV (August 16, 2021), "'Fixing The Country Movement to embark on a nationwide campaign," Accessed: December 12, 2021, https://www.youtube.com/watch?v=jDZ0hARqQ8w.

Gumede, W. "How technologies boost democracy and development in Africa," *Journal of African Media Studies*, 10, 1 (2018): 135-144.

Guttridge, W. *Military regimes in Africa* (London: Methuen, 1975).

Gyampo, R.E. "Public funding of political parties in Ghana: An outmoded concept?" *Ufahamu*, 38, 2 (2015): 3-28.

Gyampo, R. E. V. "Social media, traditional media and party politics in Ghana," *African Review*, (2017): 1-15: (2019): 1-18; DOI: 10.1080/09744053.2017.1329806

Gyampo, R. E. V. and Obeng-Odoom, F. "Yout participation in local and national development in Ghana: 1620-2013", *The Journal of Pan African Studies*, 5, 9 (2013): 129-150.

Gyekye, K. *African cultural values: An introduction* (Accra: Sankofa Publishing Co., 1996).

Gyekye, K. "Person and community in Akan thought," In Kwasi Wiredu and Kwame Gyekye (eds.), *Person and community: Ghana Philosophical Studies*, I, 101-122 (Washington: The Council for Research in Values and Philosophy, 1992).

Gyekye, K. (1997) *Tradition and modernity: Philosophical reflections on the African experience*. Oxford: Oxford University Press, p. xi.

Gyekye, K. *The unexamined life: Philosophy and the African experience* (Legon, Ghana: Sankofa Publishing Company Ltd., 2004/1996/1988).

Hanson, J. H. *The Ahmadiyya in the Gold Coast: Muslim cosmopolitans in the British empire* (Bloomington: Indiana University Press, 2017).

Harari, Y. N. (October 2018), "Why technology favors tyranny," https://edisciplinas.usp.br/pluginfile.php/4906801/mod_resource/content/1/Yuval%20Noah%20Harari%20on%20Why%20Technology%20Favors%20Tyranny%20-%20The%20Atlantic.pdf.

Harari, Y. N. *21 lessons for the 21st century* (London: Vintage, 2018).

Harari, Y. N. *Sapiens: A brief history of humankind* (London: Vintage Digital: 2016), pp. 86-87.

Hargreaves, J. D. "Towards a history of the partition of Africa," *The Journal* of African History, 1, 1 (1960): 97-109.

Hastings, A. *The construction of nationhood: Ethnicity, religion and nationalism* (Cambridge: Cambridge University Press, 1997).

Heifetz, R. A. *The practice of adaptive leadership: Tools and tactics for changing your organization* (Cambridge, MA.: Harvard University Press, 2009).

Heifetz, R. A. *Leadership on the line: Staying alive through the dangers of leading* (Harvard: Harvard Business School Press, 2002).

Heifetz, R. A. *Leadership without easy answers* (Belknap: Harvard University Press, 1994)

Hill, R. *Lord Acton* (New Haven: Yale University Press, 2000), p. xxiv.

Hilling, D. "Tema – The geography of a new port," *Geography*, 51, 2 (1966): 111-125.

Hobbes, T. *Leviathan* (edited with an intro. &. Notes by J.C.A. Gaskin) (Oxford: Oxford University Press, 1996/165).

Hochschild, A. *King Leopold's ghost: A story of greed, terror, and heroism in colonial Africa* (Boston, Mass.: Houghton Mifflin, 1998).

Holmey, O. (11 May 2020), "Ghana: John Mahama splashed by Airbus corruption affair," https://www.theafricareport.com/27714/ ghana-john-mahama-splashed-by-airbus-corruption-affair/.

Howard, P. N. *Information technology and political Islam* (Oxford: Oxford University Press, 2011).

Howard, P. N. *Pax technica: How the internet of things may set us free or lock us up.* New Haven and London: Yale University, 2015).

Isichei, E. A. *A history of Christianity in Africa: From antiquity to the present* (London: Society for Promoting Christian Knowledge, 1995).

Isin, E., and Ruppert, E. *Being digital citizens* (London: Rowman & Littlefield International Ltd., 2015).

Iwilade, A. Crisis as opportunity: youth, social media and the renegotiation of power in Africa. *Journal of Youth Studies*, 16,8(2013), 1054-1068.

Jackson, I. "Development visions in Ghana: From design schools and building research to Tema new town," *Architectural History*, 65 (2022): 293-326.

John S. Pobee. *Kwame Nkrumah and the church in Ghana, 1949-1966 (A study in the relationship between the socialist government of Nkrumah, the first Prime Minister and first President of Ghana and the Protestant Christian Churches in Ghana* (Accra: Asempa Publishers, 1988).

John, P. *A History of the American People* (London: HarperCollins

Publishers, 1997).

Jumpah, E. T.; Owusu-Arthur, J; and Ampadu-Ameyaw, R. "More youth employment programmes, less youth in work: A relook of youth employment initiatives," *Cogent Social Sciences*, 8 (2022): 1-15.

Kaku, M. *Physics of the Impossible: A Scientific Exploration into the World of Phases, Forces Field, Teleportation, and the time of Travel* (New York: Doubledy, 2008).

Kamp, M. "Introduction," in Mathias Kamp (ed), *Reality check: Assessing the impact of social media on political communication and civic engagement in Uganda*. Kampala: Konrad-Adenaur-Stifung, Uganda Programme, 2016.

Kandilige, L.; Teye, J.K. Setrana, M. and Badasu, D. M. "'They beat us with whatever is available to them': Exploitation and abuse of Ghanaian domestic workers in the Middle East," International Migration (2022): https://doi.org/10.1111/imig.13096.

Kane, O. O. (ed), *Islamic scholarship in Africa: New directions and global contexts* (New York: James Currey, 2021).

Kane, O. O. *Non-Europhone intellectuals* (Dakar/Senegal: Council for the Development of Social Science Research in Africa, 2012).

Kearney, M. D.; Chiang, S.C. and Massey, P.M. (9 October 2020), "The twitter origins and evolution of the Covid-19 'plandemic' conspiracy theory," https://misinforeview.hks.harvard.edu/article/the-twitter-origins-and-evolution-of-the-covid-19-plandemic-conspiracy-theory/.

Khaldun, Ibn. *The Muqaddimah: An introduction to history* (trans. Franz Rosenthal) (London: Routledge & K. Paul, 1958).

Kobo, O. M. "Shifting trajectories of Salafi/Ahl-Sunna reformism in Ghana," *Islamic Africa*, 6, 1-2 (2015): 60-81.

Konstan, D. *Before forgiveness: The origins of a moral idea* (Cambridge: Cambridge University Press, 2010).

Kuenyehia, A. "The impact of structural adjustment programs on women's international human rights: The example of Ghana," in Rebecca J. Cook (ed), *Human rights of women: National and international perspectives*, 422-436 (Philadelphia: University of Pennsylvania Press, 1994).

Kyei, J. R. K. O. and Berkmoes, L.H. "Political vigilante groups in Ghana: Violence or democracy," *Africa Spectrum*, 55, 3 (2020): 321-338.

Lartey, N. L. (June 8, 2021), "We're grateful for Supreme Court's ruling; we'll ensure Ghana is fixed – #FixTheCountry conveners";

Accessed: January 14, 2022; https://citinewsroom.com/2021/06/
were-grateful-for-supreme-courts-ruling-well-ensure-ghana-is-
fixed-fixthecountry-conveners/.

Lefkowitz, M.R. *Not out of Africa: How Afrocentrism became an excuse to
teach myth as history* (New York: BasicBooks, 1996).

Locke, J. *The second treaties of government in two treaties of
government* (edited by Peter Laslett) (Cambridge: University of
Cambridge, 1988/1689).

Makamani, R.; Nhemachena, A. and Mtapuri, O. (eds.), "Introduction," in

Makamani, R., Nhemachena, A. & Mtapuri, O. (eds.). *Global
capitalist's 21st century repositioning: Between Covid-19 and the
fourth industrial revolution on Africa*, 1-18 (Bamenda/Cameroon:
Langaaa Research & Publishing CIG, 2021).

Mamdani, M. *Citizen and subject: Contemporary Africa and the legacy of
late colonialism* (Princeton, N.J.: Princeton University
Press, 1996).

Manu-Osafo, M. J. "'The days of their heedless power were over and done':
Dynamics of power in the military structures of the precolonial
Asante state, 1874-1900," *The Journal of African History*, 62, 2
(2021): 254-270.

Mare, A. "State-ordered internet shutdowns and digital authoritarianism in
Zimbabwe," *International Journal of Communication*, 14 (2020):
4244-4263.

Marx, K. and Engels, F. Manifesto of the communist party (Peking: Foreign
Languages Press, 1965).

Marx, K. *Capital* Vol. I (Moscow/Russia: Progress Publishers, 1887).

Mazrui, A.A. "African Islam and comparative religion: Between revivalism
and expansion," *Third World Quarterly*, 10, 2 (1988):
499-518, p. 503.

Mazrui, A. A. *The Africans: A triple heritage* (London: BBC Publications,
1986).

Mazrui, A. A. "Nkrumah: The Leninist Czar," *Transition*, 26 (1966): 8-17.

Mazrui, A. A. "On the concept of 'We are all Africans,'" *American Political
Science Review*, 57, 1 (1963): 88-97.

McCaskie, T. C. *Asante identities: History and modernity in an African
village, 1850-1950* (Edinburgh: Edinburgh University Press, 2000).

McLeod, H. 'Secularization", *The Oxford Companion to Christian Thought*
(Oxford: Oxford University Press 2000), 653.

Mellosi, E. "'Ghetto tomatoes' and 'taxi drivers': The exploitation and
control of Sub-Saharan African migrant tomato pickers in Puglia,
Southern Italy," *Journal of Rural Studies*, 88 (2021): 491-499.

Merriman, J. *A history of modern Europe: From the renaissance to the present* (3rd edition) (New York: W. W. Norton & Company, 2010).

Meyer, B. *Translating the devil: Religion and modernity among the Ewe in Ghana* (Edinburgh: Edinburgh University Press, 1999).

Miers, S. "Slavery: A question of definition," *Slavery & Abolition*, 24, 2 (2003: 1-16.

Mill, J.S. *On liberty* (Ontario: Batoche Books Ltd., 2001).

Modernghana (15 May 2005), "'Fired' Legon V-C appeals for review," https://www.modernghana.com/news/77837/fired-legon-v-c-appeals-for-review.html.

Morrisett, L. "Technologies of freed?" in H. Jenkins and D. Thorburn (eds.). *Democracy and new media* (Cambridge, MA and London: The MIT Press, 2003).

Mutsvairo, B. "Dovetailing desires for democracy with new ICTs' potentially as platform for activism," in Bruce Mutsvairo (ed.). *Digital activism in the social media era: Critical reflections on emerging trends in sub-Saharan Africa* (Cham: Palgrave Macmillan, 2016).

Myjoyonline (13 March 2023) "Ashaiman: Police give a blow-by-blow ac count of how soldier was killed; 6 suspected nabbed," https://www.myjoyonline.com/ashaiman-police-give-blow-by-blow-account-of-how-soldier-was-killed/.

Nartey, M. and Yu, Y. "A discourse analytic study of# FixTheCountry on Ghanaian Twitter." *Social Media+ Society* 9, no. 1 (2023): 1-11.

Ndegwa, S.N. (ed), *A decade of democracy in Africa* (Leiden: Brill, 2001).

News Reporter (13 July 2021), "Akufu Addo's government is an indication that not all grey hair is a sign of wisdom – Kevin Taylor," https://loudsilencenews.com/akufo-addos-government-is-an-indication-that-not-all-grey-hair-is-a-sign-of-wisdom-kevin-taylor/.

Niekerk, B.V. "Social media and information conflict," *International Journal of Communication*, 7 (2013): 1162-1184.

Nii-Dortey, M. and Nanbigne, E. "Tabooing insults: Why the ambivalence?" *Journal of Philosophy and Culture*, 8, 1 (2020): 1-11.

Nkrumah, K. "Independence Speech," In Kwasi Konadu and Clifford C. Campbell *The Ghana Reader: History, Culture, Politics*, 301-302 (Durham/London: Duke University Press, 2016).

Nkrumah, K. "Movement for colonial freedom," *Phylon*, 16, 4 (1955): 397-409.

Nkrumah, K. Ghana: The autobiography of Kwame Nkrumah (London: Thomas Nelsons and Sons Ltd., 1957).

Nkrumah, K. *Africa must unite* (London: Heinemann, 1963).

Nkrumah, K. *Class struggle in Africa* (London: Panaf Books Ltd., 1970).

Nkrumah, K. *Dark days in Ghana* (London: Panaf Books, 1968).

Nkrumah, K. *Neo-colonialism: The last stage of imperialism* (London: Thomas Nelson & Sons, Ltd., 1965).

Nkrumah, N. *Consciencism: Philosophy and ideology for decolonization and development* (London: Heinemann, 1964).

Nkrumah, K. *Axioms of Kwame Nkrumah.* London: Hertford, 1967.

Nsiah, I. O. "'Who said we are politically inactive?: A reappraisal of the youth and political activism in Ghana 2004-2012," *Journal of Asian and African Studies*, 54, 1 (2019): 138-135.

Ntarangwi, M.; Mills, D. and Babiker, M.H.M. (eds). *African anthropologies: History, critique, and practice* (London: Zed Books, 2006).

Ntewusu, S. "Co-existence in turbulent times: Migrants and the making of Ghana's Madina," *Anno*, LXXXVI, 2 (2020): 365-382.

Nussbaum, M.C. *Women and human development: The capabilities approach* (Cambridge: Cambridge University Press, 2000).

Nussbaum, M.C. *Women and human development: The capabilities approach* (Cambridge: Cambridge University Press, 2000).

Nyamnjoh, F. B. "Incompleteness: Frontier Africa and currency of conviviality," *Journal of Asian and African Studies*, 5, 3 (2015): 253-270.

Nyamnjoh, F. B. "From bounded to flexible citizenship: Lessons from Africa," *Citizenship Studies*, 11, 1 (2007): 73-82.

Obadare, E. and Adebanwi, W. (eds.), *Governance and the crisis in contemporary Africa: Leadership in transformation* (Basingstoke, Hampshire: Palgrave Macmillan, 2016).

Odotei, I. "External influences on Ga society and culture," *Research Review*, 7, 1&2 (1991): 61-71.

Oduro-Frimpong, J. "'The fake is news': On popular visual media, fakery and legitimacy of contestation in charismatic Christianity in contemporary Ghana," *Journal of African Cultural Studies*, 33, 3 (2021): 325-343.

Oduro-Frimpong, J. "*Sakawa* rituals and cyberfraud in Ghanaian popular video movies," *African Studies Review*, 57, 2 (2014): 131-147.

Okonta, I. *The failure of leadership in Africa's development* Lanham: Lexington Books, 2020).

Okoth, M. F.; Tettey, W. J. and Banda, F. *African media and digital public sphere*. New York: Palgrave Macmillan, 2009.

Omari, P. T. *Kwame Nkrumah: The anatomy of an African dictatorship* (London: C. Hurst, 1970).

Opoku, K. A."Independence of the mind," *Journal of Black Studies*, 1, 2 (1970): 179-186.

Oquaye, M. "The process of democratisation in contemporary Ghana," *Commonwealth & Comparative Politics*, 38, 3 (2000): 53-78.

Orwell, G. *Animal farm* (London: Secker and Warburg, 1946).

Owusu-Ansah, D. "Islamic influence in a forest kingdom: The role of protective amulets in early 19th century Asante," *Transafrican Journal of History*, 12 (1983): 100-133.

Owusu, M. A. S. Nationalism in question: A study of key categories in Ghanaian history, 1863-1965 (PhD thesis submitted to Dalhousie University, 2020).

p'Bitek, O. *African religions in Western scholarship* (Nairobi: East African Literature Bureau, 1970.

Patterson, O. *The sociology of slavery; an analysis of the origins, development, and structure of Negro slavery society in Jamaica* (Rutherford, N.J.: Fairleigh Dickinson University Press, 1967).

Peil, M. "The expulsion of West African aliens," *The Journal of Modern African Studies*, 9, 2 (1971): 205-229.

Perbi, A. A. "'Who is a Ghana?' – A historical perspective," in Ghana Academy of Arts and Sciences, *National integration: Proceedings*, 2003, 29-38 (Accra: The Ghana Academy of Arts and Sciences, 2006).

Perbi, A. A. A *history of indigenous slavery in Ghana: From the 15th to the 19th century* (Accra: Sub-Saharan Publishers, 2004).

Powell, D.M. and Durojaye, E. "Constitutional resilience and the Covid-19 pandemic," In Durojaye, E. and Powell, D.M. (eds.). *Constitutional resilience and the Covid-19 pandemic: Perspective from Sub-Saharan Africa*, 1-78 (Cham: Palgrave Macmillan, 2022).

Prempeh, C. "Covid-19 and the philosophy of education: Recuperating Africa's triple heritage," *Millah: Journal of Religious Studies*, 22, 1 (2023): 95-126.

Prempeh, C. "'Food before pressure': Food and food culture in Muslim inner-city in Maamobi-Accra since the 1980s," *African Journal of Social Sciences Education*, 2, 1 (2022): 1-21.

Prempeh, C. "'Hijab is my identity': Beyond the politics of the veil: The appropriations of the veil in an inner-Muslim area of Accra (Ghana) since 1980s", *Journal of Africana Religions*, 10, 1 (2022): 20-46.

Prempeh, C. "Decolonising African divine episteme: A critical analysis of the Akan divine name of God (*Twereduampon* Kwame)," *Journal of Religion in Africa*, 52 (2022): 269-291.

Prempeh, C. "Re-imagining wasatiyyah as a socio-theological mediation of youth anger in Accra, Ghana," *Unisia*, 40, 1 (2022): 103-128.

Prempeh, C. *Nima-Maamobi in Ghana's Postcolonial Development: Migration, Islam and Social Transformation* (Bamenda/Cameroon: Langaa RPCIG, 2022).

Prempeh, C. "Dreadlocks in the Church of Pentecost: Rasta or Rastafarianism," *PentecoStudies* 2.1 (2021): 36-55, pp. 41-42.

Prempeh, C. "From offline to online imagined community: Recuperating Asante culture and history for development in Ghana" *Question*, Issue 06 (2021), pp. 36-44.

Prempeh, C. "Religion and the state in an episodic moment of COVID-19 in Ghana," *Social Sciences & Humanities Open*, Vol. 4, Issue 1 (2021), pp. 1-8.

Prempeh, C. "Religious innovations of chieftaincy in Ghana: Pentecostal Christianity and the complex persistence and transformation of Akan chieftaincy" *Religion Compass*, (2021): 1-13, DOI: 10.1111/ rec3.12426.

Prempeh, C. and Amoah, "Secular governmentality and the court of the Asante Ahemaa in 21st century: An ethnographic account of Ejisu and Juaben traditional areas". In Edmund Abaka & Kwame Osei Kwarteng (Eds.), *The Asante World*, 281-300 (London/New York: Routledge, 2021).

Prempeh, C. "African agency, human rights and issues of homosexuality: Biden and Africa" In Bob Wekesa (ed.) *Africa's Policy Towards the US: The Biden Era*, Johannesburg: African Centre for the Study of the United States, 137-157 (University of the Witwatersrand, 2021).

Prempeh, C. Christianity, Culture, and Pentecostalism in Ghana: An Ethnographic Study of Pentecostal Traditional Authorities in Contemporary Akan Society (1990s–Present) (Unpublished PhD Dissertation submitted to the University of Cambridge, 2021).

Prempeh, C. (5 August 2019), "Founders or founder? The lies and the lies we have believed for long! Enough of the lies," https:// www.modernghana.com/news/948858/founders-or-founder-the-lies-and-the-lies-we-have-believed.html.

Prempeh, C. Islamic and drugs: A study of the use of marijuana among Muslim youth in Maamobi community, Accra (MPhil unpublished thesis submitted to the Institute of African Studies, University of Ghana, 2011).

Putnam, R. D. *Bowling alone: The collapse and revival of American community* (New York: Simon & Schuster, 2000).

Quaidoo, E. The United States and the overthrow of Kwame Nkrumah (MA thesis submitted to the Fort Hays State University, 2010).

Quashigah, E.K. "Legislating religious liberty: The Ghanaian experience," *BYU Law Review*, 2, 6 (1999): 589-609.

Quayson, A. *Oxford street, Accra: City life and itineraries of transnationalism* (Durham: Duke University Press, 2014).

Rattray, R.S. *Ashanti* (Oxford: Clarendon Press, 1932); *Ashanti law and constitution* (Kumasi: Basel Mission Book Depot; London: Oxford University Press, 1923).

Riddimsghana (August 5, 2021), "Ernest Kofi Owusu Bempah Speaks On Fixing The Country Movement"; Accessed: December 10, 2021, https://riddimsghana.com/general-news/ernest-kofi-owusu-bempah-speaks-on-fixing-the-country-movement/.

Rodney, W. *How Europe underdeveloped Africa* (Nairobi: East African Educational Publishers, 1972).

Rotberg, R.I. and Mazrui, A.A. (eds), *Protest and power in black Africa* (New York: Oxford University Press, 1970).

Rousseau, J.J. *The basic political writings* (Indianapolis: IN: Hackett, 1987); Jean-Jacques Rousseau, *The basic political writings* (Indianapolis: In: Hackett, 1987).

Russell, S. "The benevolent dictatorship in Rwanda: Negative government, positive outcome?" *The Applied Anthropologist*, 32, 1 (2012):12-22.

Sallah, B. and Prempeh, C."Charismatic Christianity in Ghana: A relook at some pertinent issues," In Matthew A. Ojo (ed), *The dynamics of charismatic Christianity in Ghana and Nigeria: Essays in honour of Rev Professor Emmanuel Kingsley Larbi*, 30-56 (Accra: Pentecost Press Limited, 2022).

Sarpong, P. *Ghana in retrospect: Some aspects of Ghanaian culture* (Tema/ Ghana: Ghana Publishing Corporation, 1974).

Sartre, H. *Existentialism is humanism* (trans. Carol Macomber) (New Haven: Yale University Press, 2007).

Schildkrout, E. *People of the Zongo: The transformation of ethnic identities in Ghana* (Cambridge: Cambridge University Press, 1978).

Sebastião, S.P. "Preface," in Bogdan Pătruţ & Monica Pătruţ, *Social media in politics: Case studies on the political power of social media* (New York and Dordrecht London: N Springer Cham Heidelberg, 2014).

Shaban, ARA. (10 July 2019), "Ghana parliament drops \$200m chamber idea citing public opposition," https://www.africanews.com/2019/07/10/ghana-parliament-drops-200m-chamber-idea-citing-public-opposition//.

Sherwood, M. *Kwame Nkrumah: The years abroad 1935-1947* (Legon/Ghana: Freedom Publications, 1996).

Shipley, J. W. "Comedians, pastors, and the miraculous agency of charisma in Ghana," *Cultural Anthropology*, 24, 3 (2009): 523-552.

Sintim-Koree, S. *The God who answers by thunder: An account of Christian persecution in Nzemaland during the ban on drumming 1993-1996* (Accra: SonLife Press, 2013).

Smith, A. *An inquiry into the nature and causes of the wealth of nations*, Vol. I (Indianapolis: *LibertyClassics*, 1981), 27.

Suleiman, M. D.; Onapajo, H. and Mustapha, A. B. "Eternal influence, failed states, ungoverned spaces and small arms proliferation in Africa," in Tar, U.A. and Onwurah, C.P. (eds.), *The Palgrave handbook of small arms and conflicts in Africa*, 161-185 (Cham/Switzerland: Palgrave Macmillan, 2021).

Sundkler, B. and Steed, C. *A history of the church in Africa* (Cambridge: Cambridge University Press, 2000).

Taylor, C. *A secular age* (Cambridge, MA.: The Belknap Press of Harvard University Press, 2007).

TV3 Ghana (2017), "Prez Nana Addo's inaugural speech [Full] – 7/1/2017," https://www.youtube.com/watch?v=jUX_Z03LX3M.

Univers TV (14 May 2020), "Vetting of Supreme Court Justice Nomi nee, Prof. Henrietta J. A. N Mensah Bonsu" https://www.youtube.com/watch?v=NBuVWnXPlcY.

wa Thiong'o's, N. *Devil on the cross* (London: Heinemann, 1987).

Weber, M. *Economy and society* (A new translation by Keith Tribe) (Cambridge, Mass.: Harvard University Press, 2019).

Weber, R.H. "Politics through social networks and politics by government blocking: Do we need rules?" *International Journal of Communication*, 5 (2011): 1186-1194.

Whyte, M. K. (27 March 2005), "The Legon Vice-Chancellor must resign," https://www.modernghana.com/news/116504/the-legon-vice-chancellor-must-resign.html.

Wilks, I. "'Unity and progress': Asante politics revisited," Ghana Studies, 1 (1998): 151-179.

Wilks, I. *One nation, many histories: Ghana past and present* (Accra: Ghana Universities Press, 1996).

Wilks, I. *Asante in the nineteenth century: The structure and evolution of a political order* (Cambridge: Cambridge University Press, 1975).

Wiredu, K. "The moral foundation of an African culture," In David R. Morrow, *Moral reasoning: A text and reader on ethics and contemporary moral issues*, 216-225 (Oxford: Oxford University Press, 2018).

Woolley, S. C. and Howard, P.N. "Introduction," in Samuel C. Woolley & Philip N. Howard (eds.), *Computational propaganda: Political parties, politicians, and political manipulation on social media*. Oxford: Oxford University Press, 2019).

Yankah, K. *Speaking for the chief: Okyeame and the politics of Akan royal oratory* (Bloomington: Indiana University Press, 1995).

Yeboa-Korie, C. Y. https://dacb.org/stories/ghana/yeboa-korie-cy/.

Index